# DATE DUE

# Ultimate Rewards

# The Harvard Business Review Book Series

# Ultimate Rewards

## What Really Motivates People to Achieve

Edited with an Introduction by
**Steven Kerr**

**A Harvard Business Review Book**

The *Harvard Business Review* articles in this collection are available as
individual reprints. Discounts apply to quantity purchases. For information
and ordering contact Customer Service, Harvard Business School
Publishing, Boston, MA 02163. Telephone: (617) 495–6192, 9 A.M. to 5 P.M.
Eastern Time, Monday through Friday. Fax: (617) 495–6985, 24 hours
a day.

**Library of Congress Cataloging-in-Publication Data**

Ultimate rewards : what really motivates people to achieve / edited
   with an introduction by Steven Kerr.
      p.   cm.—(A Harvard business review book)
   Includes index.
   ISBN 0-87584-808-7
   1. Employee motivation.  2. Awards.  3. Incentive awards.
I. Kerr, Steven, 1941–  . II. Series: Harvard business review book
series.
HF5549.5.M63U45   1997
658.3'14—dc21                               97-19265
                                                CIP

The paper used in this publication meets the requirements of the American
National Standard for Permanence of Paper for Printed Library Materials
Z39.48–1984.

# Contents

# Introduction

**Steven Kerr**

Each of the articles presented here has earned the right to be included in this classic anthology. Though written at different times, indeed in different decades, the issues they deal with continue to be important today—in fact, may be more important today than ever before.

One problem with anthologies, unlike with coauthored books, is that the authors had never intended to live together, so made no arrangements for their ideas to be compatible. Consequently, the task of moving the furniture around, so to speak (ensuring that two authors' world views look good together, and that the conceptual underpinnings of one author are sufficiently sturdy to support the recommendations of another), inevitably falls to the reader and can cause an intellectual hernia.

The purpose of this introduction is to help the reader with some of the heavy lifting by identifying and elaborating the key issues being debated by these authors, and embedding these issues in a framework that may permit the reader to make some collective sense of the contents of this book.

## How Rewards Affect Performance

One of the most fundamental equations in all psychology is:

$$\text{Ability} \times \text{Motivation} = \text{Performance}$$

From this standpoint, the principal impact of competent rewards is to increase employee motivation. Some people (including Alfie Kohn,

"Why Incentive Plans Cannot Work") maintain that rewards cannot enhance ability; that if employees are inadequately prepared to do their jobs, "relying on incentives to boost productivity does nothing to address possible underlying problems and bring about meaningful change." This overstates the case, because rewards *do* affect ability by stimulating workers to focus more, study up on their jobs at home, take courses in school, and invest in better tools and information. The existence of a competent reward system can also serve to attract more qualified people to a firm, and to encourage employees to accept positional changes within a firm. However, it is true that rewards will usually have a more direct impact on employee motivation than on ability.

## Attributes of "Ultimate Rewards"

### EQUITY

Rewards should be capable of promoting both efficiency and equity. Efficiency has both subjective and objective elements, but equity is almost entirely a subjective determination, and is strongly influenced by intra-organizational and, as Michael Beer ("Rethinking Rewards") points out, national cultural forces. In many Western nations, equity means that a good reward should say thank you for the past. This is sometimes referred to as "paying for (past) performance." In other societies it means paying everyone the same, paying for length of service (seniority), or paying more to people who need more pay, as when Japanese firms award a salary increase to someone who marries or has a child. (Many of these firms also consider it equitable to pay women, especially married women, less than male employees who are doing the same job.) In still other societies, discomfort with pay for performance is based less upon philosophy than upon economic realities. Thus in countries where marginal tax rates are very high, employees are generally indifferent to financial rewards of any kind, preferring leisure time, access to vacation villages, and any perks that don't come with imputed income attached.

The above stipulations notwithstanding, we shall consider equity to mean that a person's rewards are at least approximately related to his or her job-related performance.

## EFFICIENCY

Whereas equity is often conceptualized as paying for past performance, efficiency may be thought of as invigorating future performance. Although this definition is also subject to a number of interpretations, we shall define efficiency as employees' being stimulated to work in ways that are beneficial to their organization. In theory, there is no reason why a reward that says thank you for the past can't also invigorate the future, and indeed one property of an "ultimate" reward is that it is simultaneously efficient and equitable. However, there are times when it seems that an employer must choose between the two, as when one candidate for promotion has clearly earned the job but would be a poor leader, and another has performed unevenly but would do well in the higher-level position.

For a thoughtful look at how the dimensions of equity and efficiency play off of one another, and how this tension is resolved in different types of organizations, see "What Holds the Modern Company Together?" by Rob Goffee and Gareth Jones. Using their terminology, we would expect to find that organizations high in sociability will value equity so much that they put up with quite a bit of inefficiency, whereas organizations high in solidarity will tolerate gross inequities to assure that their operations are efficient.

## MEETING FINANCIAL AND NONFINANCIAL NEEDS

Depending on whether and when you went to business school, you may have heard that "intrinsic" rewards are more important than extrinsic, that pay is at best a hygiene factor and not a motivator, and that human beings seek self-actualization and job enrichment, with money merely a kind of vestigial, low-order need that is or isn't met along the way. This point of view continues to be popular and is espoused or rebutted by various authors in this anthology.

To usefully address this controversy, perhaps we can agree on something that is not controversial—that money is absolutely unique in the enthusiasm with which it is received. Unlike all other rewards, it simply does not saturate; that is, nobody refuses it, nobody returns it, and people who have lots of it will generally do all kinds of things to get more.

Does this belief deny the validity of the arguments for self-actualization expressed in this volume? Not at all. It may well be true that human beings pursue other, loftier goals once their health, safety, and security needs are met. Even so, it is important to keep in mind, as Andrew M. Lebby ("Rethinking Rewards") and Corey Rosen and Michael Quarrey ("How Well Is Employee Ownership Working?") note, that money has the capacity to play a huge role in meeting most people's needs for recognition, status, and self-esteem. It is also possible, as in the case of philanthropists, artists (see Teresa Amabile's comments in "Rethinking Rewards"), and people who quit working to pursue some dream, for money to make it possible to pursue needs of the very highest order.

If money can play such an important role in people's lives, why do some of the authors in this anthology deny that financial rewards are a powerful motivator? Because organizations so often misuse and mismanage them! When financial rewards are disbursed equitably and efficiently, the firm purchases employee motivation and energy to pursue organizational objectives. The trouble is that money is so often distributed in ways that are neither equitable nor efficient. When this occurs, the organization hasn't purchased motivation, energy, or anything else it can use. Spending money in this way is just a foolish expense to the organization and, from the employees' standpoint, is far less likely to fulfill their high-order needs.

## AVAILABILITY

As an example of an inefficient reward practice, consider the most fundamental property of any reward—its availability. Simply put, if you don't have something, you shouldn't try to use it. This point may seem so obvious as to be not worth mentioning, but in fact it's violated all the time. Organizations with minuscule salary increase pools may spend hundreds of management hours rating, ranking, and grading employees, only to waste time, raise expectations, and ultimately produce such pitiful increases that everybody is disappointed and embarrassed. In such cases the point is *not* that financial rewards are unimportant, but that they are so insufficient that they are inefficient. If financial rewards aren't available, it's smart to accept that fact and go on to other things—in particular, to better use of nonfinancial rewards, whose availability is never limited by the budget or the boss.

Effective reliance on intrinsic rewards in an environment where financial rewards are unavailable is documented by Peter F. Drucker ("What Business Can Learn from Nonprofits").

## ELIGIBILITY

Whereas rewards may be unavailable through no one's fault or design, *ineligibility*—making various rewards available only to certain classes of people, e.g., salaried but not hourly, fulltime but not adjunct, and bonus-eligible versus bonus-ineligible—is almost always intentional and is usually done for very good reasons. Organizations typically seek to induce newer and lower-level employees to aspire to climb the organizational ladder, and consequently make many attractive rewards available only to those who reach higher levels. Common examples of such rewards include profit sharing, stock options, invitations to meetings in attractive locations, and permission to fly first class or use the company plane. Equally motivating to low-level workers is the desire to escape thankless, poorly compensated assignments. Thus graduate students work desperately to earn their Ph.D.'s, assistant professors lust for tenure, interns aspire to be full-fledged doctors, and junior employees in accounting, law, and consulting firms put in long hours to become partners.

Unfortunately, this conception of rewards was devised for an earlier time, when bigger meant better, perpetual growth seemed assured, and managers were rewarded for adding layers, staff, and budget. In today's era of de-layering and downsizing, such practices are counterproductive and are made increasingly so by an important demographic: 1996 was the year that the first wave of baby boomers turned 50, meaning that a high percentage of workers in most organizations is made up of people less than fifty years old. These workers are *not* planning to retire soon, but *are* anxious to avail themselves of the goodies that are part of the reward system for those near the top.

This combination of a larger number of people pursuing a smaller number of high-level positions means that, as both Rosabeth Moss Kanter ("New Managerial Work") and Donita S. Wolters ("Rethinking Rewards") point out, it is growing increasingly difficult to use promotions as rewards in organizations. Therefore, more and more firms today are seeking to *dismantle* some of the links between rewards and hierarchical advancement in order to help people understand that they can have a good career without rapidly ascending a hierarchy that, in today's downsized, more horizontal world, is slowly disappearing.

Beyond all these demographic and organizational realities lies the simple fact that when an organization makes people ineligible for rewards it has fewer ways to say thank you for past performance, and employees are less motivated to improve future performance. By way of illustration, consider that in most state lotteries the odds against winning are astronomical, yet millions of people buy tickets. Now imagine what would happen if it were announced that people named Jones were ineligible to win—that from now on if someone named Jones has the winning number, another number will be drawn. How likely is it that anyone named Jones will buy a ticket?

The point is that although one chance in millions and no chance at all are essentially equivalent, they produce completely different mindsets and patterns of behavior. Awarding stock options to a small number of previously ineligible employees, for example, will dramatically alter people's perceptions of these rewards, and their motivation to work harder for them. (See Jack Welch's comments on this matter in his interview with Noel Tichy and Ram Charan in "Speed, Simplicity, Self-Confidence: An Interview with Jack Welch").

However, it is essential to keep in mind that making more people eligible for rewards does *not* assure that the reward system will be viewed as more equitable. Inviting three low-level workers to an executive retreat, for example, may cause *three thousand* workers to become extremely curious about why those three were selected instead of others. Whether perceptions of equitability result depends greatly upon how credibly performance is defined and measured.

## VISIBILITY

For rewards to be equitable and efficient they must, at a minimum, be visible to those who receive them. Most rewards, but not all, are visible to recipients. For example, some organizations' descriptions of their benefits packages are couched in such actuarial doubletalk that most employees have little appreciation of their value.

In order for their impact to be substantial, rewards must also be visible to other employees besides the recipient. (If you add five hundred dollars to someone's paycheck and nobody else knows about it, the number of people you have motivated is somewhere between 0 and 1—not an effective use of company funds.)

Of all principles of effective reward, visibility is the one most often violated. Very few firms, other than public sector organizations legally required to do so, make their financial rewards public. Opposition to this notion tends to be deeply rooted, and is unlikely to be overcome by anything written here. However, two points seem worth mentioning. First, in firms where salaries are not disclosed, employees surveyed about how they're faring relative to fellow workers invariably claim to be worse off than they really are. In the absence of valid information, people share bogus data that reveal huge inequities which really don't exist. If organizations made their financial rewards visible, therefore, the dominant reaction would probably be one of relief.

Second, if they can't be convinced to publicize financial rewards, organizations should at least accept the idea of the visibility of nonfinancial rewards as desirable. Many management actions that have virtually no financial consequences—sending someone to a professional conference, for example, or inviting a team to present their proposal to the division staff or CEO, or thanking an employee in another department for working effectively across organizational boundaries—have the potential to serve as powerful rewards, but have their power substantially diminished by not being visible.

## REVERSIBILITY

One consequence of being human is that, anytime you make a decision, there's a chance you've made a bad decision. Consequently, a nice property of any decision is reversibility—the ability to undo an outcome you don't like, or at least cut your losses and prevent its repetition.

From the standpoint of organizational rewards, reversibility can be defined in two ways. Ideally it means being able to reclaim a reward, e.g., stripping someone of their title or retrieving a company car. However, it is often not possible to take back rewards once they have been disbursed. Therefore, the less rigorous definition is that the *decision* to give the reward can be reversed, so that it need not be distributed to the same individual in the future.

Some rewards are for all practical purposes irreversible; for example, try to recapture an increase in an employee's base pay. Therefore, giving a raise to an employee who shouldn't get one effectively creates a fixed annuity for the organizational life of the person. Furthermore, since future raises will probably be based on the salary that has been erroneously inflated, the error will become geometrically more expensive. That is why reversible compensation—bonuses, incentive pay, compensation at risk—is such an attractive, alternative way to distribute financial rewards. Reversible compensation also can serve as a "shock absorber," by making it possible to reduce payroll without removing people. In Japan, for example, approximately forty percent of the financial compensation of employees in most large firms is variable.

Probably the most serious difficulty with reversible rewards (including most of those in Japan) is their tendency to become calcified over time. The interval between awarding an employee a bonus and his interpretation of it as an entitlement has been scientifically determined to be exactly one hour and a half (or so it seems). Numerous companies have had to jettison their bonus plans because payouts became so taken for granted that the "incentive" component was merely another name for base pay which, when withheld for even the most legitimate of reasons, caused employees to perceive the action as a punishment. (See comments by Alfie Kohn and Michael Beer ("Rethinking Rewards") for more about this problem and suggested resolutions.)

## MULTI-SOURCED AND MULTI-DETERMINED

To this point we have focused on how to reward, and what to reward. Another key question pertains to *who* does the rewarding and the measuring. An important attribute of ultimate rewards is that they are not derived solely from the hierarchical superior. In their description of dysfunctionalities resulting from the use of performance-contingent rewards, several authors in this volume seem to take for granted that hiring, firing, rewarding, and punishing are performed solely by the hierarchical superior. In truth, as Harry Levinson ("Asinine Attitudes Toward Motivation") notes, within traditional bureaucracies this is usually the case. However, in more participative, "boundaryless" organizations (see Jack Welch's definition in his interview with Noel Tichy and Ram Charan "Speed, Simplicity, Self-Confidence: An Interview with Jack Welch"), and Rosabeth Moss Kanter ("New

Managerial Work"), authority to make decisions in key areas is delegated downward, distinctions between managers and nonmanagers begin to erode, and opportunities abound for peers, customers, subordinates, and others to contribute to the measurement and reward process. This creates the potential to greatly increase the strength of rewards without necessarily increasing the risk that resultant behaviors will be dysfunctional.

## DOING UNTO OTHERS AS THEY DO UNTO YOU

As a final example of reward-system induced inequities, consider some of the ways organizations routinely mistreat the people they are most dependent upon, namely their best performers. Across-the-board budget reductions, for example, cause little discomfort to corporate politicians (who build slack into their budgets in anticipation of such cuts) or sloppy managers (who operate with so much fat that there's plenty of room to cut). The true victims are those who are already operating with next to no slack. Similarly, poor performers can sign up for courses, attend conferences, and take their vacations whenever they want, whereas high performers are fortunate to get an occasional day off when workloads permit. And, at buyout or early retirement time in *your* organization, who is offered the more attractive package: your high performer or the person you're glad is leaving?

It is, perhaps, defensible to define equity in such a way that no special rewards accrue to the best performers. It is indefensible, however, to devise organizational practices that cause an organization's most valuable employees to be treated *worse* than everyone else.

## FINANCIAL VERSUS NONFINANCIAL REWARDS REVISITED

Having identified some of the attributes of equitable and effective rewards, let's take another look at the nonfinancial rewards, to suggest the possibility that their ultimate importance may not be that they are self-actualizing or intrinsically enriching, but rather that they possess the attributes of ultimate rewards identified here, and their distribution is therefore more likely to conform to our definitions of equity and efficiency.

For example, we noted earlier that financial rewards are often unavailable, but with nonfinancial rewards you literally can create your own supply. It is possible to give recognition, performance feedback, greater responsibility, or opportunities to participate in decision making to one individual, then give the same things to someone else or to the same person next week. All employees are typically eligible for these rewards but, if desired, more can be given to the high performers than to anyone else. There are usually no constraints upon making them visible, and they are also reversible; that is, if you inadvertently give someone more freedom, challenge, or recognition than he or she can deal with, you can take it back. You can be bold and creative with the nonfinancial rewards because the consequences of these rewards do not have to be permanent.

Whether the potential of intrinsic rewards is realized, however, depends largely upon the willingness of managers to provide them and subordinates' willingness to accept them. Though as Rosabeth Moss Kanter ("New Managerial Work") and David C. McClelland and David H. Burnham ("Power Is the Great Motivator") convincingly argue, a democratic, coaching, leadership style actually tends to *increase* managerial power and influence, Harry Levinson ("Asinine Attitudes Toward Motivation") and Ronald A. Heifetz and Donald L. Laurie ("The Work of Leadership") speak to the fear many managers have of losing power by permitting participation in decision making and delegating authority downward. Heifetz and Laurie also note that, for a variety of reasons, subordinates are often reluctant to accept such rewards.

Increased responsibility and opportunities to participate in decision making are not the only intrinsic rewards that may be unenthusiastically given or received. Increased job challenge, whether expressed in terms of Lawrence A. Bossidy's "burning platform of change" (Noel M. Tichy and Ram Charan, "The CEO as Coach: An Interview with AlliedSignal's Lawrence A. Bossidy") or Robert H. Schaffer's ("Demand Better Results—and Get Them") "pushing for major gains," is often resisted by employees. Candid performance feedback is another so-called intrinsic motivator said to be essential to healthy, well-run organizations, yet controversy exists concerning how much candor managers should offer, and how much subordinates can handle. In the three executive interviews in this text, note the insistence upon candid feedback by Jack Welch and Larry Bossidy (both interviewed by Noel Tichy and Ram Charan), in contrast with Bill Walsh's assertion (Richard Rapaport, "To Build a Winning Team: An Interview with Head Coach Bill Walsh") that "it sounds great to say that you are going to be honest and direct. But insensitive, hammer-like shots . . . delivered in the name of honesty and openness usually do the greatest damage to people."

## DESIRABLE, NEUTRAL, AND DYSFUNCTIONAL REWARDS

Another way that rewards vary is in how strongly they influence performance, and in what direction. There is an old saying that goes: If you're careful enough, nothing bad or good will ever happen to you. In this vein, it is a simple matter to create rewards that are free from the dysfunctions described by the various authors in this volume. The only side effect is that these rewards will also be inefficient, that is, will be unable to exert any favorable influence upon future perform- ance. The reward hasn't been invented that can stimulate desirable fu- ture behavior without a concomitant risk of dysfunctional behavior.

This relationship between reward strength and direction is illus- trated in Figure 1. Examples of "neutral" reward systems might in- clude: paying everyone the same; paying strictly for length of service; and making across-the-board changes, as when all Ph.D. students' annual stipends are increased by ten percent. Such practices may or may not be equitable, depending on one's definition of equity, but are inefficient in that they will not cause anything good to happen.

Therefore, the further from the neutral point a reward is located the stronger is its impact—that is, the more likely it is to stimulate both desirable and dysfunctional behaviors. It is pointless to seek rewards that induce desirable behavior at no risk of provoking dysfunctional acts, and equally pointless to lament the fact that dysfunctional con- sequences sometimes result from generally equitable and efficient re- ward systems. If these occasional negative consequences are too costly to bear, a neutral reward system should be devised, and efficiency, and by our definition equity, forsaken. In general, however, a superior strategy is to devise rewards whose effects are shown in Figure 2— likely to elicit desirable behaviors with relatively few dysfunctional side effects—while shying away from rewards whose effects are de- picted in Figure 3.

## Conclusions

There's an old, comedic definition that "an economist is someone who seeks to learn whether something that works in practice can work

*Figure 1.*

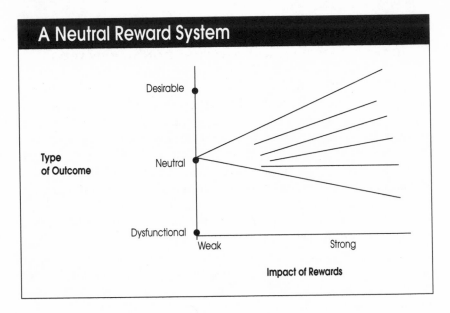

in theory." The point is that it is difficult to sell the notion that incentive plans can't work in the face of so much evidence that these plans *are* working. In this volume, you will read a description by Jerry McAdams ("Rethinking Rewards") of the success of many incentive plans—432 plans covering one million people—and an account by L. Dennis Kozlowski ("Rethinking Rewards") of the success of his own firm's plan. If you want to believe that incentive plans cannot work, you must also conclude that Kozlowski, and countless others, are deluding themselves. You also have to find an answer to the show-stopping observation by G. Bennett Stewart ("Rethinking Rewards") that "the responsiveness of ordinary citizens to incentives is demonstrated daily in our economy. Consumers cut consumption in reaction to the 'penalty' of a price increase and raise purchases in reaction to the 'bribe' of a lower price . . . can it be true . . . that people respond to monetary incentives when they *spend* their income but not when they *earn* it?"

## DESIRABLE VERSUS DYSFUNCTIONAL REWARDS REVISITED

We stated earlier that any reward that induces desirable behavior must also be capable of eliciting dysfunctional behavior. Several

*Figure 2.*

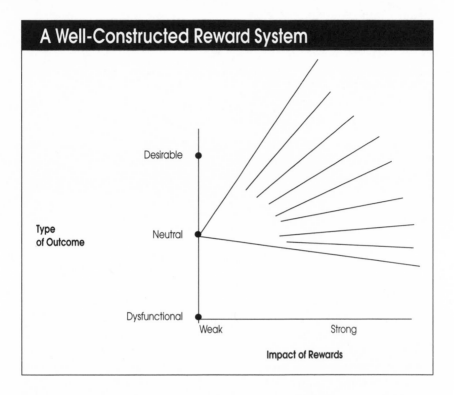

authors in the text speak to this point, referencing in particular such potentially damaging consequences as discouragement of teamwork, suppression of candor, and instigation of highly political behavior.

That this can occur is undeniable, but is it really true that these results are inevitable? In this respect, both George P. Baker III ("Rethinking Rewards") and Jerry McAdams ("Rethinking Rewards") make the critical point that by focusing on objectives rather than tasks, and on results instead of behaviors, employees will feel much less controlled, and dysfunctional consequences are far less likely to result.

If it's not possible to measure and reward results (as when results cannot be known for a long time and behavioral milestones must be established), dysfunctional consequences can still be minimized by devising rewards and punishments that are consistent with what is desired. Another old comedic routine has a patient complaining to his physician, "Doctor, Doctor, it hurts when I do that," whereupon the Doctor replies, logically enough, "Don't do that." In this vein, both

*Figure 3.*

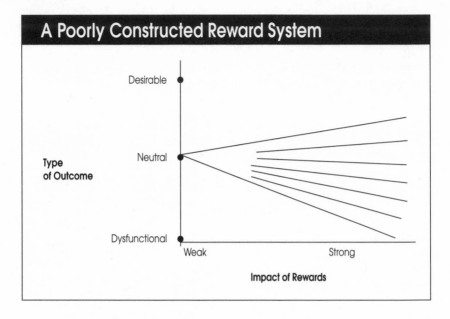

McAdams and Baker point out that rewards can be created that promote rather than discourage teamwork, and Ronald A. Heifetz and Donald L. Laurie ("The Work of Leadership") offer an excellent example of how this can happen. Similarly, both Baker and Eileen Appelbaum ("Rethinking Rewards") note that it is possible to build systems that reward people for expressing unpopular ideas, while punishing those who withhold information or engage in political behavior.

### WHAT SHOULD WE DO INSTEAD?

Probably the weakest part of the arguments against prevailing organizational reward systems is the virtual absence of alternatives by those who are most critical. Take a careful look at Harry Levinson's suggestions, for example, and see also Alfie Kohn's recommendation that, in preference to current practices, we should "pay people well and fairly, then do everything possible to help them forget about money." Does "pay well" mean paying more than competitors to people who do the same work? And if pay is not matched with performance, what on earth does "fairly" mean? As Michael Beer points out, we can't just pay everybody the same.

Kohn claims to have no preference among such criteria as need, seniority, market value, or even job responsibilities. Only pay for performance is bad. So if someone is assigned a more important job it's apparently okay to pay them more, but it's not okay to ascertain that they're actually *doing* the job they've been assigned.

## BOOK STRUCTURE

The book is divided into three parts. Part one includes five chapters that deal with individual needs and organizational rewards, and raise many of the ideas and controversies set forth in this introduction. Part two includes four chapters that portray the same issues on a broader canvas, dealing in particular with intrinsic motivation as it relates to and is derived from more participative leadership styles and more boundaryless organizational structures.

Part three includes three executive interviews—two from the world of business and one from professional sports—that raise the same issues, but explore them through the eyes of the leader-practitioner.

Finally, the last chapter in part three concludes the discussion by putting things into a situational perspective, reminding us that many of these issues have no inherent right or wrong answer, but rather depend greatly upon the "goodness of fit" between particular reward practices and the values and objectives of different organizations.

I hope you enjoy the book.

# PART

# I

# 1
# Asinine Attitudes Toward Motivation

**Harry Levinson**

In spite of the corporate efforts to promote smooth management-employee relations, events like these continue to happen:

- The top management of a large manufacturing company discovers that some of its line employees have embezzled a five-figure sum while their supervisors stood by unperturbed. The executives are dumbfounded. They had thought that the supervisors were loyal, and that they themselves were thoughtful and kindly.

- An airline purchases a fleet of hydraulic lift trucks for placing food aboard aircraft at a large New York terminal. Although these trucks cost hundreds of thousands of dollars, they sit disabled on the airport apron. Maintenance employees and technicians occasionally glance at them contemptuously as they go about their work in sullen anger. Management is dismayed that these employees seem unresponsive to its cost-reduction efforts.

- Large companies, seeking new products, acquire smaller companies. Almost invariably, the successful managements of the acquired companies are soon gone and no new products are forthcoming. The larger organizations only increase their size and managerial burdens, and the hoped-for advantages evaporate. While this happens repeatedly, executives do not seem to learn from such failures.

When these events are looked at psychologically, their underlying causes become evident.

In the *first case*, the manufacturer renegotiated its labor contract every two years. Obviously, the appropriate person to do so was the vice president in charge of labor relations. But the people who carried out the contract and knew the employees best were the first-level supervisors; no one asked them what should be in the contract and what problems they had in implementing it. By its actions, management communicated to the supervisors that they did not matter much.

Furthermore, the union let grievances pile up just before the contract came up for renewal every two years, knowing full well that, to get a contract, management would settle the grievances in the union's favor. But the supervisors were the ones who bore the brunt of the grievances, since they carried out the terms of the contract. When management gave in, the supervisors felt that they had been undercut. In effect, these people were being told that they were stupid, that they had nothing useful to contribute to policy making, and that their job was to do as they were told. So they stood by during the stealing—if management did not care about them, why should they care about management?

In the *second case*, the issue for the airlines was much the same. A purchasing officer had bought the trucks, complete with sophisticated electronic controls. What was more natural than the purchasing officer doing the buying and getting the best? But he failed to check with the mechanics and technicians who kept the trucks operating. After all, what did they know about buying, and who asks technicians anyway?

Had he asked them, he would have learned that sophisticated electronic controls were fine for Los Angeles and Phoenix, where the weather was dry and mild, but that they failed repeatedly in New York, where the trucks were exposed to variable and sometimes harsh weather. No matter how hard the technicians worked, they could not keep the trucks functioning. Like the supervisors in the previous example, they felt that they were being exploited and contemptuously treated. Ultimately, they gave up trying to keep the trucks going. Seeing how much money the company had wasted on the trucks, they had little incentive to economize in their own small ways.

In the *third case*, what happens most frequently in merger failures is that the parent (note the use of that word) company promises the newly acquired company that there will be no changes. But changes are soon forthcoming, and the first of these is likely to be in the area of accounting control systems. Obviously, controls are necessary, and, just as obviously, many small companies do not have sophisticated controls. But they tend to be flexibly innovative for that specific reason. When controls become the central thrust of management, creative people who need flexibility leave, and the parent company is left with a corporate shell. The communication to the acquired company is that it is stupid and unsophisticated and therefore the parent must control it more rigidly.

Each of the foregoing problems would be dismissed in most organizations simply as a "failure in communications." Many psychologists would advocate dealing with such difficulties by participative management. Yet beneath that glib "explanation," and unresponsive to that ready "remedy," lies a fundamental unconscious management attitude that is responsible for most contemporary management-labor problems and for what is now being called a "crisis in motivation." I call this attitude the great jackass fallacy.

Later in this article, I shall describe the fallacy in detail and offer some suggestions for correcting it. But first let us explore in more depth the motivational crisis that it has precipitated.

## Motivational Miasma

The crisis takes many forms, and its effects are easy to spot. Here are just a few examples:

- Companies are repeatedly reorganized on the advice of management consultants, but to little avail in the long run.
- New managerial devices, such as the four-day workweek and putting hourly people on salary, are loudly touted for their effect on employee motivation and morale, but the old problems soon reappear.
- Efforts to enrich jobs by giving employees more responsibility show encouraging results, but these disappear when employees seek to influence company policy and then are turned down by management.
- Business and nonprofit organizations alike are burdened by job encumbrances that result from union-management compromises.
- Increasing numbers of middle managers, engineers, teachers, and hospital personnel turn toward unionization.
- Many people in managerial ranks resign in favor of new jobs that pay less but offer greater individual freedom and initiative.

Most executives with whom I come in contact cannot understand why people do not respond to their efforts to sustain effective organizations, why people seemingly do not want to work, and why people want to leave apparently good organizations. Executives faced with these problems are often confused, angry, and hostile to their own people. The terms of office of chief executives, particularly those in educational and governmental administration, become shorter as the managerial frustrations increase.

The crisis in motivation has long been evident to students of organization, and they have offered problem-plagued executives a wide range of theories to cope with it. Suffice it to say that, by this time, thousands of executives are familiar with these theories. Many have taken part in managerial grid training, group dynamics laboratories, seminars on the psychology of management, and a wide range of other forms of training. Some have run the full gamut of training experiences; others have embraced a variety of panaceas offered by quacks.

**DISAPPOINTING REMEDIES**

The results of the aforementioned theories have not been impressive. While some companies have put them into practice with a degree of success, most have either given up their efforts as too simplistic for the complexity of organizational phenomena or have simply failed in their attempts.

There are, of course, many reasons why the remedies have failed. For one thing, executives often feel unqualified to apply the concepts. And in that feeling they are frequently right. Managers who have had little or no previous exposure to the behavioral sciences, let alone any formal training in this area, can get only the barest introductory knowledge in a brief training program. An executive would not expect a person to be able to design a complex building after a week-long training program in architecture; yet both the executive and the people who train him often expect that he will be a different person after he attends a one-week sensitivity-training laboratory.

Furthermore, it is one thing to learn to become more aware of one's own feelings; it is quite another to do something different about managing them, let alone about managing those forces that affect the feelings of other people. If everyone who had experienced psychotherapy were by that fact an expert therapist, there would be no shortage of such healers. Experience is not enough; training in a conceptual framework and supervised skill practice is also required. Many executives who have expected more of themselves and of such training have therefore been disillusioned, despite the benefits that have often resulted from even such brief experiences.

Would longer training help? Not much. Unlike marketing executives who implement marketing programs, and experts who install financial control systems, behavioral scientists (with the exception of certain kinds of psychotherapists) are not themselves expert in *doing*. While many know about the theories, and some of them practice what is called organizational development, they do not themselves change organizations. Instead they usually help people to think through alternative action possibilities and overcome communications blocks to working out their own solutions. Since most behavioral scientists are not skilled in changing organizations, then, they are not in a position to teach executives how to change them.

**POWER & FEAR:** Another reason why solutions to motivation problems do not work is that many executives are fearful of losing control of their organizations. The new theories have confronted executives with the need to distribute power in their organizations, which in turn raises questions about their authority and right to manage.

A recent study of 400 top executives in Europe indicates that they feel menaced by these new theories.[1] Most see themselves in the middle of an unsettling transition in management styles. They report that they can no longer use the authority of position; instead, they must gain their position by competition with subordinates and defend that position each step of the way. Of those interviewed, 61% spontaneously indicated that their primary problem is personnel management. Almost all of these executives have leadership problems.

Many businessmen are threatened when they must stimulate people to participate in making organizational decisions and invite people to express themselves more freely. When an executive's whole life thrust has been to obtain a position of power and control, he finds it particularly threatening to witness his power eroding as older methods of control and motivation become less effective.

Coupled with the fear of losing control is the fact that a disproportionate number of executives are characteristically insensitive to feelings. Some people, for example, pursue executive careers to obtain power over others as a way of compensating for real or fancied personal inadequacies, or as a reaction to an unconscious sense of helplessness. They are neurotically driven, and their single-minded, perpetual pursuit of control blinds them to their own subtle feelings and those of others.

Furthermore, many executives have engineering, scientific, legal, or financial backgrounds. Each of these fields places a heavy emphasis on cognitive rationality and measurable or verifiable facts. People who enter them usually are trained from childhood to suppress their feelings, to maintain a competitive, aggressive, nonemotional front. They are taught to be highly logical, and they seek to impose that kind of rationality on organizations.

As a result, they simply do not understand the power of people's feelings, and all too often they are incapable of sensing such feelings in everyday practice without considerable help. They are like tone-deaf people who, attending an opera, can understand the lyrics but cannot hear the music. Such executives are typified by a company president who was a participant in a seminar on psychological aspects of management. Halfway through the first lecture, he broke in to say, "You have already told me more about this subject than I want to know." Although he stayed to the end of the program, he simply could not grasp what was being taught.

All of these reasons, coupled with the inadequacies of contemporary motivational theory itself, explain much of the gap between theory and practice. In time, with new knowledge and better training experiences, most of the gap may be overcome. But the fact remains that much more effort could be applied now. This brings us to that unconscious assumption about motivation to which I referred earlier, one held particularly by executives in all types of organizations and reinforced by organizational theories and structures.

## Fact & Fallacy

Frequently, I have asked executives this question: What is the dominant philosophy of motivation in American management? Almost invariably, they quickly agree that it is the carrot-and-stick philosophy, reward and punishment. Then I ask them to close their eyes for a moment, and to form a picture in their mind's eye with a carrot at one end and a stick at the other. When they have done so, I then ask them to describe the central image in that picture. Most frequently they respond that the central figure is a jackass.

If the first image that comes to mind when one thinks "carrot-and-stick" is a jackass, then obviously the unconscious assumption behind the reward-punishment model is that one is dealing with jackasses who must be manipulated and controlled. Thus, unconsciously, the boss is the manipulator and controller, and the subordinate is the jackass.

The characteristics of a jackass are stubbornness, stupidity, willfulness, and unwillingness to go where someone is driving him. These, by interesting coincidence, are also the characteristics of the unmotivated employee. Thus it becomes vividly clear that the underlying assumption which managers make about motivation leads to a self-fulfilling prophecy. People inevitably respond to the carrot-and-stick by trying to get more of the carrot while protecting themselves against the stick. This predictable phenomenon has led to the formation of unions, the frequent sabotage of management's motivation efforts, and the characteristic employee suspicion of management's motivational (manipulative) techniques.

Employees obviously sense the carrot-and-stick conception behind management's attitudes and just as obviously respond with appropriate self-defending measures to the communications built around those attitudes. Of course, there is much talk about the need to improve communication in organizations. All too often, however, the problem is not that communication is inadequate but, rather, that it is already too explicit in the wrong way. When employees sense that they are being viewed as jackasses, they will automatically see management's messages as manipulative, and they will resist them, no matter how clear the type or how pretty the pictures.

### PERPETUAL POWER GAP

Since the turn of the century, numerous different philosophies of management have appeared, each emphasizing a different dimension of the management task and each advocating a new set of techniques. Although these philosophies differ from each other in many respects, all are based on reward-punishment psychology. For example, most of the contemporary psychological conceptions of motivation take a reward-punishment psychology for granted; they advocate trust and openness among employees and managers, but at the same time they acknowledge that the more powerful have a natural right to manipulate the less powerful.

As long as anyone in a leadership role operates with such a reward-punishment attitude toward motivation, he is implicitly assuming that he has (or should have) control over others and that they are in a jackass position with respect to him. This attitude is inevitably one of condescending contempt whose most blatant mask is paternalism. The result is a continuing battle between those who seek to wield power and those who are subject to it. The consequences of this battle are increased inefficiency, lowered productivity, heightened absenteeism, theft, and sometimes outright sabotage.

## BUREAUCRATIC BADLANDS

The problems resulting from the jackass fallacy are compounded further by bureaucratic organizational structures. Such structures are based on a military model that assumes complete control of the organization by those at the top. In pure form, it is a rigid hierarchy, complete with detailed job descriptions and fixed, measurable objectives.

The bureaucratic structure requires everyone at every level to be dependent on those at higher levels. Hiring, firing, promotion, demotion, reassignment, and similar actions are the prerogatives of superiors who can make decisions unilaterally. In short, one's fate is decided by a distant "they" who are beyond his influence and control.

Under such circumstances, the subordinate person becomes increasingly defensive. He must protect himself against being manipulated and against the feeling of helplessness that inevitably accompanies dependency. Rank-and-file employees have long done so by unionization; managerial and professional employees are beginning to follow suit, and this trend will continue to grow.

While the bureaucratic structure, with its heavy emphasis on internal competition for power and position, is often touted as a device for achievement, it is actually a system for defeat. Fewer people move up the pyramidal hierarchy at each step. This leaves a residual group of failures, often euphemistically called "career people," who thereafter are passed over for future promotions because they have not succeeded in the competition for managerial positions.

Most of these people feel resentful and defeated. Often they have been manipulated or judged arbitrarily. They are no longer motivated by competitive spirit, because the carrots and the sticks mean less. There is little need, in their eyes, to learn more; they simply do as they are told. They usually stay until retirement unless they are among the "deadwood" that is cleaned out when a new management takes over.

Executives new to a company or a higher-level job like to think of themselves as being effective in cleaning out such deadwood or trimming the excess managerial fat. Some take to that task with great vigor. Unfortunately, the consequences are more negative than enthusiastic executives like to recognize. In one large company, for example, management hoped that the 40-year-olds would respond with unbridled enthusiasm when the 50-year-olds were cleaned out. But the younger men failed to respond, because they saw that what was happening to the older men would be their likely fate ten years hence.

Bureaucratic structure, with its implicit power-struggle orientation, increases infighting, empire building, rivalry, and a sense of futility. It tends to magnify latent feelings that the organization is a hostile environment which people can do little to change, and it bolsters the jackass fallacy. Little wonder that many young people do not want to get caught up in such situations! Since 90% of those who work do so in organizations, most young people, too, must do so. But they would rather be in organizations that provide them an opportunity to demonstrate their competence and proficiency than in organizations that test their ability to run a managerial maze successfully.

## A FORMIDABLE CHALLENGE

The great jackass fallacy and the bureaucratic organization structure present major obstacles to organizational survival. They are essentially self-defeating if what an executive wants from employees is spontaneity, dedication, commitment, affiliation, and adaptive innovation.

As I have already indicated, many executives try to cope with the pathology of the system by introducing such new techniques as group dynamics and job enrichment. These are simply patches on the body politic of an organization. There is no way to integrate them effectively. When people are asked to express their feelings more freely and to take on greater responsibility, they soon come into conflict with power centers and power figures in a system geared to the acquisition of power. The latter soon cry, "Business is not a democracy," and disillusionment sets in once again, both on the part of managers who tried the new techniques and on the part of subordinates who were subjected to them.

Unless the fundamental assumptions of management (and behavioral scientists) about motivation are changed, and unless the organizational structure is altered to match these changed assumptions, the underlying jackass fallacy will remain visible to those who are subjected to it. Despite whatever practices the organization implements, people will avoid, evade, escape, deny, and reject both the jackass fallacy and the military-style hierarchy.

If the executive grasps the import of what I am saying, shudders uncomfortably, and wants to do something about the problem, what are his alternatives? Is he forever doomed to play with psychological gimmicks? Is he himself so much a victim of his assumptions that he cannot change them? I do not think that he necessarily is. There are constructive actions that he can take.

## The First Steps

Anyone who supervises someone else should look carefully at the assumptions he is making about motivation. He must assess the degree to which carrot-and-stick assumptions influence his own attitudes. For example, an executive might argue that if he tried to be nice to people, the stick would be softened. But even then he would merely be exhibiting paternalistic kindness. As long as his assumptions about people remain unchanged, his "being nice" is only a disguised form of carrot-and-stick which seeks to increase loyalty by creating guilt in those who are the recipients of his managerial largesse. His first priority should be to change his way of thinking about people.

After honestly and frankly facing up to one's own assumptions about what makes people tick, the next step is to look at one's organizational structure. Most organizations are constructed to fit a hierarchical model. People assume that the hierarchical organizational structure is to organizations as the spine is to human beings, that it is both a necessity and a given. As a matter of fact, it is neither a necessity nor a given.

I am arguing not against the distribution of power and control, but, rather, that this distribution need not take one particular form. Every executive should ask himself: "Is my operation organized to achieve a hierarchical structure or is it structured to accomplish the task it must do?" If it is organized more to fit the model than to fit the task, he should begin exploring more appropriate organization models.[2] To do otherwise is to invite trouble—if it has not already started.

## Conclusion

It is time for business leaders to enter a phase of more serious thinking about leadership and organizational concepts. They must do so on behalf of their own organizations as well as on behalf of society. The issue I have been discussing is critically important for society as a whole, because society increasingly is made up of organizations. The less effectively organizations carry out the work of society, the greater the cost in money and in social paralysis. The latter leads to the kind of demoralization already evident in organizations as well as in problems of transportation, health care delivery, education, and welfare.

Furthermore, we are in the midst of a worldwide social revolution, the central thrust of which is the demand of all people to have a voice in their own fate. Business leaders, many of whom have international interests and see the multiple facets of this thrust in a wide range of countries, should be in the forefront of understanding and guiding these social changes into productive channels. By applying new principles of motivation to their own organizations, they are in a position not only to sustain the vitality of those organizations but, more important, to keep them adaptive to changing circumstances.

In addition, the progressive changes that executives institute in their own organizations can then become the models for other institutional forms in a given culture. Not the least of the advantages of being on the frontier is that executives and corporations avoid the onus of being continuously compelled by angry or apathetic employees to change in ways which may be destructive to both the business and the people involved.

But leading is more than a matter of pronouncing clichés. Leading involves an understanding of motivation. It is to this understanding that business leaders must now dedicate themselves. And the way to start is by countering the great jackass fallacy in their own organizations.

## Notes

1. Frederick Harmon, "European Top Managers Struggle for Survival," *European Business,* Winter 1971, p. 14.
2. Paul R. Lawrence and Jay W. Lorsch, *Organization and Environment: Managing Differentiation and Integration* (Boston, Division of Research, Harvard Business School, 1967).

# 2
# Why Incentive Plans Cannot Work

## Alfie Kohn

It is difficult to overstate the extent to which most managers and
the people who advise them believe in the redemptive power of rewards. Certainly, the vast majority of U.S. corporations use some sort
of program intended to motivate employees by tying compensation to
one index of performance or another. But more striking is the rarely
examined belief that people will do a better job if they have been
promised some sort of incentive. This assumption and the practices
associated with it are pervasive, but a growing collection of evidence
supports an opposing view. According to numerous studies in laboratories, workplaces, classrooms, and other settings, rewards typically
undermine the very processes they are intended to enhance. The
findings suggest that the failure of any given incentive program is due
less to a glitch in that program than to the inadequacy of the psychological assumptions that ground all such plans.

## Temporary Compliance

Behaviorist theory, derived from work with laboratory animals, is
indirectly responsible for such programs as piece-work pay for factory
workers, stock options for top executives, special privileges accorded
to Employees of the Month, and commissions for salespeople. Indeed,
the livelihood of innumerable consultants has long been based on
devising fresh formulas for computing bonuses to wave in front of
employees. Money, vacations, banquets, plaques—the list of variations
on a single, simple behaviorist model of motivation is limitless. And

today even many people who are regarded as forward thinking—those who promote teamwork, participative management, continuous improvement, and the like—urge the use of rewards to institute and maintain these very reforms. What we use bribes to accomplish may have changed, but the reliance on bribes, on behaviorist doctrine, has not.

Moreover, the few articles that appear to criticize incentive plans are invariably limited to details of implementation. Only fine-tune the calculations and delivery of the incentive—or perhaps hire the author as a consultant—and the problem will be solved, we are told. As Herbert H. Meyer, professor emeritus in the psychology department at the College of Social and Behavioral Sciences at the University of South Florida, has written, "Anyone reading the literature on this subject published 20 years ago would find that the articles look almost identical to those published today." That assessment, which could have been written this morning, was actually offered in 1975. In nearly forty years, the thinking hasn't changed.

Do rewards work? The answer depends on what we mean by "work." Research suggests that, by and large, rewards succeed at securing one thing only: temporary compliance. When it comes to producing lasting change in attitudes and behavior, however, rewards, like punishment, are strikingly ineffective. Once the rewards run out, people revert to their old behaviors. Studies show that offering incentives for losing weight, quitting smoking, using seat belts, or (in the case of children) acting generously is not only less effective than other strategies but often proves worse than doing nothing at all. Incentives, a version of what psychologists call extrinsic motivators, do not alter the attitudes that underlie our behaviors. They do not create an enduring *commitment* to any value or action. Rather, incentives merely—and temporarily—change what we do.

As for productivity, at least two dozen studies over the last three decades have conclusively shown that people who expect to receive a reward for completing a task or for doing that task successfully simply do not perform as well as those who expect no reward at all. These studies examined rewards for children and adults, males and females, and included tasks ranging from memorizing facts to creative problem-solving to designing collages. In general, the more cognitive sophistication and open-ended thinking that was required, the worse people performed when working for a reward. Interestingly enough, the researchers themselves were often taken by surprise. They assumed that rewards would produce better work but discovered otherwise.

The question for managers is whether incentive plans can work when extrinsic motivators more generally do not. Unfortunately, as author G. Douglas Jenkins, Jr., has noted, most organizational studies to date—like the articles published—have tended "to focus on the effects of *variations* in incentive conditions, and not on whether performance-based pay per se raises performance levels."

A number of studies, however, have examined whether or not pay, especially at the executive level, is related to corporate profitability and other measures of organizational performance. Often they have found slight or even *negative* correlations between pay and performance. Typically, the absence of such a relationship is interpreted as evidence of links between compensation and something other than how well people do their jobs. But most of these data could support a different conclusion, one that reverses the causal arrow. Perhaps what these studies reveal is that higher pay does not produce better performance. In other words, the very idea of trying to reward quality may be a fool's errand.

Consider the findings of Jude T. Rich and John A. Larson, formerly of McKinsey & Company. In 1982, using interviews and proxy statements, they examined compensation programs at 90 major U.S. companies to determine whether return to shareholders was better for corporations that had incentive plans for top executives than it was for those companies that had no such plans. They were unable to find any difference.

Four years later, Jenkins tracked down 28 previously published studies that measured the impact of financial incentives on performance. (Some were conducted in the laboratory and some in the field.) His analysis, "Financial Incentives," published in 1986, revealed that 16, or 57%, of the studies found a positive effect on performance. However, all of the performance measures were quantitative in nature: a good job consisted of producing more of something or doing it faster. Only five of the studies looked at the quality of performance. And none of those five showed any benefits from incentives.

Another analysis took advantage of an unusual situation that affected a group of welders at a Midwestern manufacturing company. At the request of the union, an incentive system that had been in effect for some years was abruptly eliminated. Now, if a financial incentive supplies motivation, its absence should drive down production. And that is exactly what happened, at first. Fortunately, Harold F. Rothe, former personnel manager and corporate staff assistant at the Beloit Corporation, tracked production over a period of months, providing the sort of long-term data rarely collected in this field. After the initial slump, Rothe found that in the absence of incentives the welders' production quickly began to rise and eventually reached a level as high or higher than it had been before.

One of the largest reviews of how intervention programs affect worker productivity, a meta-analysis of some 330 comparisons from 98 studies, was conducted in the mid-1980s by Richard A. Guzzo, associate professor of psychology at the University of Maryland, College Park, and his colleagues at New York University. The raw numbers seemed to suggest a positive relationship between financial incentives and productivity, but because of the huge variations from one study to another, statistical tests indicated that there was no significant effect overall. What's more, financial incentives were virtually unrelated to the number of workers who were absent or who quit their jobs over a period of time. By contrast, training and goal-setting programs had a far greater impact on productivity than did pay-for-performance plans.

## Why Rewards Fail

Why do most executives continue to rely on incentive programs? Perhaps it's because few people take the time to examine the connection between incentive programs and problems with workplace productivity and morale. Rewards buy temporary compliance, so it looks like the problems are solved. It's harder to spot the harm they cause over the long term. Moreover, it does not occur to most of us to suspect rewards, given that our own teachers, parents, and managers probably used them. "Do this and you'll get that" is part of the fabric of American life. Finally, by clinging to the belief that motivational problems are due to the particular incentive system in effect at the moment, rather than to the psychological theory behind all incentives, we can remain optimistic that a relatively minor adjustment will repair the damage.

Over the long haul, however, the potential cost to any organization of trying to fine-tune reward-driven compensation systems may be considerable. The fundamental flaws of behaviorism itself doom the prospects of affecting long-term behavior change or performance improvement through the use of rewards. Consider the following six-point framework that examines the true costs of an incentive program.

**1. "Pay is not a motivator."** W. Edwards Deming's declaration may seem surprising, even absurd. Of course, money buys the things people want and need. Moreover, the less people are paid, the more concerned they are likely to be about financial matters. Indeed, several studies over the last few decades have found that when people are asked to guess what matters to their coworkers—or, in the case of managers, to their subordinates—they assume money heads the list. But put the question directly—"What do you care about?"—and pay typically ranks only fifth or sixth.

Even if people were principally concerned with their salaries, this does not prove that money is motivating. There is no firm basis for the assumption that paying people more will encourage them to do better work or even, in the long run, more work. As Frederick Herzberg, Distinguished Professor of Management at the University of Utah's Graduate School of Management, has argued, just because too little money can irritate and demotivate does not mean that more and more money will bring about increased satisfaction, much less increased motivation. It is plausible to assume that if someone's take-home pay was cut in half, his or her morale would suffer enough to undermine performance. But it doesn't necessarily follow that doubling that person's pay would result in better work.

**2. Rewards punish.** Many managers understand that coercion and fear destroy motivation and create defiance, defensiveness, and rage. They realize that punitive management is a contradiction in terms. As Herzberg wrote in HBR some 25 years ago ("One More Time: How Do You Motivate Employees?" January–February 1968), a "KITA"—which, he coyly explains, stands for "kick in the pants"—may produce movement but never motivation.

What most executives fail to recognize is that Herzberg's observation is equally true of rewards. Punishment and rewards are two sides of the same coin. Rewards have a punitive effect because they, like outright punishment, are manipulative. "Do this and you'll get that" is not really very different from "Do this or here's what will happen to you." In the case of incentives, the reward itself may be highly desired; but by making that bonus contingent on certain behaviors, managers manipulate their subordinates, and that experience of being controlled is likely to assume a punitive quality over time.

Further, not receiving a reward one had expected to receive is also indistinguishable from being punished. Whether the incentive is withheld or withdrawn deliberately, or simply not received by someone who had hoped to get it, the effect is identical. And the more desirable the reward, the more demoralizing it is to miss out.

The new school, which exhorts us to catch people doing something right and reward them for it, is not very different from the old school, which advised us to catch people doing something wrong and threaten to punish them if they ever do it again. What is essentially taking place in both approaches is that a lot of people are getting caught. Managers are creating a workplace in which people feel controlled, not an environment conducive to exploration, learning, and progress.

**3. Rewards rupture relationships.** Relationships among employees are often casualties of the scramble for rewards. As leaders of the Total Quality Management movement have emphasized, incentive programs, and the performance appraisal systems that accompany them, reduce the possibilities for cooperation. Peter R. Scholtes, senior management consultant at Joiner Associates Inc., put it starkly, "Everyone is pressuring the system for individual gain. No one is improving the system for collective gain. The system will inevitably crash." Without teamwork, in other words, there can be no quality.

The surest way to destroy cooperation and, therefore, organizational excellence, is to force people to compete for rewards or recognition or to rank them against each other. For each person who wins, there are many others who carry with them the feeling of having lost. And the more these awards are publicized through the use of memos, newsletters, and awards banquets, the more detrimental their impact can be. Furthermore, when employees compete for a limited number of incentives, they will most likely begin to see each other as obstacles to their own success. But the same result can occur with any use of rewards; introducing competition just makes a bad thing worse.

Relationships between supervisors and subordinates can also collapse under the weight of incentives. Of course, the supervisor who punishes is about as welcome to employees as a glimpse of a police car in their rearview mirrors. But even the supervisor who rewards can produce some damaging reactions. For instance, employees may be tempted to conceal any problems they might be having and present themselves as infinitely competent to the manager in control of the money. Rather than ask for help—a prerequisite for optimal performance—they might opt instead for flattery, attempting to convince the manager that they have everything under control. Very few things threaten an organization as much as a hoard of incentive-driven individuals trying to curry favor with the incentive dispenser.

**4. Rewards ignore reasons.** In order to solve problems in the workplace, managers must understand what caused them. Are employees inadequately prepared for the demands of their jobs? Is long-term growth being sacrificed to maximize short-term return? Are workers unable to collaborate effectively? Is the organization so rigidly hierarchical that employees are intimidated about making recommendations and feel powerless and burned out? Each of these situations calls for a different response. But relying on incentives to boost productivity does nothing to address possible underlying problems and bring about meaningful change.

Moreover, managers often use incentive systems as a substitute for giving workers what they need to do a good job. Treating workers well—providing useful feedback, social support, and the room for self-determination—is the essence of good management. On the other hand, dangling a bonus in front of employees and waiting for the results requires much less effort. Indeed, some evidence suggests that productive managerial strategies are less likely to be used in organizations that lean on pay-for-performance plans. In his study of welders' performance, Rothe noted that supervisors tended to "demonstrate relatively less leadership" when incentives were in place. Likewise, author Carla O'Dell reports in *People, Performance, and Pay* that a survey of 1,600 organizations by the American Productivity Center discovered little in the way of active employee involvement in organizations that used small-group incentive plans. As Jone L. Pearce, associate professor at the Graduate School of Management, University of California at Irvine, wrote in "Why Merit Pay Doesn't Work: Implications from Organization Theory," pay for performance actually "impedes the ability of managers to manage."

**5. Rewards discourage risk-taking.** "People will do precisely what they are asked to do if the reward is significant," enthused Monroe J. Haegele, a proponent of pay-for-performance programs, in "The New Performance Measures." And here is the root of the problem. Whenever people are encouraged to think about what they will get for engaging in a task, they become less inclined to take risks or explore possibilities, to play hunches or to consider incidental stimuli. In a word, the number one casualty of rewards is creativity.

Excellence pulls in one direction; rewards pull in another. Tell people that their income will depend on their productivity or performance rating, and they will focus on the numbers. Sometimes they will manipulate the schedule for completing tasks or even engage in patently unethical and illegal behavior. As Thane S. Pittman, professor and chair of the psychology department at Gettysburg College, and his colleagues point out, when we are motivated by incentives, "features such as predictability and simplicity are desirable, since the primary focus associated with this orientation is to get through the task expediently in order to reach the desired goal." The late Cornell University professor, John Condry, was more succinct: rewards, he said, are the "enemies of exploration."

Consider the findings of organizational psychologist Edwin A. Locke. When Locke paid subjects on a piece-rate basis for their work, he noticed that they tended to choose easier tasks as the payment for success increased. A number of other studies have also found that people working for a reward generally try to minimize challenge. It isn't that human beings are naturally lazy or that it is unwise to give employees a voice in determining the standards to be used. Rather, people tend to lower their sights when they are encouraged to think about what they are going to get for their efforts. "Do this and you'll get that," in other words, focuses attention on the "that" instead of the "this." Emphasizing large bonuses is the last strategy we should use if we care about innovation. Do rewards motivate people? Absolutely. They motivate people to get rewards.

**6. Rewards undermine interest.** If our goal is excellence, no artificial incentive can ever match the power of intrinsic motivation. People who do exceptional work may be glad to be paid and even more glad to be well paid, but they do not work to collect a paycheck. They work because they love what they do.

Few will be shocked by the news that extrinsic motivators are a poor substitute for genuine interest in one's job. What is far more surprising is that rewards, like punishment, may actually undermine the intrinsic motivation that results in optimal performance. The more a manager stresses what an employee can earn for good work, the less interested that employee will be in the work itself.

The first studies to establish the effect of rewards on intrinsic motivation were conducted in the early 1970s by Edward Deci, professor and chairman of the psychology department at the University of Rochester. By now, scores of experiments across the country have replicated the finding. As Deci and his colleague Richard Ryan, senior vice president of investment and training manager at Robert W. Baird and Co., Inc., wrote in their 1985 book, *Intrinsic Motivation and Self-Determination in Human Behavior,* "the research has consistently shown that any contingent payment system tends to undermine intrinsic motivation." The basic effect is the same for a variety of rewards and tasks, although extrinsic motivators are particularly destructive when tied to interesting or complicated tasks.

Deci and Ryan argue that receiving a reward for a particular behavior sends a certain message about what we have done and controls, or attempts to control, our future behavior. The more we experience being controlled, the more we will tend to lose interest in what we are doing. If we go to work thinking about the possibility of getting a bonus, we come to feel that our work is not self-directed. Rather, it is the reward that drives our behavior.

Other theorists favor a more simple explanation for the negative effect rewards have on intrinsic motivation: anything presented as a prerequisite for something else—that is, as a means toward another end—comes to be seen as less desirable. The recipient of the reward assumes, "If they have to bribe me to do it, it must be something I wouldn't want to do." In fact, a series of studies, published in 1992 by psychology professor Jonathan L. Freedman and his colleagues at the University of Toronto, confirmed that the larger the incentive we are offered, the more negatively we will view the activity for which the bonus was received. (The activities themselves don't seem to matter; in this study, they ranged from participating in a medical experiment to eating unfamiliar food.) Whatever the reason for the effect, however, any incentive or pay-for-performance system tends to make people less enthusiastic about their work and therefore less likely to approach it with a commitment to excellence.

## Dangerous Assumptions

Outside of psychology departments, few people distinguish between intrinsic and extrinsic motivation. Those who do assume that the two concepts can simply be added together for best effect. Motivation comes in two flavors, the logic goes, and both together must be better than either alone. But studies show that the real world works differently.

Some managers insist that the only problem with incentive programs is that they don't reward the right things. But these managers fail to understand the psychological factors involved and, consequently, the risks of sticking with the status quo.

Contrary to conventional wisdom, the use of rewards is not a response to the extrinsic orientation exhibited by many workers. Rather, incentives help create this focus on financial considerations. When an organization uses a Skinnerian management or compensation system, people are likely to become less interested in their work, requiring extrinsic incentives before expending effort. Then supervisors shake their heads and say, "You see? If you don't offer them a reward, they won't do anything." It is a classic self-fulfilling prophecy. Swarthmore College psychology professor Barry Schwartz has conceded that behavior theory may seem to provide us with a useful way of describing what goes on in U.S. workplaces. However, "It does this not because work is a natural exemplification of behavior theory principles but because behavior theory principles . . . had a significant hand in transforming work into an exemplification of behavior theory principles."

Managers who insist that the job won't get done right without rewards have failed to offer a convincing argument for behavioral manipulation. Promising a reward to someone who appears unmotivated is a bit like offering salt water to someone who is thirsty. Bribes in the workplace simply can't work.

# 3
# Rethinking Rewards

It is difficult to overstate the extent to which most managers—and the people who advise them—believe in the redemptive power of rewards, Alfie Kohn argues in "Why Incentive Plans Cannot Work" (September–October 1993). Certainly, the vast majority of U.S. corporations use some sort of program intended to motivate employees by tying compensation to one index of performance or another. But more striking is the rarely examined belief that people will do a better job if they have been promised some sort of incentive.

This assumption and the practices associated with it are pervasive, but a growing collection of evidence supports an opposing view. According to numerous studies in laboratories, workplaces, classrooms, and other settings, rewards typically undermine the very processes they are intended to enhance. In Kohn's view, the findings suggest that the failure of any given incentive program is due less to a glitch in that program than to the inadequacy of the psychological assumptions that ground all such plans.

Do rewards work? The answer depends on what we mean by "work." Research suggests that, by and large, rewards succeed at securing one thing only: temporary compliance. They do not create an enduring commitment to any value or action. They merely, and temporarily, change what we do. According to Kohn, incentives in the workplace simply can't work.

Nine experts consider the role of rewards in the workplace.

**G. Bennett Stewart III**
Senior Partner
Stern Stewart & Co.
New York, New York

A world without A's, praise, gold stars, or incentives? No thank you, Mr. Kohn. Communism was tried, and it didn't work.

The Soviet and Chinese economies collapsed because people were not allowed to share in the fruits of their individual efforts. With gains from personal initiative harvested as a public good, innovation ceased, and productivity froze. "They pretend to pay us, and we pretend to work" was the Russian worker's lament for the system Kohn now proposes. But for pay to mean anything, it must be linked to performance. Without that link, pay becomes nothing more than entitlement, a job nothing more than a sinecure.

Kohn is unhappy that rewarding some people necessitates penalizing others. Winston Churchill's apt aphorism is the best response. He said, "The virtue of communism is the equal sharing of its misery, and the vice of capitalism is the unequal sharing of its blessings." You can't have it both ways, Mr. Kohn. You simply can't have the equality of outcome you desire with the robust, dynamic economy we all want.

Contrary to the small-sample psychology tests Kohn cites, the responsiveness of ordinary citizens to incentives is demonstrated daily in our economy. Consumers cut consumption in reaction to the "penalty" of a price increase and raise purchases in reaction to the "bribe" of a lower price. The price system efficiently allocates scarce resources precisely because it rewards people who conserve and penalizes those who fail to respond. Can it be true, as Kohn seems to think, that people respond to monetary incentives when they *spend* their income but not when they *earn* it?

If Kohn makes a useful point, it is when he says that people won't want to be paid for doing specific tasks. But here is where we disagree: people should be rewarded for an overall job done well. To put the point in economic terms, the best incentive is having a piece of the action. Company stock, however, is not the best approach to instilling ownership, for it frequently leaves too loose a link between pay and performance.

The best approach often is to carve employees into a share of the profit contributed by their part of the company. Profit should be defined in relevant cash-flow terms after covering the cost of all capital employed, a measure that Stern Stewart & Co. calls Economic Value

Added. EVA provides employees with three clear incentives: to improve profitability, to grow profitability, and to withdraw resources from uneconomic activities. In addition, it ties their decisions and energies directly to the "net present value" of their enterprise. All key managers at Quaker Oats have been on an EVA sharing plan for several years, and Scott Paper Company introduced an EVA incentive program for all salaried employees at the beginning of 1993, to name but 2 of the 50 prominent companies that have adopted this approach.

**Eileen Appelbaum**
Associate Research Director
Economic Policy Institute
Washington, D.C.

Companies today are under intense pressure to improve efficiency and quality at a time when their resources are severely limited. Fiddling with compensation schemes appeals to many managers as a cheap way to improve their companies' performance by providing individuals with incentives to work harder. In fact, reliance on individual incentives to motivate workers and spur productivity has a long history in the United States. The U.S. human-resource model evolved in the 1950s partly in response to then-current theories of industrial psychology. By designing compensation schemes that recognize and reward individual differences, companies expected to reap the rewards of increased employee motivation and improved job performance. This idea continues to inform present managerial thinking. In his article "Why Incentive Plans Cannot Work," Alfie Kohn has performed an important service by marshaling the modern evidence on the psychological effects of incentives and by showing that rewards fail to improve, and may even reduce, performance.

We are still left, however, with questions about what improves a company's performance and what role compensation actually plays in that improvement. I would offer the following answers, based on an analysis of nearly 200 academic case studies and consultants' reports, carried out with Rosemary Batt—a doctoral candidate in labor relations and human-resource policy at MIT's Sloan School of Management—and published in *The New American Workplace: Transforming Work Systems in the United States*, published by ILR Press in 1994.

In the early part of the twentieth century, workplace innovations attempted to improve employee satisfaction and, at the same time, company performance. In contrast, the move to high-performance work systems since the mid-1980s is motivated by the need to improve quality and reduce costs simultaneously. In the mass-production model of work organization, whether the Taylorist or the U.S. HR version, improving quality raises costs—for inspection, supervision, rework, and waste. It was quite a shock to U.S. sensibilities, therefore, when Japanese auto manufacturers demonstrated that new ways of organizing work could deliver noticeably higher quality and customer satisfaction at significantly lower prices. It took nearly a decade for companies in the United States to realize that they would have to change.

Our review of the evidence indicates an acceleration of experimentation with innovative workplace practices and the emergence since the mid-1980s of two distinctly *American* high-performance models: a U.S. version of lean production that relies on employee involvement and a U.S. version of team production that relies on employee empowerment for performance gains. Productivity and performance improve the most when work is reorganized so that employees have the training, opportunity, and authority to participate effectively in decision making; when they have assurances that they will not be punished for expressing unpopular ideas; when they realize that they will not lose their jobs as a result of contributing their knowledge to improve productivity; and when they know that they will receive a fair share of any performance gains, assurances which unionized workers in high-performance companies enjoy.

Attempts to improve performance by manipulating compensation packages have proven counterproductive. However, reorganizing the work process to capitalize on employee skills and participation has improved performance, especially in combination with employment security, gainsharing, and incentives to take part in training. In this sense, then, compensation packages are an important component of the human-resource practices that are necessary to support high-performance work systems.

**Michael Beer**
Professor of Business Administration
Harvard Business School
Boston, Massachusetts

Kohn has mounted an eloquent argument, when it is considered in light of what we know about motivation and organizational effectiveness. But because certain practical considerations and cultural differences are not addressed, the argument is flawed.

Like Kohn, I have found that many managers in the United States and the United Kingdom—but not, incidentally, in continental Europe or Japan—have deeply held assumptions about the role of incentive pay in motivation. These assumptions lead them to engage compensation consultants in answering the wrong question: How should we design the incentive system in order to obtain the desired behavior? The more important question is: What role, if any, should incentive compensation play? Like Kohn, I have found that assumptions about incentive compensation have led many managers to expect incentives to solve organizational problems, when there are actually deeper underlying reasons for those problems.

Managers tend to use compensation as a crutch. After all, it is far easier to design an incentive system that will do management's work than it is to articulate a direction persuasively, develop agreement about goals and problems, and confront difficulties when they arise. The half-life of an incentive system is at best five years. When it stops paying off, employees turn against it. And the result is another dysfunctional by-product of incentive systems: precious attention, time, and money is expended on endless debates about and redesigns of the incentive system.

If incentive systems do not motivate, what should managers do about compensation? Surely, Kohn would not suggest that everyone should be paid the same. In some industries or functions—sales, for example—incentive compensation is the prevailing practice. In these areas, without paying for performance, an organization will lose its best people. Yet by paying for performance, the company runs the danger of encouraging self-interest instead of organizational commitment. This is a fundamental pay-for-performance dilemma that practicing managers confront and that Kohn neglects to address.

It is undoubtedly true that in today's competitive environment, interdependence between different business units and functions as well as the need for customer service and quality make incentive compensation less appropriate than it once was. But there are circumstances in which it is the only solution available: for example, managers of independent stores far from headquarters who don't have a motivating manager-subordinate relationship or salespeople whose performance is independent of other business units and who operate without supervision much of the time.

Managers who agree with Kohn should pay for performance but strive to use incentive systems as little as possible. Pay is an exercise in smoke and mirrors. Companies cannot stop paying for performance. However, they should avoid using incentives for all the reasons that Kohn suggests.

What can managers do? They should focus on paying people equitably, rather than using pay as an instrument of motivation. They should avoid coupling pay with yearly or quarterly performance, while promoting the top 10% or 15% of employees for outstanding long-term contributions. The poorest performers should be weeded out, while the rest should be praised for good performance and recognized through other means to promote self-esteem.

We are indebted to Kohn for ringing the alarm, but he does not provide managers with creative, practical solutions to the pay-for-performance dilemma.

**Andrew M. Lebby**
Senior Partner
The Performance Group
Washington, D.C.

The effect of rewards on motivation and performance is one of the most studied subjects in the management literature. Year after year we validate the finding that employees' perceptions of underpay result in decreased productivity, while increased pay doesn't result in increased productivity. Year after year we ask employees what motivates them, and year after year they reply: a sense of accomplishment in performing the work itself, recognition from peers and top management, career advancement, management support, and, only then, salary.

If Kohn is unable to find data that support anything but a negative relationship between financial incentives and performance, why is it that in the face of overwhelming evidence executives continue to hold onto ineffective methods? Why is it that they refuse to provide those things that employees say they want, that directly relate to increased productivity, and that have little or no financial cost?

When we stop to separate the physical nature of the reward itself from what the recipient finds rewarding, some possible answers appear. When we ask employees, "What was the last reward you received?" the most frequent response is some variant of "money." When we ask, "What did you find rewarding about money?" the most frequent response is that it was a tacit acknowledgment of the outstanding nature of their contribution. Just as it is easier for some parents to show love with gifts than with hugs, it is often easier for organizations and managers to show gratitude with money than with words.

Our current notions of pay follow naturally from our antiquated, Taylorist, mechanistic models for designing work. The work we do and how we do it have shifted significantly, but our reward and salary structures remain essentially the same. Senior managers will end financial incentives only when they rethink what work is and how it is performed. Organizations that have redesigned work to reflect cross-functional business processes or those that have implemented the actual *principles* of TQM have had to rethink pay and performance. Employees have said, "Give us the tools, the skills, the information, the support, and the respect we need." In different words, "Give us real capital, intellectual capital, and symbolic capital, and we'll increase your—and our—financial capital."

Money is an outcome of high performance. Satisfaction and respect are incentives to it.

**Teresa M. Amabile**
Professor of Psychology
Brandeis University
Waltham, Massachusetts

Kohn is absolutely right when he tells us that rewards can work against real commitment and creativity. But he doesn't tell the whole story. There are important differences between bribes and equitable compensation, and there are conditions under which rewards can *increase* involvement and creativity. What matters is what those rewards actually mean.

As Kohn points out, there is abundant evidence that interest and performance decline over the long run when people feel they are controlled by incentive systems or any other management system. What Kohn fails to point out is that people do not always feel controlled by rewards. In a recent study of professional artists, my students and I found, as Kohn would have predicted, that noncommissioned works were more creative than commissioned works. However, what mattered was not the obvious fact of contracting for reward, but the degree to which the artist felt constrained by the terms of the commission: the more constraints, the lower the creativity. In fact, some artists considered some of their commissions enabling, allowing them to create an interesting work of art that they wouldn't otherwise have had the means to do. When the reward presented the artist with new possibilities, in other words, creativity actually increased.

Intrinsic motivation—being motivated by challenge and enjoyment—is essential to creativity. But extrinsic motivation—being motivated by recognition and money—doesn't necessarily hurt. The most creative artists in our study tended to be motivated more by challenge, but they also tended to be motivated by recognition. Kohn accurately documents the evidence that rewards can undermine creativity. But he fails to mention the evidence that tangible rewards can actually enhance creativity under certain circumstances, most notably when the individual's primary focus is on the intrinsic reward of the work itself.

Bribes, as Kohn frequently notes, are bound to make people feel controlled, and he rightly points out their negative effect on people's work. But he implicitly includes salary in the same category as bribes when he argues that "pay is not a motivator." Certainly, there are some circumstances under which salary increases are perceived as bribes. A few years ago, for example, I interviewed an R&D scientist who was widely considered to be one of the three most important innovators in a large, successful company; he was also considered extremely eccentric. "They offered me a pretty large salary increase this year, but I refused it," he recounted. "Right now, my lab is my playground; I pretty much come in here and do things the way I want. But the more they pay you, the more they think they own you."

A much more common reaction, however, was the feeling expressed by other scientists that their salary increases recognized their creative contributions. Generous compensation, including company-wide profit sharing, need not be seen as a bribe, particularly when it is presented as the equitable outcome of creative competence.

Although Kohn's article is clear about what managers should avoid, it has little to say about alternatives to incentives. There is much that can be said about redesigning work and the work environment so that extrinsic motivators become less central. Managers need to know how to use these alternative techniques before they can be expected to abandon the incentive systems on which they have relied for so long.

If Kohn can convince even a few managers that incentive plans are not the keys to innovative, high-quality performance, he will have made a significant contribution. But it would be a mistake to believe that reward and recognition must always have a negative effect on performance or that creative people cannot be motivated by both money and interest in the work itself. As the poet Anne Sexton once said, "I am in love with money, so don't be mistaken. But first I want to write good poems. After that, I am anxious as hell to earn money and fame and bring the stars all down."

**Jerry McAdams**
Vice President, Performance Improvement Resources
Maritz Inc.
Director
Consortium for Alternative Reward Strategies Research
St. Louis, Missouri

A few years ago, Kohn did the business community a service with his book, *No Contest: The Case Against Competition*, which argues that competition is for the *marketplace* rather than the *workplace*. The book makes a compelling argument for focusing on teamwork instead of pitting one employee against another. The key to success, Kohn maintains, is to create an atmosphere of cooperation, channeling employees' creativity and energy to affect the business objectives of the organization positively. Competition between individuals, on the other hand, only gets in the way.

Now Kohn argues that rewards get in the way as well. On the basis of my 20 years of researching and designing reward plans for sales and nonsales employees, I disagree. Appropriate rewards for improved performance have always made good sense, intuitively and practically. They aren't wrong. They aren't intrinsically demotivating. Data show they make good business sense.

Of course, there is always a market for speeches, books, and articles that profess, through highly selective academic research, that what is working really *isn't*. Kohn's article is a provocative exercise in attention-getting, niche marketing. Unfortunately, Kohn's article will probably be used by some to deny performance-improvement opportunities.

I do agree with Kohn's point regarding the negative aspects of the reinforcement of tasks, particularly when the reinforcement plan is piece-rate or merit-pay based. Measuring and rewarding on an individual level (sales excepted) does tend to become controlling. The focus should be on business objectives, not tasks. The study, *Capitalizing on Human Assets*, covering one-million employees and 432 compensation plans and sponsored by the nonprofit Consortium for Alternative Reward Strategies Research (CARS), shows that rewarding groups of employees, usually whole plants and offices, is a powerful business strategy. According to the study, this strategy pays off a median three-to-one return on the cost of the rewards. Employees earn from 2% to 15% of their base pay in incentives or noncash awards. No lay-offs appear to result from the improved performance. Interviews and extensive data analysis of the 432 plans show positive employee-management cooperation and improved information sharing and employee involvement.

Rewards are not bribes. Bribes are payments for behavior that may be in the organization's best interest but are clearly *not* in the individual's. Rewards reinforce a "win-win" environment. The objective of a reward plan is not to "control or manipulate," as Kohn contends. It is to provide focus and reward improved performance.

Tom Peters was right when he wrote about Kohn's thesis, "What we need is a lot *more* positive reinforcement, and a lot less of the negative kind, throughout the corporate landscape. And far from cautioning companies about the dangers of incentives, we should be applauding those that offer their employees a bigger piece of the action" (INC, April 1988). The CARS research has done just that, looking at more plans in greater depth than any other study. The bottom line is simple: reward plans work when properly designed and supported; there can be something in it for everyone.

I think it is time to focus on the productive use of people as assets to business not on the counterproductive theories in Kohn's article.

## L. Dennis Kozlowski
Chairman and CEO
Tyco Laboratories, Inc.
Exeter, New Hampshire

I'll accept that elephants cannot fly and that fish cannot walk, but Kohn's argument that incentive plans cannot work defies the laws of nature at Tyco Laboratories. Tyco provides a compelling case study that incentives *can* and *do* work for both managers and shareholders. In fact, we believe our incentive compensation program is at the heart of our company's success.

We view the relationship between Tyco's management and its shareholders as very straightforward: management works for the shareholders. It is our mission to create value for them through stock-price appreciation. In fact, our share price has closely tracked our earnings curve for many years, lending considerable weight to our determination to encourage earnings growth in a prudent and consistent manner. Our compensation program, in turn, was designed to align the financial interests of our executives with those of our shareholders. The basic rule is this: the more the executives earn for the shareholders, the more they earn for themselves.

Tyco's 250 profit centers fall into four major businesses. Within the context of a few corporate financial controls, we tell each profit-center manager to run the business as if he or she owned it. A decentralized approach lets us put the financial resources of a $3-billion corporation behind the entrepreneurial spirit, drive, and resourcefulness of managers who think and act like owners. It's the best of both worlds. Profit-center autonomy and responsibility go hand in hand. We encourage each unit's management team to share the unit's profits. The more profits the business unit earns for the shareholders, the more compensation the management team earns for itself.

Our incentive plan has several important and unique features. For one, incentive compensation is directly tied to each business unit's performance and not to corporate results or other factors beyond any individual's control. In addition, the awards are not based on how units perform against a budget or any other preset goal. Instead, awards constitute a preestablished percentage of earnings. Since we adopted this approach, the quality of the budgeting process has substantially improved. Finally, award opportunities are uncapped, and, as a result, they encourage the entrepreneurial spirit that we value.

When designed effectively and integrated thoroughly into the management process, executive incentive programs work well for management and shareholders alike.

**George P. Baker III**
Associate Professor
Harvard Business School
Boston, Massachusetts

The problem is not that incentives can't work but that they work all too well. Kohn's analysis of the unintended and unwanted side effects of many incentive plans is perfectly apt; plans that provide incentives for the wrong behavior will produce the wrong results. However, Kohn's solution to abandon incentive plans entirely is misguided. Rather, managers must learn how to harness and use the power of incentives to drive individual motivation and organizational effectiveness.

In several places, Kohn's assertions about the weakness of incentive plans only serve to highlight the power of such plans to influence behavior. What Kohn says is absolutely true: if teamwork and cooperation are desired, and the incentive plan rewards only individual results, then the plan will generate counterproductive results. However, a well-designed incentive plan that rewards team productivity not only will avoid such unproductive behavior but also will induce employee cooperation. This is the logical basis for the majority of profit-sharing and employee stock-ownership plans, whose effectiveness mounting evidence supports.

Similarly, Kohn's observation that incentive plans cause employees to curry favor with the boss and withhold information about poor performance is often accurate. But the solution is not to eliminate the boss's ability to reward employees. Instead, supervisors should be trained to ignore or punish politicking. It is precisely because incentives are so powerful that Kohn can predict that if managers reward politicking, politicking will result.

Reward plans need not be controlling, as Kohn seems to imply. Consider the store-manager incentive plan at Au Bon Pain. Store managers are given a profitability target and are allowed to keep a substantial fraction of any profits they earn above this target. The chain puts few constraints on how they achieve or exceed their targets. The plan has hardly been "the enemy of exploration." Rather, it has resulted in an explosion of entrepreneurial experimentation and innovation. Notice, however, that the Au Bon Pain plan is not, in Kohn's words, "contingent on behavior." It is contingent on results, and herein lies the crucial difference. Plans that are contingent on behavior will encourage the prescribed behavior and stifle initiation. However, plans that reward desired results are likely to stimulate innovation.

Perhaps the most disturbing omission from Kohn's article is his failure to suggest an alternative to the use of incentive plans. If companies are to abandon extrinsic incentives as a way to motivate employees, what are they to use instead? Is Kohn recommending that we live with the loss of individual motivation and lack of organizational innovation and flexibility that characterizes companies and societies without extrinsic incentives? Without some level of extrinsic incentive to supplement the intrinsic drive of individuals, organizations become unwieldy and inflexible. As a general prescription for the management of organizations, Kohn's approach is naive and utopian. In the real world, organizations must manage incentives if they are to be flexible, innovative, and directed.

**Donita S. Wolters**
Manager of Human Resources
JMM Operational Services, Inc.
Denver, Colorado

While Kohn makes a number of valid points with respect to the dangers of incentive plans, his summary execution of incentives is unwarranted. Incentives are neither all good nor all bad. Although not the right answer in all cases, they can be highly effective motivational tools and should be employed under the appropriate circumstances.

Without a doubt, financial rewards can be, and have been, both overused and misused. Implementing a poorly designed or ill-suited incentive plan can do more harm than good because employees will inevitably receive mixed, even conflicting, messages from the organization about its values and priorities, leading to confusion and frustration. Incentives are no substitute for good management and should not be used indiscriminately to remedy problems when more effective solutions exist. Kohn mentions training and goal setting as examples of effective strategies for improving productivity, and his advice is well-taken. Incentives cannot improve performance if employees are not properly trained to perform their tasks or have no idea what is expected of them. But something more is often needed to elicit the necessary effort. The job-rate pay systems that typify unionized blue-collar environments—where mediocrity and lack of innovation are the hallmarks, and employees do just enough to get by—illustrate the point.

I have observed, as a veteran of many employee-counseling sessions, that employees are more apt to become disillusioned with incentive plans when they feel exploited because the expected rewards are not forthcoming, not when they are rewarded for something they were inclined to do in the first place. To avoid perceptions of exploitation and manipulation, however, two design features of the incentive program are imperative.

First, the criteria for and the actual evaluation of performance must be seen as objective and within the performer's control. This means that anyone should be able to predict the reward consistently and reliably based on given actions and results. The reward should not be determined through highly subjective processes, such as a supervisor's individual opinion. Kohn seems to support this view when he states that "not receiving a reward one had expected to receive is . . . indistinguishable from being punished."

Second, the recipient should consider the reward equal to the effort that produced it. Too insignificant and the incentive will be insulting and thus ineffective; overdone and the balance of fairness will be upset. Insufficient attention to these dynamics may underlie the apparent failure of many executive incentive plans, which could more accurately be termed entitlement programs.

Kohn goes on to decry the inability of incentives to "create an enduring *commitment* to any value or action." I question the relevance of this criticism. The purpose of incentives is not to change employees' values but to direct their behavior in ways that will benefit the organization and the employees themselves. More telling is Kohn's failure to identify a viable alternative to incentives. Of course, the intrinsic rewards he praises are extremely motivating where they happen to exist, but they are not always present and cannot usually be created.

The current trend in organizations is toward less hierarchy and more teamwork. For employees, this means that fewer promotions are available and greater cooperation among coworkers is required. For employers, this means that maximum versatility and productivity must be summoned from all members. The use of incentive plans represents one strategy for aligning organizational and individual goals by treating employees as partners in both the risks and the successes of the business. Kohn recognizes that the majority of companies in the United States utilize some sort of incentive plan. Indeed, his assertions are being tested on the firing line and disproved by a persuasive cross section of U.S. business.

### Alfie Kohn Responds: "I believe incentive plans *must* fail."

The average U.S. company has come to resemble a game show: "Tell our employees about the fabulous prizes we have for them if their productivity improves!" None of my respondents doubts the pervasiveness of this mentality. In fact, several profess incredulity that anyone would question the value of dangling rewards in front of people. In my experience, this reaction most often comes from the consultants who make their living selling incentive programs. What I hear around the country from people with no axe to grind is a frank acknowledgment that incentive plans rarely work.

Consider the following.

- A human-resource executive at a major U.S. auto company recently surveyed her colleagues in various industries; they told her that, at best, their incentive plans didn't do *too* much damage.
- *Training Magazine* ran a cover story entitled: "Why No One Likes Your Incentive Program."
- As Michael Beer observes, pay-for-performance programs are typically tossed out a few years after they are begun.
- To the best of my knowledge, no controlled study has ever found long-term improvement in the quality of performance as a result of extrinsic rewards.

Of course, it is comforting to believe that incentives fail only for incidental reasons, such as that they are "misused," as Donita Wolters would have it, or that they are offered "for the wrong behavior," as George Baker claims. But I believe incentive plans *must* fail, because they are based on a patently inadequate theory of motivation. Trying to undo the damage by adopting a new pay-for-performance scheme is rather like trying to cure alcoholism by switching from vodka to gin. This argument makes a lot of people angry, as seems clear from Jerry McAdam's unpleasant speculations about my ulterior motives and from the amusing, if predictable, mutterings about communism by G. Bennett Stewart. If the attachment to carrot-and-stick psychology—or any dogma—is deep enough, questioning simply isn't permitted.

W. Edwards Deming, and others before him, have been telling us for years that money is not a motivator. Judging from Teresa Amabile's response, however, I may not have been clear enough about the difference between compensation in general and pay-for-performance in particular. Neither can produce quality, but only the latter is positively harmful. I agree with Amabile that "generous compensation . . . need not be seen as a bribe," but I disagree that "people do not always feel controlled by rewards." Richard Ryan and his colleagues at the University of Rochester, pioneers in researching this question, have concluded that "rewards in general appear to have a controlling significance to some extent and thus in general run the risk of undermining intrinsic motivation." Offering good things to people on the condition that they do what you tell them is, almost by definition, a way of trying to exert control.

But even someone who insists that it's possible in theory to devise a noncontrolling reward has to concede that control is what incentive plans in the real world are all about. Just listen to the defenders of these programs: the whole idea is to "direct [employees'] behavior," as Wolters says. No wonder the evidence shows that incentives do not "supplement the intrinsic drive of individuals," as Baker believes, but tend to supplant it. As a rule, the more salient the extrinsic motivator, the more intrinsic motivation evaporates.

One could say, as Baker does, that incentives work too well, in the sense that they are destructive of excellence and interest. But one cannot conclude from this that the problem is merely one of implementation. Baker errs in assuming that just because rewards undermine cooperation it follows that they can also create it. If something has the power to hurt, that doesn't mean more of it will motivate. Again, think of money: less of it can demotivate, but that doesn't mean that more of it will motivate. I think Baker also misunderstands why employees try so hard to convince their reward-dispensing supervisors that everything is under control. It's not because the latter are deliberately rewarding such behavior. Rather, the use of rewards and the extrinsic orientation they produce inexorably lead people to focus on pleasing those in charge of handing out the goodies. Fine-tuning the incentive plan cannot solve the problem.

Finally, a number of correspondents are understandably curious about my views on what should replace incentive plans. If a discussion on this point was conspicuously absent from the article, which was an excerpt from my book *Punished by Rewards*, it was due to limited space. I do grapple at length with alternatives to incentives in another chapter, "Thank God It's Monday." Here, a few words will have to suffice.

On compensation, my advice is this: pay people well and fairly, then do everything possible to help them forget about money. I have no objection to profit-sharing: it seems sensible enough that the people who made the profit ought to have it. Nor am I keen to promote one criterion for compensation over another: for example, need, seniority, job responsibilities, training, market value. My concern is primarily to convince managers to stop manipulating employees with rewards and punishments and to stop pushing money into their faces.

My other concern is to emphasize the futility of fiddling with compensation schemes. This is not the road to quality. Andrew Lebby, a consultant, and Eileen Appelbaum, a researcher, corroborate this, and each offers a way of thinking about where excellence actually comes from. I find it useful to think in terms of three C's: choice, collaboration, and content. Choice means that employees should be able to participate in making decisions about what they do every day. Collaboration denotes the need to structure teams in order to facilitate an exchange of ideas and a climate of support. Content refers to what people are asked to do: as Frederick Herzberg said, "If you want people motivated to do a good job, give them a good job to do."

An organization that provides these three ingredients in place of artificial inducements like incentive plans will not "lose its best people," as Beer worries. Innovation and excellence are the natural results of helping people experience intrinsic motivation. But intrinsic motivation cannot survive in an organization that treats its employees like pets.

# 4

# How Well Is Employee Ownership Working?

Corey Rosen and Michael Quarrey

Ever since 1974, when Congress enacted the first of a series of tax measures designed to encourage employee stock ownership plans (ESOPs), the number of employee-owned (or partially owned) companies has grown from about 1,600 to 8,100, and the number of employees owning stock has jumped from 250,000 to more than eight million.[1] Employee-owners publish the *Milwaukee Journal,* bag groceries at Publix Supermarkets, roll tin plate at Weirton Steel, and create high-tech products at W.L. Gore Associates. How well are these companies doing?

Underlying worker ownership is a radically democratic, Jeffersonian ideal—one we strongly endorse. Every American wants to own some property, to have a stake. We all want to know that we are working "for ourselves."

Still, the ultimate test of employee ownership is how well ESOPs affect corporate performance. If the only way to keep a company competitive is to distance employees from the managerial prerogatives of ownership, so be it. When a ship sinks, it is no consolation to the surviving hands that they own a piece of the wreck.

We have recently completed a major study of ESOP companies that should put an end to talk about wrecks. Not only have workers gained financially, but we can prove that ESOP companies have grown much faster than they would have without their ownership plans. We have found, moreover, that ESOP companies grow fastest when ownership is combined with a program for worker participation. A synergy emerges between the two: ownership provides a strong incentive for employees to work productively, and opportunities for participation enhance productivity by providing channels for workers' ideas and talents.


## How Do ESOPs Work?

The tax incentives have proven so attractive to companies, it's little wonder that the number of ESOPs has grown. The 1986 tax reform act has only made ESOPs more agreeable. Businesses can still deduct contributions to ESOPs from corporate income taxes. If an ESOP buys stock in a closely held firm, the owner can defer taxation on the sale. Other laws—there have been 17 in all—allow an ESOP to borrow money and use the loan to buy company stock; the company can make tax-deductible contributions to the ESOP to pay off the loan. The 1986 act permits banks to continue to deduct 50% of the interest income they receive from ESOP debt. Estates of owners of closely held companies can exclude 50% of their taxable income from a sale to the company's ESOP, up to a maximum benefit of $750,000.

Nor is it particularly difficult for a company to set up an ESOP. You begin with a trust fund. You then contribute new shares of company stock to the plan or contribute cash—again, this is tax deductible—for the ESOP to buy existing stock. You can help the ESOP borrow to purchase either kind of share.

Employees, meanwhile, acquire a gradually increasing right to company shares through vesting. For example, if an employee is qualified to receive 100 shares after seven years, he or she will receive, say, 20 shares after three years, 70 shares after five years, and so on. They are entitled to receive the entire cash value of their stock at separation or retirement.

While it is true that some ESOPs have been used as a last-ditch effort to save failing businesses, prevent hostile takeovers, or even induce employees to make wage concessions, the U.S. General Accounting Office reports that such cases account for only about 3% of all company plans. Only about 8% terminated pension plans to create their ESOPs, and about 40% of all ESOP companies have at least one other kind of retirement plan. Of the more than 100 ESOP companies we have studied, only one had required wage concessions; managers at the rest said their wage and benefit packages were competitive quite apart from the ESOPs.

By and large, then, ESOPs are started for the purposes Congress intended—such as allowing employees to become owners of profitable, closely held companies when a principal owner retires (such cases account for about half of all plans) or as an additional employee benefit. The typical ESOP owns a 10% to 40% interest in the company, with 10% to 15% of the plans owning a majority. At least one-third of all plans will eventually afford workers the chance to acquire a controlling interest. And companies, public and private, have instituted ESOPs for other positive reasons—to borrow capital, to divest subsidiaries, or simply to buttress a corporate commitment to having workers share in managerial decisions.

## How Do We Judge Performance?

Nearly all previous studies of employee ownership have found that ESOP companies do respectably well.[2] Unfortunately, all these studies look at ESOP companies only *after* the plans have been set up. As a result, it has been impossible to say whether employee ownership is the cause of better corporate performance or simply that the more successful companies were the ones to set up plans in the first place.

We determined to avoid this ambiguity in our research. In 1986, we studied 45 ESOP companies, looking at data for each during the five years before it instituted the plan and the five years after. We might well have simply compared pre-ESOP figures with post-ESOP figures for each company. But this could prove misleading. Suppose the business climate had brightened—which it did for many industries—during the latter five years? Could the gains be credited to ESOPs? You can't tell how the Yankees are doing merely by comparing this year's stats with last year's. You have to consider the team's standing among other American League teams. (Weirton Steel, perhaps the most familiar ESOP company—which we excluded from our study because it could not meet our ten-year requirement—registered impressive gains after adopting its plan in 1984. Were the gains due to an industrywide recovery or to changes within the company?)

We decided to compare the performance of ESOP companies with the performance of other similar companies. The pivotal year remained the one in which the companies' ESOPs took effect. But we were careful to consider company performance in the context of industry trends. Of the ESOP companies we studied, 20 were from an earlier survey for which we had sufficient data; we excluded companies that had had ESOPs from the start. To provide an adequate sample, we looked at an additional 25 companies. We then chose at least five comparison companies for every ESOP company from *Dun & Bradstreet*, for a total of 238. These were comparable to the ESOP companies in terms of business line, size, and, where possible, location. We excluded from our ESOP sample companies with business line combinations for which there were no comparison companies.

## ESOP Companies Grow Faster

Once we had our two samples, we collected data on sales and employment growth. We then compared the growth rates of each ESOP company with its five or more comparison companies, calculating the differences in performance before and after the ESOP was established.

If an ESOP company's growth was consistent and significantly higher than its comparison companies' growth, we ascribed this to the "ESOP effect." An ESOP company might well have outperformed the comparison companies before it set up its ESOP. We registered an ESOP effect only if the company's performance was even more impressive after it set up its plan.

The results of this analysis proved striking. During the five years before instituting their ESOPs, the 45 companies had, on average, grown moderately faster than the 238 comparison companies: annual employment growth was 1.21% faster, and sales growth, 1.89% faster. During the five years after these companies instituted ESOPs, however, their annual employment growth outstripped that of the comparison companies by 5.05%, while sales growth was 5.4% faster. Moreover, 73% of the ESOP companies in our sample significantly improved their performance after they set up their plans.

Incidentally, it would obviously have been preferable to judge the performance of ESOP companies by profit, not growth. Failing companies can grow—at least for a while. But most of the companies in our sample have remained closely held, and we knew in advance that unvarnished profit statements would not be available to us. The next best thing, we reckoned, was to look at growth over a sustained period. Again, we looked at only stable companies whose performance we could track for a minimum of ten years.

Finally, we wondered if there might be other factors involved in setting up an ESOP that might account for improved performance— a change in management, perhaps, or an extraordinary use of ESOP tax breaks. We tested for these and other factors and found no relationship.

## Added Value of Participation

The data show that ESOPs exert a positive influence on corporate performance. But the question remains whether any one aspect of employee ownership can be thought the key to higher productivity.

When we looked at the ESOP companies alone, our most interesting finding was the impact of worker participation. Regardless of company size, or the size of employee contributions, or even the percentage of the company owned by the ESOP, the most salient correlation was between corporate performance and workers' perceptions of their managers' attitudes toward worker participation. ESOP companies that instituted participation plans grew at a rate three to four times faster than ESOP companies that did not. Also impressive was the correlation between performance and the actual routines of participation—for example, the number of meetings held in which workers and management could develop corporate plans and resolve difficulties.

One virtue of these data is that they are intuitively satisfying. Most people work better when they enjoy what they're doing. Our data suggest that employees enjoy their work most when they feel they have some say about the conditions of their work day. At Cost Cutter Stores, a grocery chain based in Bellingham, Washington, the mere establishment of an ownership plan raised employee expectations about their role in the company, forcing management to get employees more involved. After a series of meetings between management and employees, managers began interviewing employees one-on-one. The productivity of Cost Cutter has gone up so much that Associated Grocers, which measures such things for its members, reported that the company was "off its charts." Cost Cutter executives are the first to say that the transition to a different and more participative management style was difficult and would not have been made without the impetus provided by employee ownership.

Or consider, once more, Weirton Steel. In 1984, Weirton's 7,000 employees bought the company to keep it from closing. As 100% owners of a steel mill (which could be worth $1 billion in good times), Weirton's workers suffered from no lack of entrepreneurial spirit. Weirton set up intensive three-day training programs to teach employees to run employee involvement teams on their own; it installed television monitors throughout the plant to keep employees informed of developments, and it shares detailed financial and production data, good and bad, with employee-owners. After 3 1/2 years, Weirton now employs 8,500 people and has made a profit for 14 straight quarters, a record unmatched among integrated steelmakers.[3]

Given these findings, companies might well decide they should implement participation programs without necessarily ceding ownership to workers. That conclusion would be unwarranted. Data on participation's impact on non-ESOP companies is at best mixed, while ownership alone has a modest but important effect. Ownership and participation together have considerable impact. There is no escaping the conclusion that American workers sense a difference between working for their own benefit and merely being employed for the company's benefit; a difference between participation by right and participation at the sufferance of managers.

## Having a Stake

Clearly, feeling like a participant is critical to a worker's greater contribution to a company after it establishes an ESOP. But it is important not to define participation too narrowly. For a worker to feel like a participant-owner, there must be a tangible financial benefit and a process of consultation, not just abstract prestige.

In 1985, we conducted a study of 108 randomly selected ESOPs, looking at how much workers had profited from them during the previous four years. The average contribution was the equivalent of 10.1% of workers' pay, and the average annual gain in stockholders' equity was 11.5% (compared, incidentally, with about 6% for the Dow Jones industrial average during that time).

Using these figures and applying conservative assumptions about how quickly workers' shares are vested, we calculated that an employee making the 1983 median wage of $18,000 would accumulate $31,000 over the next 10 years and $120,000 over 20 years.

This may not sound like a great deal of money. Yet in 1983, the median net financial assets of a family at retirement, aside from home equity, amounted to only $11,000. Americans are clearly not in the habit of saving. Of course, by putting aside 10% to 15% of their yearly pay into other retirement or forced savings plans, workers could accumulate a sum equal to the value of ESOP shares. But *would* they elect to put this much aside?

And if ESOPs are a hedge against feeling strapped at retirement, they matter as much to workers for the way they can improve life before retirement. We surveyed 2,800 employees in 37 representative ESOP companies across the country. While our data show clearly that employees react to ownership primarily in financial terms—the larger the annual company contribution to their accounts, the more motivated they claim to be—workers nevertheless say they cherish the demonstrated commitment of management to worker ownership and participation.

In fact, such basics as company size, lines of business, and workforce characteristics do not affect employee attitudes much. Not even employee voting rights correlated with higher morale, though in about 15% of private ESOP companies employees can vote their shares on all issues. (By law, employees in private ESOP companies must be able to vote on issues involving sale, liquidation, relocation, or merger. In public companies, workers have the right to vote on all issues.)

Again, employees are enthusiastic about companies that engage their ideas and talents, whether in an informal open-door meeting with the president or at a random meeting with a supervisor. The best companies, they say, regularly hold sessions in which managers and workers can thrash out problems. But employees attached little importance to the formal trappings of corporate control, such as having representation on the board.

Workers may well appreciate the money they get by owning company stock. But their enthusiasm won't do much for corporate performance unless it can be channeled into creative enterprise. Employees ought to feel that they can share new ideas, devise new ways to work together more efficiently, take on responsibility for customer satisfaction.

The lessons for management are clear. Give employees an opportunity to acquire a significant share of the company and develop opportunities for them to participate as owners. This course is remarkably effective, remarkably exciting, and remarkably different from the one the vast majority of American companies travel.

## Notes

1. In her article, "The Attack on Pay," HBR March–April 1987, Rosabeth Moss Kanter correctly cites our book (with Joseph Blasi), *Taking Stock: Employee Ownership at Work* to the effect that 11 million workers have

participated in stock ownership plans. That number includes the 3 million workers who had participated in payroll stock ownership plans (or PAYSOPs), which were not intended to encourage ownership and were in any case eliminated by the 1986 tax reform act.

2. See, for example, Michael Conte and Arnold Tannenbaum, *Employee Ownership* (Ann Arbor: University of Michigan Survey Research Center, 1980); Thomas Marsh and Dale McAlister, "ESOP's Tables," *Journal of Corporation Law,* Spring 1981, p. 612; Matthew Trachman and Corey Rosen, "Report to the National Venture Capital Association of the Relationship of Employee Ownership and Corporate Growth in High-Tech Firms," unpublished paper, 1985.

3. For an earlier look at Weirton Steel, see William E. Fruhan, "Management, Labor, and the Golden Goose," HBR September–October 1985, p. 131.

# 5

# What Business Can Learn from Nonprofits

**Peter F. Drucker**

The Girl Scouts, the Red Cross, the pastoral churches—our non-profit organizations—are becoming America's management leaders. In two areas, strategy and the effectiveness of the board, they are practicing what most American businesses only preach. And in the most crucial area—the motivation and productivity of knowledge work-ers—they are truly pioneers, working out the policies and practices that business will have to learn tomorrow.

Few people are aware that the nonprofit sector is by far America's largest employer. Every other adult—a total of 80 million plus peo-ple—works as a volunteer, giving on average nearly five hours each week to one or several nonprofit organizations. This is equal to 10 million full-time jobs. Were volunteers paid, their wages, even at minimum rate, would amount to some $150 billion, or 5% of GNP. And volunteer work is changing fast. To be sure, what many do requires little skill or judgment: collecting in the neighborhood for the Community Chest one Saturday afternoon a year, chaperoning young-sters selling Girl Scout cookies door to door, driving old people to the doctor. But more and more volunteers are becoming "unpaid staff," taking over the professional and managerial tasks in their organiza-tions.

Not all nonprofits have been doing well, of course. A good many community hospitals are in dire straits. Traditional churches and syna-gogues of all persuasions—liberal, conservative, evangelical, funda-mentalist—are still steadily losing members. Indeed, the sector overall has not expanded in the last 10 or 15 years, either in terms of the money it raises (when adjusted for inflation) or in the number of volunteers. Yet in its productivity, in the scope of its work and in its contribution to American society, the nonprofit sector has grown tremendously in the last two decades.

The Salvation Army is an example. People convicted to their first prison term in Florida, mostly very poor black or Hispanic youths, are now paroled into the Salvation Army's custody—about 25,000 each year. Statistics show that if these young men and women go to jail the majority will become habitual criminals. But the Salvation Army has been able to rehabilitate 80% of them through a strict work program run largely by volunteers. And the program costs a fraction of what it would to keep the offenders behind bars.

Underlying this program and many other effective nonprofit endeavors is a commitment to management. Twenty years ago, management was a dirty word for those involved in nonprofit organizations. It meant business, and nonprofits prided themselves on being free of the taint of commercialism and above such sordid considerations as the bottom line. Now most of them have learned that nonprofits need management even more than business does, precisely because they lack the discipline of the bottom line. The nonprofits are, of course, still dedicated to "doing good." But they also realize that good intentions are no substitute for organization and leadership, for accountability, performance, and results. Those require management and that, in turn, begins with the organization's mission.

As a rule, nonprofits are more money-conscious than business enterprises are. They talk and worry about money much of the time because it is so hard to raise and because they always have so much less of it than they need. But nonprofits do not base their strategy on money, nor do they make it the center of their plans, as so many corporate executives do. "The businesses I work with start their planning with financial returns," says one well-known CEO who sits on both business and nonprofit boards. "The nonprofits start with the performance of their mission."

Starting with the mission and its requirements may be the first lesson business can learn from successful nonprofits. It focuses the organization on action. It defines the specific strategies needed to attain the crucial goals. It creates a disciplined organization. It alone can prevent the most common degenerative disease of organizations, especially large ones: splintering their always limited resources on things that are "interesting" or look "profitable" rather than concentrating them on a very small number of productive efforts.

The best nonprofits devote a great deal of thought to defining their organization's mission. They avoid sweeping statements full of good intentions and focus, instead, on objectives that have clear-cut implications for the work their members perform—staff and volunteers both. The Salvation Army's goal, for example, is to turn society's rejects—alcoholics, criminals, derelicts—into citizens. The Girl Scouts help youngsters become confident, capable young women who respect themselves and other people. The Nature Conservancy preserves the diversity of nature's fauna and flora. Nonprofits also start with the environment, the community, the "customers" to be; they do not, as American businesses tend to do, start with the inside, that is, with the organization or with financial returns.

Willowcreek Community Church in South Barrington, Illinois, outside Chicago, has become the nation's largest church—some 13,000 parishioners. Yet it is barely 15 years old. Bill Hybels, in his early twenties when he founded the church, chose the community because it had relatively few churchgoers, though the population was growing fast and churches were plentiful. He went from door to door asking, "Why don't you go to church?" Then he designed a church to answer the potential customers' needs: for instance, it offers full services on Wednesday evenings because many working parents need Sunday to spend with their children. Moreover, Hybels continues to listen and react. The pastor's sermon is taped while it is being delivered and instantly reproduced so that parishioners can pick up a cassette when they leave the building because he was told again and again, "I need to listen when I drive home or drive to work so that I can build the message into my life." But he was also told: "The sermon always tells me to change my life but never how to do it." So now every one of Hybels's sermons ends with specific action recommendations.

A well-defined mission serves as a constant reminder of the need to look outside the organization not only for "customers" but also for measures of success. The temptation to content oneself with the "goodness of our cause"—and thus to substitute good intentions for results—always exists in nonprofit organizations. It is precisely because of this that the successful and performing nonprofits have learned to define clearly what changes *outside* the organization constitute "results" and to focus on them.

The experience of one large Catholic hospital chain in the Southwest shows how productive a clear sense of mission and a focus on results can be. Despite the sharp cuts in Medicare payments and hospital stays during the past eight years, this chain has increased revenues by 15% (thereby managing to break even) while greatly expanding its services and raising both patient-care and medical standards. It has done so because the nun who is its CEO understood that she and her staff are in the business of delivering health care (especially to the poor), not running hospitals.

As a result, when health care delivery began moving out of hospitals for medical rather than economic reasons about ten years ago, the chain promoted the trend instead of fighting it. It founded ambulatory surgery centers, rehabilitation centers, X-ray and lab networks, HMOs, and so on. The chain's motto was: "If it's in the patient's interest, we have to promote it; it's then our job to make it pay." Paradoxically, the policy has filled the chain's hospitals; the freestanding facilities are so popular they generate a steady stream of referrals.

This is, of course, not so different from the marketing strategy of successful Japanese companies. But it is very different indeed from the way most Western businesses think and operate. And the difference is that the Catholic nuns—and the Japanese—start with the mission rather than with their own rewards, and with what they have to make happen outside themselves, in the marketplace, to deserve a reward.

Finally, a clearly defined mission will foster innovative ideas and help others understand why they need to be implemented—however much they fly in the face of tradition. To illustrate, consider the Daisy Scouts, a program for five-year-olds which the Girl Scouts initiated a few years back. For 75 years, first grade had been the minimum age for entry into a Brownie troop, and many Girl Scout councils wanted to keep it that way. Others, however, looked at demographics and saw the growing numbers of working women with "latch key" kids. They also looked at the children and realized that they were far more sophisticated than their predecessors a generation ago (largely thanks to TV).

Today the Daisy Scouts are 100,000 strong and growing fast. It is by far the most successful of the many programs for preschoolers that have been started these last 20 years, and far more successful than any of the very expensive government programs. Moreover, it is so far the only program that has seen these critical demographic changes and children's exposure to long hours of TV viewing as an opportunity.

Many nonprofits now have what is still the exception in business—a functioning board. They also have something even rarer: a CEO who is clearly accountable to the board and whose performance is reviewed annually by a board committee. And they have what is rarer still: a board whose performance is reviewed annually against preset performance objectives. Effective use of the board is thus a second area in which business can learn from the nonprofit sector.

In U.S. law, the board of directors is still considered the "managing" organ of the corporation. Management authors and scholars agree that strong boards are essential and have been writing to that effect for more than 20 years, beginning with Myles Mace's pioneering work.[1] Nevertheless, the top managements of our large companies have been whittling away at the directors' role, power, and independence for more than half a century. In every single business failure of a large company in the last few decades, the board was the last to realize that things were going wrong. To find a truly effective board, you are much better advised to look in the nonprofit sector than in our public corporations.

In part, this difference is a product of history. Traditionally, the board has run the shop in nonprofit organizations—or tried to. In fact, it is only because nonprofits have grown too big and complex to be run by part-time outsiders, meeting for three hours a month, that so many have shifted to professional management. The American Red Cross is probably the largest nongovernmental agency in the world and certainly one of the most complex. It is responsible for worldwide disaster relief; it runs thousands of blood banks as well as the bone and skin banks in hospitals; it conducts training in cardiac and respiratory rescue nationwide; and it gives first-aid courses in thousands of schools. Yet it did not have a paid chief executive until 1950, and its first professional CEO came only with the Reagan era.

But however common professional management becomes—and professional CEOs are now found in most nonprofits and all the bigger ones—nonprofit boards cannot, as a rule, be rendered impotent the way so many business boards have been. No matter how much nonprofit CEOs would welcome it—and quite a few surely would—nonprofit boards cannot become their rubber stamp. Money is one reason. Few directors in publicly held corporations are substantial shareholders, whereas directors on nonprofit boards very often contribute large sums themselves, and are expected to bring in donors as well. But also, nonprofit directors tend to have a personal commitment to the organization's cause. Few people sit on a church vestry or on a school board unless they deeply care about religion or education. Moreover, nonprofit board members typically have served as volunteers themselves for a good many years and are deeply knowledgeable about the organization, unlike outside directors in a business.

Precisely because the nonprofit board is so committed and active, its relationship with the CEO tends to be highly contentious and full of potential for friction. Nonprofit CEOs complain that their board "meddles." The directors, in turn, complain that management "usurps" the board's function. This has forced an increasing number of nonprofits to realize that neither board nor CEO is "the boss." They are colleagues, working for the same goal but each having a different task. And they have learned that it is the CEO's responsibility to define the tasks of each, the board's and his or her own.

For example, a large electric co-op in the Pacific Northwest created ten board committees, one for every member. Each has a specific work assignment: community relations, electricity rates, personnel, service standards, and so on. Together with the co-op's volunteer chairman and its paid CEO, each of these one-person committees defines its one-year and three-year objectives and the work needed to attain them, which usually requires five to eight days a year from the board member. The chairman reviews each member's work and performance every year, and a member whose performance is found wanting two years in a row cannot stand for reelection. In addition, the chairman, together with three other board members, annually reviews the performance of the entire board and of the CEO.

The key to making a board effective, as this example suggests, is not to talk about its function but to organize its work. More and more nonprofits are doing just that, among them half a dozen fair-sized liberal arts colleges, a leading theological seminary, and some large research hospitals and museums. Ironically, these approaches reinvent the way the first nonprofit board in America was set up 300 years ago: the Harvard University Board of Overseers. Each member is assigned as a "visitor" to one area in the university—the Medical School, the Astronomy Department, the investment of the endowment—and acts both as a source of knowledge to that area and as a critic of its performance. It is a common saying in American academia that Harvard has the only board that makes a difference.

The weakening of the large corporation's board would, many of us predicted (beginning with Myles Mace), weaken management rather than strengthen it. It would diffuse management's accountability for performance and results; and indeed, it is the rare big-company board that reviews the CEO's performance against preset business objectives. Weakening the board would also, we predicted, deprive top management of effective and credible support if it were attacked. These predictions have been borne out amply in the recent rash of hostile takeovers.

To restore management's ability to manage we will have to make boards effective again—and that should be considered a responsibility of the CEO. A few first steps have been taken. The audit committee in most companies now has a real rather than a make-believe job responsibility. A few companies—though so far almost no large ones—have a small board committee on succession and executive development, which regularly meets with senior executives to discuss their performance and their plans. But I know of no company so far where there are work plans for the board and any kind of review of the board's performance. And few do what the larger nonprofits now do routinely: put a new board member through systematic training.

Nonprofits used to say, "We don't pay volunteers so we cannot make demands upon them." Now they are more likely to say, "Volunteers must get far greater satisfaction from their accomplishments and make a greater contribution precisely because they do not get a paycheck." The steady transformation of the volunteer from well-meaning amateur to trained, professional, unpaid staff member is the most significant development in the nonprofit sector—as well as the one with the most far-reaching implications for tomorrow's businesses.

A Midwestern Catholic diocese may have come furthest in this process. It now has fewer than half the priests and nuns it had only 15 years ago. Yet it has greatly expanded its activities—in some cases, such as help for the homeless and for drug abusers, more than doubling them. It still has many traditional volunteers like the Altar Guild members who arrange flowers. But now it is also being served by some 2,000 part-time unpaid staff who run the Catholic charities, perform administrative jobs in parochial schools, and organize youth activities, college Newman Clubs, and even some retreats.

A similar change has taken place at the First Baptist Church in Richmond, Virginia, one of the largest and oldest churches in the Southern Baptist Convention. When Dr. Peter James Flamming took over five years ago, the church had been going downhill for many years, as is typical of old, inner-city churches. Today it again has 4,000 communicants and runs a dozen community outreach programs as well as a full complement of in-church ministries. The church has only nine paid full-time employees. But of its 4,000 communicants, 1,000 serve as unpaid staff.

This development is by no means confined to religious organizations. The American Heart Association has chapters in every city of any size throughout the country. Yet its paid staff is limited to those at national headquarters, with just a few traveling troubleshooters serving the field. Volunteers manage and staff the chapters, with full responsibility for community health education as well as fund raising.

These changes are, in part, a response to need. With close to half the adult population already serving as volunteers, their overall number is unlikely to grow. And with money always in short supply, the nonprofits cannot add paid staff. If they want to add to their activities—and needs are growing—they have to make volunteers more productive, have to give them more work and more responsibility. But the major impetus for the change in the volunteer's role has come from·the volunteers themselves.

More and more volunteers are educated people in managerial or professional jobs—some preretirement men and women in their fifties, even more baby-boomers who are reaching their mid-thirties or forties. These people are not satisfied with being helpers. They are knowledge workers in the jobs in which they earn their living, and they want to be knowledge workers in the jobs in which they contribute to society—that is, their volunteer work. If nonprofit organizations want to attract and hold them, they have to put their competence and knowledge to work. They have to offer meaningful achievement.

Many nonprofits systematically recruit for such people. Seasoned volunteers are assigned to scan the newcomers—the new member in a church or synagogue, the neighbor who collects for the Red Cross—to find those with leadership talent and persuade them to try themselves in more demanding assignments. Then senior staff (either a full-timer on the payroll or a seasoned volunteer) interviews the newcomers to assess their strengths and place them accordingly. Volunteers may also be assigned both a mentor and a supervisor with whom they work out their performance goals. These advisers are two different people, as a rule, and both, ordinarily, volunteers themselves.

The Girl Scouts, which employs 730,000 volunteers and only 6,000 paid staff for 3 1/2 million girl members, works this way. A volunteer typically starts by driving youngsters once a week to a meeting. Then a more seasoned volunteer draws her into other work—accompanying Girl Scouts selling cookies door-to-door, assisting a Brownie leader on a camping trip. Out of this step-by-step process evolve the volunteer boards of the local councils and, eventually, the Girl Scouts governing organ, the National Board. Each step, even the very first, has its own compulsory training program, usually conducted by a woman who is herself a volunteer. Each has specific performance standards and performance goals.

What do these unpaid staff people themselves demand? What makes them stay—and, of course, they can leave at any time. Their first and most important demand is that the nonprofit have a clear mission, one that drives everything the organization does. A senior vice president in a large regional bank has two small children. Yet she just took over as chair of the state chapter of Nature Conservancy, which finds, buys, and manages endangered natural ecologies. "I love my job," she said, when I asked her why she took on such heavy additional work, "and of course the bank has a creed. But it doesn't really know what it contributes. At Nature Conservancy, I know what I am here for."

The second thing this new breed requires, indeed demands, is training, training, and more training. And, in turn, the most effective way to motivate and hold veterans is to recognize their expertise and use them to train newcomers. Then these knowledge workers demand responsibility—above all, for thinking through and setting their own performance goals. They expect to be consulted and to participate in making decisions that affect their work and the work of the organization as a whole. And they expect opportunities for advancement, that is, a chance to take on more demanding assignments and more responsibility as their performance warrants. That is why a good many nonprofits have developed career ladders for their volunteers.

Supporting all this activity is accountability. Many of today's knowledge-worker volunteers insist on having their performance reviewed against preset objectives at least once a year. And increasingly, they expect their organizations to remove nonperformers by moving them to other assignments that better fit their capacities or by counseling them to leave. "It's worse than the Marine Corps boot camp," says the priest in charge of volunteers in the Midwestern diocese, "but we have 400 people on the waiting list." One large and growing Midwestern art museum requires of its volunteers—board members, fundraisers, docents, and the people who edit the museum's newsletter—that they set their goals each year, appraise themselves against these goals each year, and resign when they fail to meet their goals two years in a row. So does a fair-sized Jewish organization working on college campuses.

These volunteer professionals are still a minority, but a significant one—perhaps a tenth of the total volunteer population. And they are growing in numbers and, more important, in their impact on the nonprofit sector. Increasingly, nonprofits say what the minister in a large pastoral church says: "There is no laity in this church; there are only pastors, a few paid, most unpaid."

This move from nonprofit volunteer to unpaid professional may be the most important development in American society today. We hear a great deal about the decay and dissolution of family and community and about the loss of values. And, of course, there is reason for concern. But the nonprofits are generating a powerful countercurrent. They are forging new bonds of community, a new commitment to active citizenship, to social responsibility, to values. And surely what the nonprofit contributes to the volunteer is as important as what the volunteer contributes to the nonprofit. Indeed, it may be fully as important as the service, whether religious, educational, or welfare related, that the nonprofit provides in the community.

This development also carries a clear lesson for business. Managing the knowledge worker for productivity is the challenge ahead for American management. The nonprofits are showing us how to do that. It requires a clear mission, careful placement and continuous learning and teaching, management by objectives and self-control, high demands but corresponding responsibility, and accountability for performance and results.

There is also, however, a clear warning to American business in this transformation of volunteer work. The students in the program for senior and middle-level executives in which I teach work in a wide diversity of businesses: banks and insurance companies, large retail chains, aerospace and computer companies, real estate developers, and many others. But most of them also serve as volunteers in non-profits—in a church, on the board of the college they graduated from, as scout leaders, with the YMCA or the Community Chest or the local symphony orchestra. When I ask them why they do it, far too many give the same answer: Because in my job there isn't much challenge, not enough achievement, not enough responsibility; and there is no mission, there is only expediency.

## Note

1. A good example is Myles Mace, "The President and the Board of Directors," HBR March–April 1972, p. 37.

# PART
# II

# 1
# Power Is the Great Motivator

David C. McClelland and David H. Burnham

This article was originally published in March–April 1976. It won the McKinsey Award for excellence and has consistently been one of the best-selling HBR reprints. For its republication as an HBR Classic, David C. McClelland has written a retrospective commentary.

What makes or motivates a good manager? The question is enormous in scope. Some people might say that a good manager is one who is successful—and by now most business researchers and businesspeople know what motivates people who successfully run their own small businesses. The key to their success has turned out to be what psychologists call the need for achievement, the desire to do something better or more efficiently than it has been done before. Any number of books and articles summarize research studies explaining how the achievement motive is necessary for a person to attain success.

But what has achievement motivation got to do with good management? There is no reason on theoretical grounds why a person who has a strong need to be more efficient should make a good manager. While it sounds as if everyone ought to have the need to achieve, in fact, as psychologists define and measure achievement motivation, the need to achieve leads people to behave in ways that do not necessarily engender good management.

For one thing, because they focus on personal improvement and doing things better by themselves, achievement-motivated people

---

*Authors' note*: All the names and case material in this article are disguised.

want to do things themselves. For another, they want concrete short-term feedback on their performance so that they can tell how well they are doing. Yet managers, particularly in large, complex organizations, cannot perform by themselves all the tasks necessary for success. They must manage others to perform for the organization. And they must be willing to do without immediate and personal feedback since tasks are spread among many people.

The manager's job seems to call more for someone who can influence people than for someone who does things better alone. In motivational terms, then, we might expect the successful manager to have a greater *need for power* than a need to achieve. But there must be other qualities besides the need for power that go into the makeup of a good manager. We will discuss here just what these qualities are and how they interrelate.

To measure the motivations of managers, we studied a number of them in different large U.S. corporations who were participating in management workshops designed to improve their managerial effectiveness. (See the insert "Workshop Techniques.") We concluded that the top manager of a company must possess a high need for power, that is, a concern for influencing people. However, this need must be disciplined and controlled so that it is directed toward the benefit of the institution as a whole and not toward the manager's personal aggrandizement. Moreover, the top manager's need for power ought to be greater than his or her need for being liked.

## Measuring Managerial Effectiveness

What does it mean when we say that a good manager has a greater need for power than for achievement? Consider the case of Ken Briggs, a sales manager in a large U.S. corporation who joined one of our managerial workshops. About six years ago, Ken Briggs was promoted to a managerial position at headquarters, where he was responsible for salespeople who service his company's largest accounts.

In filling out his questionnaire at the workshop, Ken showed that he correctly perceived what his job required of him, namely, that he should influence others' success more than achieve new goals himself or socialize with his subordinates. However, when asked with other members of the workshop to write a story depicting a managerial situation, Ken unwittingly revealed through his fiction that he did not share those concerns. Indeed, he discovered that his need for achievement was very high—in fact, over the ninetieth percentile—and his need for power was very low, in about the fifteenth percentile. Ken's high need to achieve was no surprise—after all, he had been a very successful salesman—but obviously his motivation to influence others was much less than his job required. Ken was a little disturbed but thought that perhaps the measuring instruments were not accurate and that the gap between the ideal and his score was not as great as it seemed.

Then came the real shocker. Ken's subordinates confirmed what his stories revealed: he was a poor manager, having little positive impact on those who worked for him. They felt they had little responsibility delegated to them, he never rewarded but only criticized them, and the office was not well organized but was confused and chaotic. On all those scales, his office rated in the tenth to fifteenth percentile relative to national norms.

As Ken talked the results of the survey over privately with a workshop leader, he became more and more upset. He finally agreed, however, that the results confirmed feelings he had been afraid to admit to himself or others. For years, he had been miserable in his managerial role. He now knew the reason: he simply did not want, and he had not been able, to influence or manage others. As he thought back, he realized he had failed every time he had tried to influence his staff, and he felt worse than ever.

Ken had responded to failure by setting very high standards—his office scored in the ninety-eighth percentile on this scale—and by trying to do most things himself, which was close to impossible; his own activity and lack of delegation consequently left his staff demoralized. Ken's experience is typical of those who have a strong need to achieve but low power motivation. They may become very successful salespeople and, as a consequence, may be promoted into managerial jobs for which they, ironically, are unsuited.

If achievement motivation does not make a good manager, what motive does? It is not enough to suspect that power motivation may be important; one needs hard evidence that people who are better managers than Ken Briggs is do in fact possess stronger power motivation and perhaps score higher in other characteristics as well. But how does one decide who is the better manager?

Real-world performance measures are hard to come by if one is trying to rate managerial effectiveness in production, marketing, finance, or research and development. In trying to determine who the better managers were in Ken Briggs's company, we did not want to rely only on their superiors. For a variety of reasons, superiors' judgments of their subordinates' real-world performance may be inaccurate. In the absence of some standard measure of performance, we decided that the next best index of a manager's effectiveness would be the climate he or she creates in the office, reflected in the morale of subordinates.

Almost by definition, a good manager is one who, among other things, helps subordinates feel strong and responsible, rewards them properly for good performance, and sees that things are organized so that subordinates feel they know what they should be doing. Above all, managers should foster among subordinates a strong sense of team spirit, of pride in working as part of a team. If a manager creates and encourages this spirit, his or her subordinates certainly should perform better.

In the company Ken Briggs works for, we have direct evidence of a connection between morale and performance in the one area where performance measures are easy to find—namely, sales. In April 1973, at least three employees from this company's 16 sales districts filled out questionnaires that rated their office for organizational clarity and team spirit. Their scores were averaged and totaled to give an overall morale score for each office. The percentage gains or losses in sales for each district in 1973 were compared with those for 1972. The difference in sales figures by district ranged from a gain of nearly 30% to a loss of 8%, with a median gain of about 14%. The graph "The Link Between Morale and Sales" shows how, in Ken Briggs's company, at least, high morale at the beginning of the year became a good index of how well the sales division would actually perform throughout the year. Moreover, it seems likely that the manager who can create high morale among salespeople can also do the same for employees in other areas (production, design, and so on), which leads to better overall performance. What characteristics, then, does a manager need to create that kind of morale?

## The Power Factor

In examining the motive scores of more than 50 managers of both high- and low-morale units in all sections of the same large company, we found that most of the managers—more than 70%—were high in power motivation compared with the average person. This finding confirms that power motivation is important for management. (Re-

*Exhibit I.*

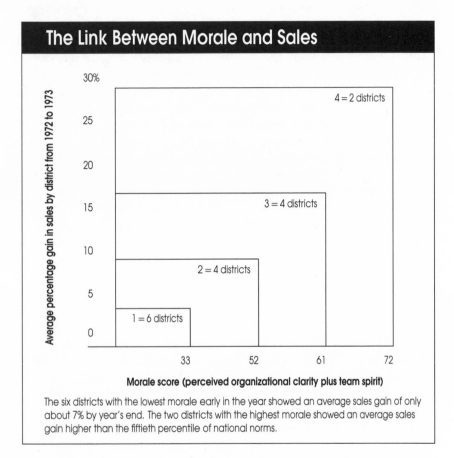

## The Link Between Morale and Sales

The six districts with the lowest morale early in the year showed an average sales gain of only about 7% by year's end. The two districts with the highest morale showed an average sales gain higher than the fiftieth percentile of national norms.

member that, as we use the term, *power motivation* refers not to dictatorial behavior but to a desire to have impact, to be strong and influential.) The better managers, as judged by the morale of those working for them, tended to score even higher in power motivation. But the most important determining factor of high morale turned out to be not how their power motivation compared with their need to achieve but whether it was higher than their need to be liked. This relationship existed for 80% of the better sales managers as compared with only 10% of the poorer managers. And the same held true for other managers in nearly every part of the organization.

In the research, product development, and operations divisions,

73% of the better managers had a stronger need for power than a need to be liked, as compared with only 22% of the poorer managers, who tended to be what we term *affiliative managers*—whose strongest drive is to be liked. Why should this be so? Sociologists have long argued that for a bureaucracy to function effectively, those who manage it must apply rules universally; that is, if they make exceptions for the particular needs of individuals, the whole system will break down.

The manager with a high need to be liked is precisely the one who wants to stay on good terms with everybody and, therefore, is the one most likely to make exceptions for particular needs. If an employee asks for time off to stay home and look after a sick spouse and the kids, the affiliative manager agrees almost without thinking, out of compassion for the employee's situation.

When former President Gerald Ford remarked in pardoning Richard Nixon that Nixon had "suffered enough," he was responding as an affiliative manager would because he was empathizing primarily with Nixon's needs and feelings. Sociological theory and our findings both argue, however, that the person whose need for affiliation is high does not make a good manager. This kind of person creates low morale because he or she does not understand that other people in the office will tend to regard exceptions to the rules as unfair to themselves, just as many U.S. citizens felt that it was unfair to let Nixon off and punish others who were less involved than he was in the Watergate scandal.

So far, our findings are a little alarming. Do they suggest that the good manager is one who cares for power and is not at all concerned about the needs of other people? Not quite, for the good manager has other characteristics that must still be taken into account.

Above all, the good manager's power motivation is not oriented toward personal aggrandizement but toward the institution that he or she serves. In another major research study, we found that the signs of controlled action or inhibition that appear when a person exercises imagination in writing stories tell a great deal about the kind of power that person needs.[1] We discovered that if a high power-motive score is balanced by high inhibition, stories about power tend to be altruistic. That is, the heroes in the story exercise power on behalf of someone else. This is the socialized face of power as distinguished from the concern for personal power, which is characteristic of individuals whose stories are loaded with power imagery but show no sign of inhibition or self-control. In our earlier study, we found ample evidence that the latter individuals exercise their power impulsively. They are more often rude to other people, they drink too much, they try to exploit others sexually, and they collect symbols of personal prestige such as fancy cars or big offices.

Individuals high in power and in control, on the other hand, are more institution minded; they tend to get elected to more offices, to control their drinking, and to have a desire to serve others. Not surprisingly, we found in the workshops that the better managers in the corporation also tend to score high on both power and inhibition.

## Three Kinds of Managers

Let us recapitulate what we have discussed so far and have illustrated with data from one company. The better managers we studied—what we call *institutional managers*—are high in power motivation, low in affiliation motivation, and high in inhibition. They care about institutional power and use it to stimulate their employees to be more productive. Now let us compare them with *affiliative managers* (those in whom the need for affiliation is higher than the need for power) and with the *personal power managers* (those in whom the need for power is higher than for affiliation but whose inhibition score is low).

In the sales division of the company we chose to use as an illustration, there were managers who matched the three types fairly closely. The chart "Which Manager Was Most Effective?" shows how their subordinates rated the offices they worked in on responsibility, organizational clarity, and team spirit. Managers who are concerned about being liked tend to have subordinates who feel that they have little personal responsibility, that organizational procedures are not clear, and that they have little pride in their work group.

In short, as we expected, affiliative managers make so many ad hominem and ad hoc decisions that they almost totally abandon orderly procedures. Their disregard for procedure leaves employees feeling weak, irresponsible, and without a sense of what might happen next, of where they stand in relation to their manager, or even of what they ought to be doing. In this company, the group of affiliative managers portrayed in the chart were below the thirtieth percentile in morale scores.

The managers who are motivated by a need for personal power are somewhat more effective. They are able to create a greater sense of responsibility in their divisions and, above all, a greater team spirit. They can be thought of as managerial equivalents of successful tank commanders such as General George Patton, whose own daring in-

*Exhibit II.*

## Which Manager Was Most Effective?

Percentile ranking of average scores (national norms)

| 0 | 10 | 20 | 30 | 40 | 50 | 60 |

**Sense of responsibility**

**Organizational clarity**

**Team spirit**

Scores for at least three subordinates of:

☐ Affiliative managers (affiliation greater than power, high inhibition)

■ Personal power managers (power greater than affiliation, low inhibition)

▨ Institutional managers (power greater than affiliation, high inhibition)

Average scores on selected dimensions by subordinates of managers with different motive profiles.

spired admiration in his troops. But notice how in the chart these people are still only in the fortieth percentile in the amount of organizational clarity that they create, as compared with the high-power, low-affiliation, high-inhibition managers—institutional managers.

Managers motivated by personal power are not disciplined enough to be good institution builders, and often their subordinates are loyal to them as individuals rather than to the institution they serve. When a personal power manager leaves, disorganization often follows. The strong group spirit that the manager has personally inspired deflates. The subordinates do not know what to do for themselves.

Of the managerial types, the institutional manager is the most successful in creating an effective work climate. Subordinates feel that they have more responsibility. Also, those kinds of managers create high morale because they produce the greatest sense of organizational clarity and team spirit. If such a manager leaves, he or she can be more readily replaced by another because the employees have been encouraged to be loyal to the institution rather than to a particular person.

Since it seems undeniable that a manager with a power orientation creates better morale in subordinates than one with a people orientation, we must consider that a concern for power is essential to good management. Our findings seem to fly in the face of a long and influential tradition of organizational psychology, which insists that authoritarian management is what is wrong with most businesses in the United States. Let us say frankly that we think the bogeyman of authoritarianism has been wrongly used to downplay the importance of power in management. After all, management is an influence game. Some proponents of democratic management seem to have forgotten this fact, urging managers to be more concerned with people's personal needs than with helping them to get things done.

But much of the apparent conflict between our findings and those of other behavioral scientists in this area stems from the fact that we are talking about *motives*, and behaviorists are often talking about *actions*. What we are saying is that managers must be interested in playing the influence game in a controlled way. That does not necessarily mean that they are or should be authoritarian in action. On the contrary, it appears that power-motivated managers make their subordinates feel strong rather than weak. The true authoritarian in action would have the reverse effect, making people feel weak and powerless.

Thus another important ingredient in the profile of a manager is managerial style. In the illustrative company, 63% of the better managers (those whose subordinates had higher morale) scored higher on the democratic or coaching styles of management as compared with only 22% of the poorer managers, a statistically significant difference. By contrast, the latter scored higher on authoritarian or coercive management styles. Since the better managers were also higher in power motivation, it seems that in action they express their power motivation in a democratic way, which is more likely to be effective.

To see how motivation and style interact, consider the case of George Prentice, a manager in the sales division of another company. George had exactly the right combination of motives to be an institutional manager. He was high in the need for power, low in the need for affiliation, and high in inhibition. He exercised his power in a controlled, organized way. The stories he wrote reflected this fact. In one story, for instance, he wrote, "The men sitting around the table were feeling pretty good; they had just finished plans for reorganizing the company; the company has been beset with a number of organizational problems. This group, headed by a hard-driving, brilliant young executive, has completely reorganized the company structurally with new jobs and responsibilities. . . ."

This described how George himself was perceived by the company, and shortly after the workshop, he was promoted to vice president in charge of all sales. But George was also known to his colleagues as a monster, a tough guy who would "walk over his grandmother" if she stood in the way of his advancement. He had the right motive combination and, in fact, was more interested in institutional growth than he was in personal power, but his managerial style was all wrong. Taking his cue from some of the top executives in the corporation, he told people what they had to do, and he threatened them with dire consequences if they did not do it.

When George was confronted with his authoritarianism in a workshop, he recognized that this style was counterproductive—in fact, in another part of the study we found that it was associated with low morale—and he subsequently changed to acting more like a coach, which was the scale on which he scored the lowest initially. George saw more clearly that his job was not to force other people to do things but rather to help them to figure out ways of getting their jobs done better for the company.

## Profile of the Institutional Manager

One reason it was easy for George Prentice to change his managerial style was that, as we saw in his imaginative stories, he was already having thoughts about helping others, characteristic of people with the institution-building motivational pattern. In further examining institution builders' thoughts and actions, we found they have four major characteristics:

- Institution managers are more organization minded; that is, they tend to join more organizations and to feel responsible for building up those organizations. Furthermore, they believe strongly in the importance of centralized authority.

- They report that they like to work. This finding is particularly interesting because our research on achievement motivation has led many commentators to argue that achievement motivation promotes the "Protestant work ethic." Almost the precise opposite is true. People who have a high need to achieve like to *reduce* their work by becoming more efficient. They would like to see the same result obtained in less time or with less effort. But managers who have a need for institutional power actually seem to like the discipline of work. It satisfies their need for getting things done in an orderly way.

- They seem quite willing to sacrifice some of their own self-interest for the welfare of the organization they serve.

- They have a keen sense of justice. It is almost as if they feel that people who work hard and sacrifice for the good of the organization should and will get a just reward for their effort.

It is easy to see how each of these four concerns helps a person become a good manager, concerned about what the institution can achieve.

We discovered one more fact in studying the better managers at George Prentice's company. They were more mature. Mature people can be most simply described as less egotistic. Somehow their positive self-image is not at stake in their jobs. They are less defensive, more willing to seek advice from experts, and have a longer-range view. They accumulate fewer personal possessions and seem older and wiser. It is as if they have awakened to the fact that they are not going to live forever and have lost some of the feeling that their own personal future is all that important.

Many U.S. businesspeople fear this kind of maturity. They suspect that it will make them less hard driving, less expansion minded, and less committed to organizational effectiveness. Our data do not support their fears.

Those fears are exactly the ones George Prentice had before he went to the workshop. Afterward, he was a more effective manager, not despite his loss of some of the sense of his own importance but because of it. The reason is simple: his subordinates believed afterward that he was genuinely more concerned about the company than he was about himself. Whereas once they respected his confidence but feared him, they now trust him. Once, he supported their image of him as a "big man" by talking about the new Porsche and Honda he had bought; when we saw him recently, he said, almost as an aside, "I don't buy things anymore."

## Altering Managerial Style

George Prentice was able to change his managerial style after learning more about himself. But does self-knowledge generally improve managerial behavior?

Consider the results shown in the chart "Managers *Can* Change Their Style," where "before" and "after" workshop training scores are compared. To judge by their subordinates' responses, the managers were clearly more effective after coming to terms with their style. The subordinates felt that they received more rewards, that the organizational procedures were clearer, and that morale was higher.

But what do those differences mean in human terms? How did the managers change? Sometimes they decided they should get into another line of work. This happened to Ken Briggs, for example, who found that the reason he was doing so poorly as a manager was because he had almost no interest in influencing others. He understood how he would have to change in order to do well in his present job, but in the end decided, with the help of management, that he would prefer to work back into his first love, sales.

Ken Briggs moved into remaindering, helping retail outlets for his company's products get rid of last year's stock so that they can take on each year's new styles. He is very successful in this new role; he has cut costs, increased dollar volume, and in time has worked himself into an independent role selling some of the old stock on his own in a way that is quite satisfactory to the business. And he does not have to manage anybody anymore.

In George Prentice's case, less change was needed. He obviously was a very competent manager with the right motive profile for a top company position. When he was promoted, he performed even more successfully than he had previously because he realized that he needed to become more positive in his approach and less coercive in his managerial style.

But what about a person who does not want to change jobs and discovers that he or she does not have the right motive profile to be a manager? The case of Charlie Blake is instructive. Charlie was as low in power motivation as Ken Briggs, his need to achieve was about average, and his affiliation motivation was above average. Thus he had

*Exhibit III.*

## Managers *Can* Change Their Style

Percentile ranking of average scores (national norms)

| 0 | 10 | 20 | 30 | 40 | 50 | 60 |
|---|----|----|----|----|----|----|

**Sense of responsibility**

**Rewards received**

**Organizational clarity**

**Team spirit**

☐ Before manager training

■ After manager training

Average scores on selected dimensions by more than
50 salespeople before and after their managers were trained.

the affiliative-manager profile, and, as expected, the morale among his subordinates was very low. When Charlie learned that his subordinates' sense of responsibility and perception of a reward system were in the tenth percentile and that team spirit was in the thirtieth, he was shocked. When shown a film depicting three managerial climates, Charlie said he preferred what turned out to be the authoritarian climate. He became angry when the workshop trainer and other members in the group pointed out the limitations of this managerial style. He became obstructive in the group process and objected strenuously to what was being taught.

In an interview conducted much later, Charlie said, "I blew my cool. When I started yelling at you for being all wrong, I got even madder when you pointed out that, according to my style questionnaire, you bet that that was just what I did to my salespeople. Down underneath, I knew something must be wrong. The sales performance for my division wasn't so good. Most of it was due to me anyway and not to my salespeople. Obviously, their reports that they felt I delegated very little responsibility to them and didn't reward them at all had to mean something. So I finally decided to sit down and try to figure what I could do about it. I knew I had to start being a manager instead of trying to do everything myself and blowing my cool at others because they didn't do what I thought they should. In the end, after I calmed down on the way back from the workshop, I realized that it is not so bad to make a mistake; it's bad not to learn from it."

After the course, Charlie put his plans into effect. Six months later, his subordinates were asked to rate him again. He attended a second workshop to study the results and reported, "On the way home, I was nervous. I knew I had been working with those guys and not selling so much myself, but I was afraid of what they would say about how things were going in the office. When I found out that the team spirit and some of those other low scores had jumped from around the thirtieth to the fifty-fifth percentile, I was so delighted and relieved that I couldn't say anything all day long."

When he was asked how he acted differently from before, Charlie said, "In previous years when corporate headquarters said we had to make 110% of our original goal, I had called the salespeople in and said, in effect, 'This is ridiculous; we are not going to make it, but you know perfectly well what will happen if we don't. So get out there and work your tails off.' The result was that I worked 20 hours a day and they did nothing.

"This time I approached the salespeople differently. I told them three things. First, they were going to have to do some sacrificing for the company. Second, working harder is not going to do much good because we are already working about as hard as we can. What will be required are special deals and promotions. You are going to have to figure out some new angles if we are to make it. Third, I'm going to back you up. I'm going to set a realistic goal with each of you. If you make that goal but don't make the company goal, I'll see to it that you are not punished. But if you do make the company goal, I'll see to it that you will get some kind of special rewards."

When the salespeople challenged Charlie, saying he did not have enough influence to give them rewards, rather than becoming angry,

Charlie promised rewards that were in his power to give—such as longer vacations.

Note that Charlie has now begun to behave in a number of ways that we found to be characteristic of the good institutional manager. He is, above all, higher in power motivation—the desire to influence his salespeople—and lower in his tendency to try to do everything himself. He asks people to sacrifice for the company. He does not defensively chew them out when they challenge him but tries to figure out what their needs are so that he can influence them. He realizes that his job is more one of strengthening and supporting his subordinates than of criticizing them. And he is keenly interested in giving them just rewards for their efforts.

The changes in his approach to his job have certainly paid off. The sales figures for his office in 1973 were up more than 16% over 1972 sales and up still further in 1974 over 1973 sales. In 1973, his gain over the previous year ranked seventh in the nation; in 1974, it ranked third. And he wasn't the only one in his company to change managerial styles. Overall sales at his company were up substantially in 1973 compared with 1972 sales, an increase that played a large part in turning the overall company performance around from a $15 million loss in 1972 to a $3 million profit in 1973. The company continued to improve its performance in 1974 with an 11% further gain in sales and a 38% increase in profits.

## Workshop Techniques

We derived the case studies and data used in this article from a number of workshops we conducted, during which executives learned about their managerial styles and abilities as well as how to change them. The workshops also provided an opportunity for us to study which motivation patterns in people make for the best managers.

At the workshops and in this article, we use the technical terms *need for achievement, need for affiliation*, and *need for power*. The terms refer to measurable factors indicating motivation in groups and individuals. Briefly, those characteristics are measured by coding managers' spontaneous thoughts according to how often they think about doing something better or more efficiently than before (need for achievement), about establishing or maintaining friendly relations with others (need for affiliation), or about having an impact on others (need for power). When we talk about power, we are not talking about dictatorial power but about the need to be strong and influential.

When the managers first arrived at the workshops, they were asked to fill out a questionnaire about their jobs. Each participant analyzed his or her job, explaining what he or she thought it required. The managers were asked to write a number of stories about pictures of various work situations we showed them. The stories were coded according to how concerned an individual was with achievement, affiliation, or power, as well as for the amount of inhibition or self-control they revealed. We then compared the results against national norms. The differences between a person's job requirements and his or her motivational patterns can often help assess whether the person is in the right job, is a candidate for promotion to another job, or is likely to be able to adjust to fit the present position.

To find out what kind of managerial style the participants had, we then gave them a questionnaire in which they had to choose how they would handle various realistic work situations in office settings. We divided their answers into six management styles or ways of dealing with work situations. The styles were democratic, affiliative, pacesetting, coaching, coercive, and authoritarian. The managers were asked to comment on the effectiveness of each style and to name the style they preferred.

One way to determine how effective managers are is to ask the people who work for them. Thus, to isolate the characteristics that good managers have, we asked at least three subordinates of each manager at the workshop questions about their work situations that revealed characteristics of their supervisors according to six criteria: (1) the amount of conformity to rules the supervisor requires, (2) the amount of responsibility they feel they are given, (3) the emphasis the department places on standards of performance, (4) the degree to which rewards are given for good work compared with punishment when something goes wrong, (5) the degree of organizational clarity in the office, and (6) its team spirit.[1] The managers who received the highest morale scores (organizational clarity plus team spirit) from their subordinates were determined to be the best managers, possessing the most desirable motive patterns.

We also surveyed the subordinates six months later to see if morale scores rose after managers completed the workshop.

We measured participants on one other characteristic deemed important for good management: maturity. By coding the stories that the managers wrote, which revealed their attitudes toward authority and the kinds of emotions displayed over specific issues, we were able to pinpoint managers at one of four stages in the progress toward maturity. People in Stage I are dependent on others for guidance and strength. Those in Stage II are interested primarily in autonomy. In Stage III, people want to manipulate others. In Stage IV, they lose their egotistic desires and wish to serve others selflessly.[2]

The conclusions we present in this article are based on workshops attended by more than 500 managers from some 25 U.S. corporations. We drew the examples in the charts from one of those companies.

1. Based on G.H. Litwin and R.A. Stringer's *Motivation and Organizational Climate* (Boston: Division of Research, Harvard Business School, 1966).

2. Based on work by Abigail Stewart, as reported in David C. McClelland's *Power: The Inner Experience* (New York: Irvington Publishers, 1975).

Of course, not everyone can be reached by a workshop. Henry Carter managed a sales office for a company that had very low morale (around the twentieth percentile) before he went for training. When morale was checked some six months later, it had not improved. Overall sales gain subsequently reflected this fact—only 2% above the previous year's figures.

Oddly enough, Henry's problem was that he was so well liked by everybody that he felt little pressure to change. Always the life of the party, he is particularly popular because he supplies other managers with special hard-to-get brands of cigars and wines at a discount. He uses his close ties with everyone to bolster his position in the company, even though it is known that his office does not perform well compared with others.

His great interpersonal skills became evident at the workshop when he did very poorly at one of the business games. When the discussion turned to why he had done so badly and whether he acted that way on the job, two prestigious participants immediately sprang to his defense, explaining away Henry's failure by arguing that the way he did things was often a real help to others and the company. As a result, Henry did not have to cope with such questions at all. He had so successfully developed his role as a likable, helpful friend to everyone in management that, even though his salespeople performed badly, he did not feel under any pressure to change the way he managed people.

What have we learned from Ken Briggs, George Prentice, Charlie Blake, and Henry Carter? We have discovered what motives make an effective manager—and that change is possible if a person has the right combination of qualities.

Oddly enough, the good manager in a large company does not have a high need for achievement, as we define and measure that motive, although there must be plenty of that motive somewhere in his or her organization. The top managers shown here have a high need for power and an interest in influencing others, both greater than their interest in being liked by people. The manager's concern for power should be socialized—controlled so that the institution as a whole, not only the individual, benefits. People and nations with this motive profile are empire builders; they tend to create high morale and to expand the organizations they head. But there is also danger in this motive profile; as in countries, empire building can lead to imperialism and authoritarianism in companies.

The same motive pattern that produces good power management can also lead a company to try to dominate others, ostensibly in the interests of organizational expansion. Thus it is not surprising that big business has had to be regulated periodically by federal agencies.

Similarly, the best managers possess two characteristics that act as regulators—a greater emotional maturity, where there is little egotism, and a democratic, coaching managerial style. If an institutional power motivation is checked by maturity, it does not lead to an aggressive, egotistic expansiveness. That means managers can control their subordinates and influence others around them without having to resort to coercion or to an authoritarian management style.

Summarized in this way, what we have found out through empirical and statistical investigations may sound like good common sense. But it is more than common sense; now we can say objectively what the characteristics of the good manager are. Managers of corporations can select those who are likely to be good managers and train those already in managerial positions to be more effective with more confidence.

### Retrospective Commentary by David C. McClelland

Two important changes have occurred in the workplace since David H. Burnham and I wrote "Power Is the Great Motivator" in 1976. The big, old-fashioned hierarchical organizations we studied have flattened out. And female managers have entered the workplace in full force.

Yet our findings about management style still hold true, regardless of a manager's gender, for the type of hierarchical organization we observed in the article. Successful managers—what we called institutional managers—have a strong need for power (that is, for influencing others) that is greater than their need to be liked, and they exhibit self-control.

That finding was confirmed through subsequent research, including a study of people who were promoted up the managerial ranks at AT&T. Of people who joined AT&T between 1956 and 1960, the institutional managers had been promoted 16 years later to a higher level much more often than other types of managers, we found. We also discovered that the same managerial characteristics predicted future success for both men and women who entered the AT&T system between 1976 and 1980.

However, in a recent study of PepsiCo, a large, decentralized company, we found that having a high need for *achievement* contributes more to success than does a high interest in influencing other people. In fact, the need for power was often a handicap in that company. That confirms earlier convincing evidence that a constant concern for improvement, for growing the business in a cost-efficient way, characterizes successful managers of *small* companies, which is what many subsidiaries of PepsiCo essentially function as.

To show conclusively how women manage, we still need much more information. But the AT&T follow-up research did provide an opportunity to observe the subtleties in style differences between the best female and male managers. Using an objective coding system to analyze the stories managers wrote about hypothetical situations, Ruth Jacobs, a principal at McBer and Company, and I found the women much more consensus oriented than the men. In particular, the women seemed to think about power as a resource that can be used to influence outcomes on the job and to focus the competencies of the people who work for them. Men in the study, on the other hand, tended to think of power more as an end in itself, as something they can use to react against or take power away from others in authority. Men saw power as a way to supersede others in power; women rarely did.

Since 1976, my work focus has returned to a lifelong interest in *competencies* in management. That has meant taking a close look at people who are outstanding managers and trying to break down exactly how they go about work vis-à-vis the way less effective managers do. The work developed as a reaction to studies that seem to resurface every 25 years or so (as they have done again recently) asserting a link between intelligence and overall competence. Intelligence, those studies claim, is a hereditary factor that cannot be altered and is therefore the only relevant measure of a person's "competence."

My work has shown the opposite to be true. In fact, results of the

Scholastic Aptitude Test given to college-bound students, among others, relate little to how competently those people manage in the workplace later in life. People who scored exceptionally well on SATs often later functioned poorly as managers, and people with only average scores often made the best managers. It is not intelligence that separates the best people from the worst when it comes to job performance. To measure competency levels, I coded interviews with managers about everyday work situations for specific behaviors, including self-control, self-confidence, an ability to get a consensus from people, and strong motivations for achievement, power, or both.

Indeed, such motivational characteristics (as illustrated by the institutional managers in our article) continually emerge as what separates world-class managers from mediocre ones. That is as true today as when we wrote the article, and it applies to women as well as to men. What has happened in the meantime is that we have a better idea of what combinations of motives and other competencies that we can measure in interviews create managerial success in the new decentralized organizations.

## Notes

1. David C. McClelland, William N. Davis, Rudolf Kalin, and Eric Warner, *The Drinking Man* (New York: The Free Press, 1972).

# 2
# Demand Better Results—and Get Them

**Robert H. Schaffer**

One of the most dramatic, large-scale productivity improvements I am familiar with occurred in a regulated public utility—an industry not noted for such performance breakthroughs. In the early 1960s, this company's productivity was about average among 20 similar companies in North America, as both work load and work force were rapidly rising. In 1966, the trend shifted: the work load continued to rise, but the number of employees began to drop. By 1968, the company's productivity ranked among the best in its industry. The difference between average and best performance was worth savings of more than $40 million a year—well over one-third of its net income at that time.

What produced this gain? Neither new technology nor labor-saving machinery was a significant factor. No significant change in management took place. The company was not reorganized. Nor were programs incorporating management by objectives, organizational development, mathematical modeling, or management information systems responsible for the shift. The key to the turnaround was a decision by the principal operating officer (with backing from the chief executive) that the company must and could make substantial productivity gains. Naturally, many supportive programs and activities were necessary to translate this determination into results. These activities, however, would have produced little if a clear demand for improved

This article, which originally appeared in the *Harvard Business Review* in 1974, includes a retrospective commentary by the author.

performance had not been placed on the company's management team.

Most organizations have the potential for as great—or greater—gains. Very few, however, ever realize them. Few managers possess the capacity—or feel compelled—to establish high performance-improvement expectations in ways that elicit results. Indeed, the capacity for such demand making could be the most universally underdeveloped management skill.

## Why Demands Aren't Made

Pushing for major gains can appear very risky to managers, and these perceived risks exert tremendous inhibition on performance expectations. If the newly installed manager asserts that significant gains are possible, he may threaten his predecessor and current boss—and thus arouse their antagonism—by implying that they had settled for less. Even if he has been in the job for a while, he subjects himself to the same estrangement.

Great demands increase the risk of resistance from subordinates and of the embarrassment of failing to reach ambitious goals. Managers who set unusually high demands may be challenged by others. They must therefore be sure of their facts and clear about directions. The struggle to upgrade performance may expose their uncertainties, weaknesses, and inadequate knowledge. More modest expectations reduce all these risks.

In addition, establishing well-defined and unequivocal expectations for superior performance creates the worry that the failure of subordinates to produce will require drastic action. Musing out loud about a long-needed productivity improvement effort, the vice president of a manufacturing operation asked, "What would happen if we set specific targets and my people didn't meet them? I'd have to do something—maybe let some of them go. Then I'd have to bring in people I trusted even less." Before even determining whether he could create an effective strategy, this man was paralyzed by the anticipated consequences of failure.

The fear of rejection is also a powerful motivator. Asking subordinates to do much more than they assert they can do runs the risk, at least in a manager's mind, of earning their resentment, if not their dislike. Many managers have been only too eager to adopt the model of the manager portrayed by the human relations movements of the

1950s and 1960s—the loving, understanding, and supportive father figure. The model of the stern, demanding manager was portrayed as a villain.

Although many exponents of human relations did emphasize the importance of high expectations and tough goals, managers frequently overlooked those parts of the message. They saw that high expectations for performance could lead to psychological rejection by subordinates. The prevailing opinion was that by adopting the right techniques, managers could avoid confronting subordinates on performance expectations and asking them to produce much more than the managers estimated they were likely to give anyhow.

Are managers conscious of the discrepancy between the performance they are requiring and what might be possible? To an extent, they are. Most sense that their organizations could achieve more, but their vision is obstructed. To avoid the uneasiness and guilt brought on by too clear a vision of performance gaps, managers unconsciously employ a variety of psychological mechanisms for obstructing the truth.

## EVASION THROUGH RATIONALIZATION

Managers may escape having to demand better performance by convincing themselves that they have done all they can to establish expectations. For instance, they may claim that everyone already knows what must be accomplished. When asked whether they have made the goals clear to their people, these managers respond with a variation of "If they don't know what the goals of this outfit are by now, they don't belong in their jobs."

Sincere in their belief that their subordinates are doing their best, managers frequently look for substandard performance elsewhere. Do the following statements sound familiar?

"We can reduce back orders, but you're going to have to pay for plenty of overtime."

"If you want us to cut inventories any further, be prepared for delayed shipments."

"Ever since they trimmed our maintenance budget, we haven't been able to keep this plant operating properly."

Performance improvements always seem to call for an expansion of resources or an increase in authority. Overlooking the possibility of obtaining greater yields from available resources, managers often fail to impose greater demands and expectations on their employees. And when managers do try to demand more, their subordinates are quick to point out that they are doing all that can be done. Thus all levels of management may share the illusion of operating at the outer limit when, in fact, they are far from it.

To avoid having to impose new requirements on subordinates, a manager may decide to take on the job herself. She reassures herself that her people are already overloaded or that they lack some qualification that she possesses. At the other extreme is the manager who covers up his reluctance to make demands with toughness, gruffness, or arbitrariness. He may threaten or needle subordinates without actually specifying requirements and deadlines for results. In the folklore of management, such toughness of manner is equated with a preoccupation with achievement.

## RELIANCE ON PROCEDURES

Managers can avoid the necessity of demand making by putting their chips on a variety of management programs, procedures, and innovations that they hope will produce better results. But while such mechanisms may help an organization respond to demands, they are no substitute for good management.

For example, a manager may try an incentive system aimed at seducing subordinates into better performance through the promise of "goodies." Many top officers are perpetually preoccupied with new kinds of salary, profit-sharing, and stock-option plans and with promotions, titles, and other so-called incentives. Management assumes that if the right carrots are held out, managers and employees will run like rabbits.

Infusions of new managerial technology also may appear to be the key to performance improvements. Management will install information systems, mathematical planning models, industrial engineering studies, training programs, or any of dozens of other programs offered by technical staff or outside consultants. Top management may even reorganize the company—or parts of it. Perhaps convinced of the magic in their medicines, even the best-trained staff technicians and management consultants become the unwitting coconspirators of managers who fail to establish higher performance requirements for subordinates. In one well-known international company, an internal consulting group put together a mathematical planning model to maximize corporate profits in interdivisional negotiations. But the president used a flimsy excuse to escape from the struggle of requiring his division heads to operate within the framework of the models.

## ATTACKS THAT SKIRT THE TARGET

A manager may set tough goals and insist they be achieved—and yet fail to produce a sense of accountability in subordinates. For example, managers often define even significant goals in vague or general terms that make accountability impossible. The R&D director is told that she "must get more new products out this year"; the personnel director hears that "turnover must be reduced"; management at a transportation company insists that "safety is our number one objective." When reporting time comes, who can say whether these objectives have been met?

Similarly, a manager may establish goals but insist that subordinates can't be held accountable because they lack the authority to get the job done. The case of a petrochemical plant whose product quality was well below par illustrates this point. Quality depended on how well a number of interdependent departments processed components. Top management charged department heads to improve operations and monitored these activities, but it failed to hold any individuals responsible for the quality of the end product on the grounds that none of them was in sufficient control of all the factors. The quality improvements failed to meet expectations.

Sometimes, when pressed by superiors, a manager will establish expectations in a way that tells subordinates that he is merely following instructions from above. In fact, he unconsciously hopes that his subordinates' performance will fall short, "proving," as he has asserted all along, that the new stretch goals cannot be attained.

Ironically, management-by-objectives programs often create heavy paper snowstorms in which managers can escape from demand making. In many MBO programs, as lists of goals get longer and documents get thicker, the focus becomes diffused, bulk is confused with quality, and energy is spent on the mechanics rather than on results. A manager challenged on the performance of her group can safely point to the packet of papers and assert, "My managers have spent many hours developing their goals for the year."

## Strategy for Action

The avoidance mechanisms just described act as powerful deterrents to dramatic performance improvement—but they do not have to. There are ways to accelerate progress.

If management is willing to invest time and energy, there is a way it can expect more and get more. I have seen the process work in a variety of organizations: in a refinery that expanded its output while reducing its force by half; in a large, urban teaching hospital that shifted its mission and direction radically; in a poorly maintained detergent and foodstuffs plant that became more competitive without more investment; and in school systems where determined leaders generated innovation despite the inertia of tradition.

The essence of the five-step strategy outlined here is to make a successful initial attempt at upgrading expectations and obtaining a response and then to use this achievement as the foundation for increasingly ambitious steps. A series of demands, initially limited, then more ambitious—each supported by careful plans, controls, and persistence—makes success more likely than does a big plunge involving demands for sweeping changes.

### SELECT THE GOAL

Start with an urgent problem. Are the costs of one department too high? Is a budget being seriously overrun? Is a quality specification being consistently missed? Is there a shortfall in meeting a sales quota? Beginning with problems like these is essential to generating the feeling that achievement of the goal is imperative, not merely desirable.

As you select the goal, assemble the information needed to frame the performance demand. You need this information not only to define the need and specify the target but also to convince people why performance improvement is essential.

It is also a good idea to sound out your subordinates on the opportunities for improvement; their responses will give you a sense of their readiness. To illustrate, the management at a newspaper publishing plant tried to launch a comprehensive improvement effort. The needs were so great and resistance by managers at lower levels so strong that very little was accomplished. Interviews with the composing room supervisors, however, revealed that they shared upper management's distress over the number of typographical errors in news and advertising matter. This information made it possible to design an initial project mobilizing supporters of change.

The more participation by subordinates in determining goals, the better. Managers should not, however, permit their dedication to the participatory process to mean abdication of their own responsibilities.

## SPECIFY THE MINIMUM EXPECTATION OF RESULTS

Broad, far-reaching, or amorphous goals should be narrowed to one or two specific, measurable ones. A manager may protest with "I have too many things that have to get done to concentrate on only one or two of them." But the fragmentation of a manager's attention in trying to push them all ahead can keep her perpetually trapped in the same defense mechanisms from which she is trying to escape. Whether the first-step goal is a modest advance or a bold one, it must focus the energy of the organization on one or two sharply defined targets.

For example, one company, in treading a path between mass production and tailored engineering, was losing money because it could not clarify its proper place in the market and develop the appropriate products. Top management spent hundreds of hours conferring and making studies to define the business, the product line, and the pricing strategy. This produced more frustration than progress.

The undertaking was transformed, however, when the president asked the executives to select from a dozen new products the one they agreed would most likely be profitable and conform to their vision of the business. He directed them to sketch out a market plan and pricing policy for this product. They were to draw from this effort some generalizations that could be applied to policy determination. The president was convinced that the group could produce the result in a short time. And he was confident that the initial step would provide insights into the next steps to clarify the company's direction.

## COMMUNICATE YOUR EXPECTATIONS CLEARLY

Share with the persons responsible, both orally and in writing, the determination of the goal, the locus of responsibility, the timetable, and the constraints. Make clear that you are not asking for permission to set the goal, not securing their advice on whether the goal is attainable, and not implying that if they do not meet the target, you will nevertheless appreciate their efforts. Make sure they understand that this is not a goal that *should* be achieved; it is one that *must* be achieved.

## MONITOR THE PROJECT, BUT DELEGATE RESPONSIBILITY

Work-planning disciplines are essential to preventing these projects from fading into the ether. Trying to keep the goals, commitments, and plans only in your mind is sure to undermine the project; rather, have the manager responsible for each goal or subgoal provide you with a written work plan of steps to be taken to reach the goal. This plan should also specify how progress will be measured and how it will be reported to you.

Moreover, assign responsibility for achieving each goal to one person, even though the contributions of many may be essential for success. Consider the case of a company whose technically complex new product was failing to perform as promised. The president talked about the problem with her marketing, engineering, and manufacturing vice presidents; each claimed that his function was doing its job and that the problems originated elsewhere. After spending much more time than usual with her subordinates, the president was still able to effect only a slight improvement.

The turnaround came when she told her department heads that it was unwise for her to get involved in trying to solve the problem. That was *their* job. She gave them full responsibility for reducing the frequency of unacceptable products to a target level within three months. She assigned to one executive the responsibility for shaping an integrated plan and for making certain it was adequate to achieve the result. In addition, the president requested that each of the other managers produce a plan specifying his or her own functions, contributions, and timetable. After many months of struggling for a solution, the company for the first time pinpointed a goal to be achieved, established responsibilities for achievement, and introduced work-planning disciplines to manage the process in an orderly way.

When responsibility for results is not explicitly assigned, subordinates tend to "delegate" it upward, especially if the boss tries to play a helpful role in the project. Top management must ensure that project members clearly understand their responsibility and must not permit them to turn offers of help and support into opportunities to pass the buck.

## EXPAND AND EXTEND THE PROCESS

Once some success has been achieved on a first set of demands, it should be possible to repeat the process on new goals or on an extension of the first. This will lead to further expansion.

Consider the efforts of a large railway express terminal that handled tens of thousands of shipments daily. It was performing very poorly on many counts: costs were high, productivity was low, and delivery deadlines were often missed. Studies had identified the potential for saving hundreds of thousands of dollars, but those savings were illusive. Then the head of the terminal and his boss ceased talking about what was going wrong and all the improvements that were needed. Instead, they identified the most crucial short-term goals.

From these few they selected one: getting *all* of one category of shipments out on time each day. It was not an easy goal, but it was clear and understandable; it could be sharply defined and measured, and action steps could be quickly identified. Meeting that target was the all-important first success that launched the terminal on an ambitious improvement program. Once the first traffic category was under control, top management planned a series of slightly more ambitious improvement programs. Gradually, the terminal's managers gained confidence in asking for more, and their staffs gained confidence that they could respond. Eventually, many of the sizable savings promised in the earlier studies were realized.

# Psychodynamics of Action

While moving ahead through successive sets of demands, top management has some essential work to do on the psychological front as well. The methods and procedures for negotiating goals with subordinates are well known; almost overlooked but more significant are the often unconscious negotiations that managers carry on with themselves. They frequently bargain themselves down to comfortable expectation levels long before they confront subordinates. They must learn to share the risk taking that they want their subordinates to assume. They may have to live with the "testing" subordinates subject them to, and they may need to engage in consciousness-raising to make sure they do not slip into rationalizations for failing to see that their directives are carried out.

Managers often unintentionally ensure that they will share in the glory of their subordinates' successes but that lower levels will take the blame for failures. For example, a plant manager had been pressuring the head of maintenance to realign the responsibilities of supervisors and workers as a way to increase efficiency. The step would make a number of persons redundant. Low-level managers and supervisors resisted the move, warning of various disasters that would befall the plant.

The deadlock was broken only when the plant manager—through transfers, early retirements, and a very modest layoff—reduced the maintenance force to the level needed after the proposed reorganization. Once the most painful step had been taken, maintenance management quickly installed the new structure. Instead of insisting self-righteously that the key to action was overcoming the resistance of maintenance management, the plant manager assumed the risk and reduced the staff.

When managers expect better results, subordinates may express their own lack of self-confidence in the form of tests. For example, they may continue to do exactly what they have been doing, suggesting that they heard the boss's words but disbelieve the message. Or they may imply that "it can't be done." Some subordinates may advise managers that for their own good—considering the high risks involved—they should lower their sights. They may even withdraw their affection and approval from their managers.

Such testing is usually an expression of subordinates' anxiety over whether they can actually achieve the goal; it is a way to seek reassurance from the boss. If the boss is as anxious as they are, he will be upset by the testing and may react against what he perceives as defiance. If he has self-confidence, he will accept the testing for what it is and try to help his subordinates deal with the problem—without lowering his expectations.

In breaking out of productiveness-limiting traps, consciousness-raising may be needed to help managers assess more objectively their approach to establishing demands. Consultants—inside or outside—can help managers gain the necessary perspective. Or several managers who are working through the same process may join forces, since each can be more detached about the others' behavior than about his or her own. They may meet periodically to probe such questions as: Have you adequately assessed the potential for progress? Have you made the performance requirements clear to your associates? Are these goals ambitious enough? Are you providing your subordinates with enough help? Are you sharing the risks with them? How well are you standing up to testing? Have you defined goals that at least some of your subordinates can see as exciting and achievable?

Perhaps the most important function of consciousness-raising has to do with getting started. It is very difficult to alter the pattern of relationships between superiors and subordinates, especially if they have been working together for a long time. You cannot take the first step without worrying that your people may say (or think), "Oh, come off it. We know who you are!"

## The Rewards Are There

The strategy for demanding better performance—and getting it—begins with a focus on one or two vital goals. Management assesses readiness and then defines the goal. The organization receives clearly stated demands and unequivocally stated expectations. Management assigns the responsibility for results to individuals, and work-planning discipline provides the means for self-control and assessment of progress. Management keeps wired in, tenaciously pushing the project forward. Early successes provide the reinforcement to shoot for more ambitious targets, which may be extensions of the first goal or additional goals.

There is no limit to the pace or scope of expansion. As this process expands, a shift in management style and organizational dynamics gradually takes place: sophisticated planning techniques, job redesign, closer line and staff collaboration, and other advances will come about naturally.

With clearly conveyed, "nonnegotiable" expectations and a step-by-step expansion strategy, you may find that the anticipated difficulties and dangers never materialize. If your subordinates are like most, they will respond to the higher demands. They will be able to accomplish what is expected—or most of it. And despite a bit of testing or hazing, most of them will enjoy working in a more results-oriented environment. Thus you will be creating greater job satisfaction and mutual respect, better relationships among levels, and a multiplied return on the organization's human and material resources.

## Retrospective Commentary

In company after company, I have asked managers to estimate how much more their organizations would produce if overlapping functions were eliminated, if units began to work more in sync with each other, if people worked more closely to their real potential, and if they dissipated less energy in political hassles, self-aggrandizing behavior, useless meetings, and projects that go nowhere. Not surprisingly, almost everyone has selected the "25 to 50%" and the "over 50%" categories.

With all this latent potential evident, why hasn't there been more progress toward meeting the global competitive challenge? I am as convinced as I was 17 years ago that the principal reason is that "few managers possess the capacity—or feel compelled—to establish high performance-improvement expectations in ways that elicit results." This capacity continues to be the most universally underdeveloped managerial skill.

There is no doubt that companies today are more impressed with the need for performance improvement than they were in 1974. They are making vast investments in new tools, new plants, and new technology. They have cranked up massive programs in continuous improvement, customer service, total quality, and culture change that dwarf the efforts of the 1960s and 1970s. Senior executives, corporate staff groups, university professors, and consulting firms have thrown themselves into the battle. The Malcolm Baldrige National Quality Award furnishes a national rallying point.

If these programs were put under the spotlight, however, they would be discovered to serve frequently as convenient escape mechanisms for managers avoiding the struggle of radically upgrading their organizations' performance.

Ironically, the "thinkers" who have invented the latest organizational effectiveness strategies unwittingly provide new busywork escapes. By putting so much emphasis on processes and techniques, they have slighted the importance of results. Thousands of employees are trained in seven-step problem solving and statistical quality control; thousands of managers are "empowered"; and thousands of creative reward and communications systems are in place. In the absence of compelling requirements for measurable improvement, however, little improvement occurs.

For example, teams of consultants and social scientists set up more than 40 different programs in a large international corporation in an effort to make it a "total quality company." In publicizing this undertaking, the company proudly asserted that it did not expect significant results until the *fourth* year.

Companies will never achieve competitive performance levels as long as their executives believe that the right training and development activities, applied with enough diligence, will eventually be rewarded with the right bottom-line results. That is a siren song for all those managers who don't have the stomach for the necessary personal struggle. No combination of programs and training can inject the required experience, skill, and confidence.

Contrary to the mythology, setting high-performance imperatives does not conflict with empowering people. Empowerment comes as people rise to the challenge of tough demands and, through effort, meet them. Listen to two Motorola employees describe their experience on a project to turn out a product for Nippon Telephone and Telegraph:

"The customer came and told us that nothing except absolute excellence would be accepted. The team was really turned on by the challenge of doing something that was considered impossible."

"People were challenged every day. There was a strong drive to succeed in this program. It was the most exciting time of my life."

Those are empowered people.

To create this kind of environment, managers have to personally experiment with demand making on some urgently needed improvement, like accelerating the development of new products, making far-reaching gains in quality, or improving customer relationships. Demand making can enliven organizations with the challenge of tough goals and the gratification that comes with success. Without an ever-sharpening demand framework, improvement programs and activities are merely diversions from the real work of making our corporations more competitive worldwide.

—Robert H. Schaffer

# 3
# The New Managerial Work

## Rosabeth Moss Kanter

Managerial work is undergoing such enormous and rapid change that many managers are reinventing their profession as they go. With little precedent to guide them, they are watching hierarchy fade away and the clear distinctions of title, task, department, even corporation, blur. Faced with extraordinary levels of complexity and interdependency, they watch traditional sources of power erode and the old motivational tools lose their magic.

The cause is obvious. Competitive pressures are forcing corporations to adopt new flexible strategies and structures. Many of these are familiar: acquisitions and divestitures aimed at more focused combinations of business activities, reductions in management staff and levels of hierarchy, increased use of performance-based rewards. Other strategies are less common but have an even more profound effect. In a growing number of companies, for example, horizontal ties between peers are replacing vertical ties as channels of activity and communication. Companies are asking corporate staffs and functional departments to play a more strategic role with greater cross-departmental collaboration. Some organizations are turning themselves nearly inside out—buying formerly internal services from outside suppliers, forming strategic alliances and supplier-customer partnerships that bring external relationships inside where they can influence company policy and practice. I call these emerging practices "postentrepreneurial" because they involve the application of entrepreneurial creativity and flexibility to established businesses.

Such changes come highly recommended by the experts who urge organizations to become leaner, less bureaucratic, more entrepreneurial. But so far, theorists have given scant attention to the dramatically altered realities of managerial work in these transformed corporations. We don't even have good words to describe the new relationships. "Superiors" and "subordinates" hardly seem accurate, and even "bosses" and "their people" imply more control and ownership than managers today actually possess. On top of it all, career paths are no longer straightforward and predictable but have become idiosyncratic and confusing.

Some managers experience the new managerial work as a loss of power because much of their authority used to come from hierarchical position. Now that everything seems negotiable by everyone, they are confused about how to mobilize and motivate staff. For other managers, the shift in roles and tasks offers greater personal power. The following case histories illustrate the responses of three managers in three different industries to the opportunities and dilemmas of structural change.

**Hank is vice president and chief engineer for a leading heavy equipment manufacturer** that is moving aggressively against foreign competition. One of the company's top priorities has been to increase the speed, quality, and cost-effectiveness of product development. So Hank worked with consultants to improve collaboration between manufacturing and other functions and to create closer alliances between the company and its outside suppliers. Gradually, a highly segmented operation became an integrated process involving project teams drawn from component divisions, functional departments, and external suppliers. But along the way, there were several unusual side effects. Different areas of responsibility overlapped. Some technical and manufacturing people were co-located. Liaisons from functional areas joined the larger development teams. Most unusual of all, project teams had a lot of direct contact with higher levels of the company.

Many of the managers reporting to Hank felt these changes as a loss of power. They didn't always know what their people were doing, but they still believed they ought to know. They no longer had sole input into performance appraisals; other people from other functions had a voice as well, and some of them knew more about employees' project performance. New career paths made it less important to please direct superiors in order to move up the functional line.

Moreover, employees often bypassed Hank's managers and interacted directly with decision makers inside and outside the company. Some of these so-called subordinates had contact with division executives and senior corporate staff, and sometimes they sat in on high-level strategy meetings to which their managers were not invited.

At first Hank thought his managers' resistance to the new process was just the normal noise associated with any change. Then he began to realize that something more profound was going on. The reorganization was challenging traditional notions about the role and power of managers and shaking traditional hierarchy to its roots. And no one could see what was taking its place.

**When George became head of a major corporate department in a large bank holding company**, he thought he had arrived. His title and rank were unmistakable, and his department was responsible for determining product-line policy for hundreds of bank branches and the virtual clerks—in George's eyes—who managed them. George staffed his department with MBAs and promised them rapid promotion.

Then the sand seemed to shift beneath him. Losing market position for the first time in recent memory, the bank decided to emphasize direct customer service at the branches. The people George considered clerks began to depart from George's standard policies and to tailor their services to local market conditions. In many cases, they actually demanded services and responses from George's staff, and the results of their requests began to figure in performance reviews of George's department. George's people were spending more and more time in the field with branch managers, and the corporate personnel department was even trying to assign some of George's MBAs to branch and regional posts.

To complicate matters, the bank's strategy included a growing role for technology. George felt that because he had no direct control over the information systems department, he should not be held fully accountable for every facet of product design and implementation. But fully accountable he was. He had to deploy people to learn the new technology and figure out how to work with it. Furthermore, the bank was asking product departments like George's to find ways to link existing products or develop new ones that crossed traditional categories. So George's people were often away on cross-departmental teams just when he wanted them for some internal assignment.

Instead of presiding over a tidy empire the way his predecessor had, George presided over what looked to him like chaos. The bank said senior executives should be "leaders, not managers," but George didn't know what that meant, especially since he seemed to have lost control over his subordinates' assignments, activities, rewards, and careers. He resented his perceived loss of status.

The CEO tried to show him that good results achieved the new way would bring great monetary rewards, thanks to a performance-based bonus program that was gradually replacing more modest yearly raises. But the pressures on George were also greater, unlike anything he'd ever experienced.

**For Sally, purchasing manager at an innovative computer company**, a new organizational strategy was a gain rather than a loss, although it changed her relationship with the people reporting to her. Less than ten years out of college, she was hired as an analyst—a semiprofessional, semiclerical job—then promoted to a purchasing manager's job in a sleepy staff department. She didn't expect to go much further in what was then a well-established hierarchy. But after a shocking downturn, top management encouraged employees to rethink traditional ways of doing things. Sally's boss, the head of purchasing, suggested that "partnerships" with key suppliers might improve quality, speed innovation, and reduce costs.

Soon Sally's backwater was at the center of policy-making, and Sally began to help shape strategy. She organized meetings between her company's senior executives and supplier CEOs. She sent her staff to contribute supplier intelligence at company seminars on technical innovation, and she spent more of her own time with product designers and manufacturing planners. She led senior executives on a tour of supplier facilities, traveling with them in the corporate jet.

Because some suppliers were also important customers, Sally's staff began meeting frequently with marketing managers to share information and address joint problems. Sally and her group were now also acting as internal advocates for major suppliers. Furthermore, many of these external companies now contributed performance appraisals of Sally and her team, and their opinions weighed almost as heavily as those of her superiors.

As a result of the company's new direction, Sally felt more personal power and influence, and her ties to peers in other areas and to top management were stronger. But she no longer felt like a manager directing subordinates. Her staff had become a pool of resources deployed by many others besides Sally. She was exhilarated by her personal opportunities but not quite sure the people she managed should have the same freedom to choose their own assignments. After all, wasn't that a manager's prerogative?

Hank's, George's, and Sally's very different stories say much about the changing nature of managerial work. However hard it is for managers at the very top to remake strategy and structure, they themselves will probably retain their identity, status, and control. For the managers below them, structural change is often much harder. As work units become more participative and team oriented, and as professionals and knowledge workers become more prominent, the distinction between manager and nonmanager begins to erode.

## The New Managerial Quandaries

- At American Express, the CEO instituted a program called "One Enterprise" to encourage collaboration between different lines of business. One Enterprise has led to a range of projects where peers from different divisions work together on such synergistic ventures as cross-marketing, joint purchasing, and cooperative product and market innovation. Employees' rewards are tied to their One Enterprise efforts. Executives set goals and can earn bonuses for their contributions to results in other divisions.
- But how do department managers control their people when they're working on cross-departmental teams? And who determines the size of the rewards when the interests of more than one area are involved?

- At Security Pacific National Bank, internal departments have become forces in the external marketplace. For example, the bank is involved in a joint venture with local auto dealers to sell fast financing for car purchases. And the MIS department is now a profit center selling its services inside and outside the bank.
- But what is the role of bank managers accountable for the success of such entrepreneurial ventures? And how do they shift their orientation from the role of boss in a chain of command to the role of the customer?

- At Digital Equipment Corporation, emphasis on supplier partnerships to improve quality and innovation has multiplied the need for cross-functional as well as cross-company collaboration. Key suppliers are included on product planning teams with engineering, manufacturing, and purchasing staff. Digital uses its human resources staff to train and do performance appraisals of its suppliers, as if they were part of the company. In cases where suppliers are also customers, purchasing and marketing departments also need to work collaboratively.
- But how do managers learn enough about other functions to be credible, let alone influential, members of such teams? How do they maintain adequate communication externally while staying on top of what their own departments are doing? And how do they handle the extra work of responding to projects initiated by other areas?

- At Banc One, a growing reliance on project teams spanning more than 70 affiliated banks has led the CEO to propose eliminating officer titles because of the lack of correlation between status as measured by title and status within the collaborative team.

○ But then what do "rank" and "hierarchy" mean anymore, especially for people whose careers consist of a sequence of projects rather than a sequence of promotions? What does "career" mean? Does it have a shape? Is there a ladder?

• At Alcan, which is trying to find new uses and applications for its core product, aluminum, managers and professionals from line divisions form screening teams to consider and refine new-venture proposals. A venture manager, chosen from the screening team, takes charge of concepts that pass muster, drawing on Alcan's worldwide resources to build the new business. In one case of global synergy, Alcan created a new product for the Japanese market using Swedish and American technology and Canadian manufacturing capacity.

○ But why should senior managers release staff to serve on screening and project teams for new businesses when their own businesses are making do with fewer and fewer people? How do functionally oriented managers learn enough about worldwide developments to know when they might have something of value to offer someplace else? And how do the managers of these new ventures ever go back to the conventional line organization as middle managers once their venture has been folded into an established division?

• At IBM, an emphasis on customer partnerships to rebuild market share is leading to practices quite new to the company. In some cases, IBM has formed joint development teams with customers, where engineers from both companies share proprietary data. In others, the company has gone beyond selling equipment to actually managing a customer's management information system. Eastman Kodak has handed its U.S. data center operations to IBM to consolidate and manage, which means lower fixed costs for Kodak and greater ability to focus on its core businesses rather than on ancillary services. Some 300 former Kodak people still fill Kodak's needs as IBM employees, while two committees of IBM and Kodak managers oversee the partnership.

○ But who exactly do the data center people work for? Who is in charge? And how do traditional notions of managerial authority square with such a complicated set of relationships?

To understand what managers must do to achieve results in the postentrepreneurial corporation, we need to look at the changing picture of how such companies operate. The picture has five elements:

1. There are a greater number and variety of channels for taking action and exerting influence.

2. Relationships of influence are shifting from the vertical to the horizontal, from chain of command to peer networks.

3. The distinction between managers and those managed is diminishing, especially in terms of information, control over assignments, and access to external relationships.

4. External relationships are increasingly important as sources of internal power and influence, even of career development.

5. As a result of the first four changes, career development has become less intelligible but also less circumscribed. There are fewer assured routes to success, which produces anxiety. At the same time, career paths are more open to innovation, which produces opportunity.

To help companies implement their competitive organizational strategies, managers must learn new ways to manage, confronting changes in their own bases of power and recognizing the need for new ways to motivate people.

## The Bases of Power

The changes I've talked about can be scary for people like George and the managers reporting to Hank, who were trained to know their place, to follow orders, to let the company take care of their careers, to do things by the book. The book is gone. In the new corporation, managers have only themselves to count on for success. They must learn to operate without the crutch of hierarchy. Position, title, and authority are no longer adequate tools, not in a world where subordinates are encouraged to think for themselves and where managers have to work synergistically with other departments and even other companies. Success depends increasingly on tapping into sources of good ideas, on figuring out whose collaboration is needed to act on those ideas, on working with both to produce results. In short, the new managerial work implies very different ways of obtaining and using power.

The postentrepreneurial corporation is not only leaner and flatter, it also has many more channels for action. Cross-functional projects, business-unit joint ventures, labor-management forums, innovation funds that spawn activities outside mainstream budgets and reporting lines, strategic partnerships with suppliers or customers—these are all overlays on the traditional organization chart, strategic pathways that ignore the chain of command.

Their existence has several important implications. For one thing, they create more potential centers of power. As the ways to combine resources increase, the ability to command diminishes. Alternative paths of communication, resource access, and execution erode the authority of those in the nominal chain of command. In other words, the opportunity for greater speed and flexibility undermines hierarchy. As more and more strategic action takes place in these channels, the jobs that focus inward on particular departments decline in power.

As a result, the ability of managers to get things done depends more on the number of networks in which they're centrally involved than on their height in a hierarchy. Of course, power in any organization always has a network component, but rank and formal structure used to be more limiting. For example, access to information and the ability to get informal backing were often confined to the few officially sanctioned contact points between departments or between the company and its vendors or customers. Today these official barriers are disappearing, while so-called informal networks grow in importance.

In the emerging organization, managers add value by deal making, by brokering at interfaces, rather than by presiding over their individual empires. It was traditionally the job of top executives or specialists to scan the business environment for new ideas, opportunities, and resources. This kind of environmental scanning is now an important part of a manager's job at every level and in every function. And the environment to be scanned includes various company divisions, many potential outside partners, and large parts of the world. At the same time, people are encouraged to think about what they know that might have value elsewhere. An engineer designing windshield wipers, for example, might discover properties of rubber adhesion to glass that could be useful in other manufacturing areas.

Every manager must think cross-functionally because every department has to play a strategic role, understanding and contributing to other facets of the business. In Hank's company, the technical managers and staff working on design engineering used to concentrate only on their own areas of expertise. Under the new system, they have to keep in mind what manufacturing does and how it does it. They need to visit plants and build relationships so they can ask informed questions.

One multinational corporation, eager to extend the uses of its core product, put its R&D staff and laboratory personnel in direct contact with marketing experts to discuss lines of research. Similarly, the superior economic track record of Raytheon's New Products Center—dozens of new products and patents yielding profits many times their development costs—derives from the connections it builds between its inventors and the engineering and marketing staffs of the business units it serves.

This strategic and collaborative role is particularly important for the managers and professionals on corporate staffs. They need to serve as integrators and facilitators, not as watchdogs and interventionists. They need to sell their services, justify themselves to the business units they serve, literally compete with outside suppliers. General Foods recently put overhead charges for corporate staff services on a pay-as-you-use basis. Formerly, these charges were either assigned uniformly to users and nonusers alike, or the services were mandatory. Product managers sometimes had to work through as many as eight layers of management and corporate staff to get business plans approved. Now these staffs must prove to the satisfaction of their internal customers that their services add value.

By contrast, some banks still have corporate training departments that do very little except get in the way. They do no actual training, for example, yet they still exercise veto power over urgent divisional training decisions and consultant contracts.

As managers and professionals spend more time working across boundaries with peers and partners over whom they have no direct control, their negotiating skills become essential assets. Alliances and partnerships transform impersonal, arm's-length contracts into relationships involving joint planning and joint decision making. Internal competitors and adversaries become allies on whom managers depend for their own success. At the same time, more managers at more levels are active in the kind of external diplomacy that only the CEO or selected staffs used to conduct.

In the collaborative forums that result, managers are more personally exposed. It is trust that makes partnerships work. Since collaborative ventures often bring together groups with different methods, cultures, symbols, even languages, good deal making depends on empathy—the ability to step into other people's shoes and appreciate their goals. This applies not only to intricate global joint ventures but also to the efforts of engineering and manufacturing to work together more effectively. Effective communication in a cooperative effort rests on more than a simple exchange of information; people must be adept at anticipating the responses of other groups. "Before I get too excited about our department's design ideas," an engineering manager told me, "I'm learning to ask myself, 'What's the marketing position on this? What will manufacturing say?' That sometimes forces me to make changes before I even talk to them."

An increase in the number of channels for strategic contact within the postentrepreneurial organization means more opportunities for people with ideas or information to trigger action: salespeople encouraging account managers to build strategic partnerships with customers, for example, or technicians searching for ways to tap new-venture funds to develop software. Moreover, top executives who have to spend more time on cross-boundary relationships are forced to delegate more responsibility to lower level managers. Delegation is one more blow to hierarchy, of course, since subordinates with greater responsibility are bolder about speaking up, challenging authority, and charting their own course.

For example, it is common for new-venture teams to complain publicly about corporate support departments and to reject their use in favor of external service providers, often to the consternation of more orthodox superiors. A more startling example occurred in a health care company where members of a task force charged with finding synergies among three lines of business shocked corporate executives by criticizing upper management behavior in their report. Service on the task force had created collective awareness of a shared problem and had given people the courage to confront it.

The search for internal synergies, the development of strategic alliances, and the push for new ventures all emphasize the political side of a leader's work. Executives must be able to juggle a set of constituencies rather than control a set of subordinates. They have to bargain, negotiate, and sell instead of making unilateral decisions and issuing commands. The leader's task, as Chester Barnard recognized long ago, is to develop a network of cooperative relationships among all the people, groups, and organizations that have something to contribute to an economic enterprise. Postentrepreneurial strategies magnify the complexity of this task. After leading Teknowledge, a producer of expert systems software, through development alliances with six corporations including General Motors and Procter & Gamble, company chairman Lee Hecht said he felt like the mayor of a small city. "I have a constituency that won't quit. It takes a hell of a lot of balancing." The kind of power achieved through a network of stakeholders is very different from the kind of power managers wield in a traditional bureaucracy. The new way gets more done, but it also takes more time. And it creates an illusion about freedom and security.

The absence of day-to-day constraints, the admonition to assume responsibility, the pretense of equality, the elimination of visible status markers, the prevalence of candid dialogues across hierarchical levels—these can give employees a false sense that all hierarchy is a thing of the past. Yet at the same time, employees still count on hierarchy to shield them when things go wrong. This combination would create the perfect marriage of freedom and support—freedom when people want to take risks, support when the risks don't work out.

In reality, less benevolent combinations are also possible, combinations not of freedom and support but of insecurity and loss of control. There is often a pretense in postentrepreneurial companies that status differences have nothing to do with power, that the deference paid to top executives derives from their superior qualifications rather than from the power they have over the fates of others. But the people at the top of the organization chart still wield power—and sometimes in ways that managers below them experience as arbitrary. Unprecedented individual freedom also applies to top managers, who are now free to make previously unimaginable deals, order unimaginable cuts, or launch unimaginable takeovers. The reorganizations that companies undertake in their search for new synergies can uncover the potential unpredictability and capriciousness of corporate careers. A man whose company was undergoing drastic restructuring told me, "For all of my ownership share and strategic centrality and voice in decisions, I can still be faced with a shift in direction not of my own making. I can still be reorganized into a corner. I can still be relocated into oblivion. I can still be reviewed out of my special project budget."

These realities of power, change, and job security are important because they affect the way people view their leaders. When the illusion of simultaneous freedom and protection fades, the result can be a loss of motivation.

## Sources of Motivation

One of the essential, unchanging tasks of leaders is to motivate and guide performance. But motivational tools are changing fast. More and more businesses are doing away with the old bureaucratic incentives and using entrepreneurial opportunity to attract the best talent. Managers must exercise more leadership even as they watch their bureaucratic power slip away. Leadership, in short, is more difficult yet more critical than ever.

Because of the unpredictability of even the most benign restructuring, managers are less able to guarantee a particular job—or any job at all—no matter what a subordinate's performance level. The reduction in hierarchical levels curtails a manager's ability to promise promotion. New compensation systems that make bonuses and raises dependent on objective performance measures and on team appraisals deprive managers of their role as the sole arbiter of higher pay. Cross-functional and cross-company teams can rob managers of their right to direct or even understand the work their so-called subordinates do. In any case, the shift from routine work, which was amenable to oversight, to "knowledge" work, which often is not, erodes a manager's claim to superior expertise. And partnerships and ventures that put lower level people in direct contact with each other across departmental and company boundaries cut heavily into the managerial monopoly on information. At a consumer packaged-goods manufacturer that replaced several levels of hierarchy with teams, plant team members in direct contact with the sales force often had data on product ordering trends before the higher level brand managers who set product policy.

As if the loss of carrots and sticks was not enough, many managers can no longer even give their people clear job standards and easily mastered procedural rules. Postentrepreneurial corporations seek problem-solving, initiative-taking employees who will go the unexpected extra mile for the customer. To complicate the situation further still, the complexities of work in the new organization—projects and relationships clamoring for attention in every direction—exacerbate the feeling of overload.

With the old motivational tool kit depleted, leaders need new and more effective incentives to encourage high performance and build commitment. There are five new tools:

*Mission.* Helping people believe in the importance of their work is essential, especially when other forms of certainty and security have disappeared. Good leaders can inspire others with the power and excitement of their vision and give people a sense of purpose and pride in their work. Pride is often a better source of motivation than the traditional corporate career ladder and the promotion-based reward system. Technical professionals, for example, are often motivated most effectively by the desire to see their work contribute to an excellent final product.

*Agenda Control.* As career paths lose their certainty and companies' futures grow less predictable, people can at least be in charge of their own professional lives. More and more professionals are passing up jobs with glamour and prestige in favor of jobs that give them greater control over their own activities and direction. Leaders give their subordinates this opportunity when they give them release time to work on pet projects, when they emphasize results instead of procedures, and when they delegate work and the decisions about how to do it. Choice of their next project is a potent reward for people who perform well.

*Share of Value Creation.* Entrepreneurial incentives that give teams a piece of the action are highly appropriate in collaborative companies. Because extra rewards are based only on measurable results, this approach also conserves resources. Innovative companies are experimenting with incentives like phantom stock for development of new ventures and other strategic achievements, equity participation in project returns, and bonuses pegged to key performance targets. Given the cross-functional nature of many projects today, rewards of this kind must sometimes be systemwide, but individual managers can also ask for a bonus pool for their own areas, contingent, of course, on meeting performance goals. And everyone can share the kinds of rewards that are abundant and free—awards and recognition.

*Learning.* The chance to learn new skills or apply them in new arenas is an important motivator in a turbulent environment because it's oriented toward securing the future. "The learning organization" promises to become a 1990s business buzzword as companies seek to learn more systematically from their experience and to encourage continuous learning for their people. In the world of high technology, where people understand uncertainty, the attractiveness of any company often lies in its capacity to provide learning and experience. By this calculus, access to training, mentors, and challenging projects is more important than pay or benefits. Some prominent companies—General Electric, for example—have always been able to attract top talent, even when they could not promise upward mobility, because people see them as a training ground, a good place to learn, and a valuable addition to a resume.

*Reputation.* Reputation is a key resource in professional careers, and the chance to enhance it can be an outstanding motivator. The professional's reliance on reputation stands in marked contrast to the bureaucrat's anonymity. Professionals have to make a name for themselves, while traditional corporate managers and employees stayed behind the scenes. Indeed, the accumulation of reputational "capital" provides not only an immediate ego boost but also the kind of publicity that can bring other rewards, even other job offers. Managers can enhance reputation—and improve motivation—by creating stars, by providing abundant public recognition and visible awards, by crediting the authors of innovation, by publicizing people outside their own departments, and by plugging people into organizational and professional networks.

The new, collaborative organization is predicated on a logic of flexible work assignments, not of fixed job responsibilities. To promote innovation and responsiveness, two of today's competitive imperatives, managers need to see this new organization as a cluster of activity sets, not as a rigid structure. The work of leadership in this new corporation will be to organize both sequential and synchronous projects of varying length and breadth, through which varying combinations of people will move, depending on the tasks, challenges, and opportunities facing the area and its partners at any given moment.

Leaders need to carve out projects with tangible accomplishments, milestones, and completion dates and then delegate responsibility for these projects to the people who flesh them out. Clearly delimited projects can counter overload by focusing effort and can provide short-term motivation when the fate of the long-term mission is uncertain. Project responsibility leads to ownership of the results and sometimes substitutes for other forms of reward. In companies where product development teams define and run their own projects, members commonly say that the greatest compensation they get is seeing the advertisements for their products. "Hey, that's mine! I did that!" one engineer told me he trumpeted to his family the first time he saw a commercial for his group's innovation.

This sense of ownership, along with a definite time frame, can spur higher levels of effort. Whenever people are engaged in creative or problem-solving projects that will have tangible results by deadline dates, they tend to come in at all hours, to think about the project in their spare time, to invest in it vast sums of physical and emotional energy. Knowing that the project will end and that completion will be an occasion for reward and recognition makes it possible to work much harder.

Leaders in the new organization do not lack motivational tools, but the tools are different from those of traditional corporate bureaucrats. The new rewards are based not on status but on contribution, and they consist not of regular promotion and automatic pay raises but of excitement about mission and a share of the glory and the gains of success. The new security is not employment security (a guaranteed job no matter what) but *employability* security—increased value in the internal and external labor markets. Commitment to the organization still matters, but today managers build commitment by offering project opportunities. The new loyalty is not to the boss or to the company but to projects that actualize a mission and offer challenge, growth, and credit for results.

The old bases of managerial authority are eroding, and new tools of leadership are taking their place. Managers whose power derived from hierarchy and who were accustomed to a limited area of personal control are learning to shift their perspectives and widen their horizons. The new managerial work consists of looking outside a defined area of responsibility to sense opportunities and of forming project teams drawn from any relevant sphere to address them. It involves communication and collaboration across functions, across divisions, and across companies whose activities and resources overlap. Thus rank, title, or official charter will be less important factors in success at the new managerial work than having the knowledge, skills, and sensitivity to mobilize people and motivate them to do their best.

# 4

# The Work of Leadership

## Ronald A. Heifetz and Donald L. Laurie

To stay alive, Jack Pritchard had to change his life. Triple bypass surgery and medication could help, the heart surgeon told him, but no technical fix could release Pritchard from his own responsibility for changing the habits of a lifetime. He had to stop smoking, improve his diet, get some exercise, and take time to relax, remembering to breathe more deeply each day. Pritchard's doctor could provide sustaining technical expertise and take supportive action, but only Pritchard could adapt his ingrained habits to improve his long-term health. The doctor faced the leadership task of mobilizing the patient to make critical behavioral changes; Jack Pritchard faced the adaptive work of figuring out which specific changes to make and how to incorporate them into his daily life.

Companies today face challenges similar to the ones confronting Pritchard and his doctor. They face *adaptive challenges*. Changes in societies, markets, customers, competition, and technology around the globe are forcing organizations to clarify their values, develop new strategies, and learn new ways of operating. Often the toughest task for leaders in effecting change is mobilizing people throughout the organization to do adaptive work.

Adaptive work is required when our deeply held beliefs are challenged, when the values that made us successful become less relevant, and when legitimate yet competing perspectives emerge. We see adaptive challenges every day at every level of the workplace—when companies restructure or reengineer, develop or implement strategy, or merge businesses. We see adaptive challenges when marketing has difficulty working with operations, when cross-functional teams don't work well, or when senior executives complain, "We don't seem to be able to execute effectively." Adaptive problems are often systemic problems with no ready answers.

Mobilizing an organization to adapt its behaviors in order to thrive in new business environments is critical. Without such change, any company today would falter. Indeed, getting people to do adaptive work is the mark of leadership in a competitive world. Yet for most senior executives, providing leadership and not just authoritative expertise is extremely difficult. Why? We see two reasons. First, in order to make change happen, executives have to break a long-standing behavior pattern of their own: providing leadership in the form of solutions. This tendency is quite natural because many executives reach their positions of authority by virtue of their competence in taking responsibility and solving problems. But the locus of responsibility for problem solving when a company faces an adaptive challenge must shift to its people. Solutions to adaptive challenges reside not in the executive suite but in the collective intelligence of employees at all levels, who need to use one another as resources, often across boundaries, and learn their way to those solutions.

Second, adaptive change is distressing for the people going through it. They need to take on new roles, new relationships, new values, new behaviors, and new approaches to work. Many employees are ambivalent about the efforts and sacrifices required of them. They often look to the senior executive to take problems off their shoulders. But those expectations have to be unlearned. Rather than fulfilling the expectation that they will provide answers, leaders have to ask tough questions. Rather than protecting people from outside threats, leaders should allow them to feel the pinch of reality in order to stimulate them to adapt. Instead of orienting people to their current roles, leaders must disorient them so that new relationships can develop. Instead of quelling conflict, leaders have to draw the issues out. Instead of maintaining norms, leaders have to challenge "the way we do business" and help others distinguish immutable values from historical practices that must go.

Drawing on our experience with managers from around the world, we offer six principles for leading adaptive work: "getting on the balcony," identifying the adaptive challenge, regulating distress, maintaining disciplined attention, giving the work back to people, and protecting voices of leadership from below. We illustrate those principles with an example of adaptive change at KPMG Netherlands, a professional-services firm.

## Get on the Balcony

Earvin "Magic" Johnson's greatness in leading his basketball team came in part from his ability to play hard while keeping the whole game situation in mind, as if he stood in a press box or on a balcony above the field of play. Bobby Orr played hockey in the same way. Other players might fail to recognize the larger patterns of play that performers like Johnson and Orr quickly understand, because they are so engaged in the game that they get carried away by it. Their attention is captured by the rapid motion, the physical contact, the roar of the crowd, and the pressure to execute. In sports, most players simply may not see who is open for a pass, who is missing a block, or how the offense and defense work together. Players like Johnson and Orr watch these things and allow their observations to guide their actions.

Business leaders have to be able to view patterns as if they were on a balcony. It does them no good to be swept up in the field of action. Leaders have to see a context for change or create one. They should give employees a strong sense of the history of the enterprise and what's good about its past, as well as an idea of the market forces at work today and the responsibility people must take in shaping the future. Leaders must be able to identify struggles over values and power, recognize patterns of work avoidance, and watch for the many other functional and dysfunctional reactions to change.

Without the capacity to move back and forth between the field of action and the balcony, to reflect day to day, moment to moment, on the many ways in which an organization's habits can sabotage adaptive work, a leader easily and unwittingly becomes a prisoner of the system. The dynamics of adaptive change are far too complex to keep track of, let alone influence, if leaders stay only on the field of play.

We have encountered several leaders, some of whom we discuss in this article, who manage to spend much of their precious time on the balcony as they guide their organizations through change. Without that perspective, they probably would have been unable to mobilize people to do adaptive work. Getting on the balcony is thus a prerequisite for following the next five principles.

## Identify the Adaptive Challenge

When a leopard threatens a band of chimpanzees, the leopard rarely succeeds in picking off a stray. Chimps know how to respond to this kind of threat. But when a man with an automatic rifle comes near, the routine responses fail. Chimps risk extinction in a world of poachers unless they figure out how to disarm the new threat. Similarly, when businesses cannot learn quickly to adapt to new challenges, they are likely to face their own form of extinction.

Consider the well-known case of British Airways. Having observed the revolutionary changes in the airline industry during the 1980s, then chief executive Colin Marshall clearly recognized the need to transform an airline nicknamed Bloody Awful by its own passengers into an exemplar of customer service. He also understood that this ambition would require more than anything else changes in values, practices, and relationships throughout the company. An organization whose people clung to functional silos and valued pleasing their bosses more than pleasing customers could not become The World's Favourite Airline. Marshall needed an organization dedicated to serving people, acting on trust, respecting the individual, and making teamwork happen across boundaries. Values had to change throughout British Airways. People had to learn to collaborate and to develop a collective sense of responsibility for the direction and performance of the airline. Marshall identified the essential adaptive challenge: creating trust throughout the organization. He is one of the first executives we have known to make "creating trust" a priority.

To lead British Airways, Marshall had to get his executive team to understand the nature of the threat created by dissatisfied customers: Did it represent a technical challenge or an adaptive challenge? Would expert advice and technical adjustments within basic routines suffice, or would people throughout the company have to learn new ways of doing business, develop new competencies, and begin to work collectively?

Marshall and his team set out to diagnose in more detail the organization's challenges. They looked in three places. First, they listened to the ideas and concerns of people inside and outside the organization—meeting with crews on flights, showing up in the 350-person reservation center in New York, wandering around the baggage-handling area in Tokyo, or visiting the passenger lounge in whatever airport they happened to be in. Their primary questions were, Whose values, beliefs, attitudes, or behaviors would have to change in order for progress to take place? What shifts in priorities, resources, and power were necessary? What sacrifices would have to be made and by whom?

Second, Marshall and his team saw conflicts as clues—symptoms of adaptive challenges. The way conflicts across functions were being expressed were mere surface phenomena: the underlying conflicts had to be diagnosed. Disputes over seemingly technical issues such as procedures, schedules, and lines of authority were in fact proxies for underlying conflicts about values and norms.

Third, Marshall and his team held a mirror up to themselves, recognizing that they embodied the adaptive challenges facing the organization. Early in the transformation of British Airways, competing values and norms were played out on the executive team in dysfunctional ways that impaired the capacity of the rest of the company to collaborate across functions and units and make the necessary trade-offs. No executive can hide from the fact that his or her team reflects the best and the worst of the company's values and norms, and therefore provides a case in point for insight into the nature of the adaptive work ahead.

Thus, identifying its adaptive challenge was crucial in British Airways' bid to become The World's Favourite Airline. For the strategy to succeed, the company's leaders needed to understand themselves, their people, and the potential sources of conflict. Marshall recognized that strategy development itself requires adaptive work.

## Regulate Distress

Adaptive work generates distress. Before putting people to work on challenges for which there are no ready solutions, a leader must realize that people can learn only so much so fast. At the same time, they must feel the need to change as reality brings new challenges. They cannot learn new ways when they are overwhelmed, but eliminating stress altogether removes the impetus for doing adaptive work. Because a leader must strike a delicate balance between having people feel the need to change and having them feel overwhelmed by change, leadership is a razor's edge.

A leader must attend to three fundamental tasks in order to help maintain a productive level of tension. Adhering to these tasks will allow him or her to motivate people without disabling them.

First, a leader must create what can be called a holding environment. To use the analogy of a pressure cooker, a leader needs to regulate the pressure by turning up the heat while also allowing some steam to escape. If the pressure exceeds the cooker's capacity, the cooker can blow up. However, nothing cooks without some heat.

In the early stages of corporate change, the holding environment can be a temporary "place" in which a leader creates the conditions for diverse groups to talk to one another about the challenges facing them, to frame and debate issues, and to clarify the assumptions behind competing perspectives and values. Over time, more issues can be phased in as they become ripe. At British Airways, for example, the shift from an internal focus to a customer focus took place over four or five years and dealt with important issues in succession: building a credible executive team, communicating with a highly fragmented organization, defining new measures of performance and compensation, and developing sophisticated information systems. During that time, employees at all levels learned to identify what and how they needed to change.

Thus a leader must sequence and pace the work. Too often, senior managers convey that everything is important. They start new initiatives without stopping other activities or they start too many initiatives at the same time. They overwhelm and disorient the very people who need to take responsibility for the work.

Second, a leader is responsible for direction, protection, orientation, managing conflict, and shaping norms. (See the table "Adaptive Work Calls for Leadership.") Fulfilling these responsibilities is also important for a manager in technical or routine situations. But a leader engaged in adaptive work uses his authority to fulfill them differently. A leader provides direction by identifying the organization's adaptive challenge and framing the key questions and issues. A leader protects people by managing the rate of change. A leader orients people to new roles and responsibilities by clarifying business realities and key values. A leader helps expose conflict, viewing it as the engine of creativity and learning. Finally, a leader helps the organization maintain those norms that must endure and challenge those that need to change.

Third, a leader must have presence and poise; regulating distress is perhaps a leader's most difficult job. The pressures to restore equilibrium are enormous. Just as molecules bang hard against the walls of a pressure cooker, people bang up against leaders who are trying to sustain the pressures of tough, conflict-filled work. Although leadership demands a deep understanding of the pain of change—the fears and sacrifices associated with major readjustment—it also requires the ability to hold steady and maintain the tension. Otherwise, the pressure escapes and the stimulus for learning and change is lost.

A leader has to have the emotional capacity to tolerate uncertainty, frustration, and pain. He has to be able to raise tough questions

### Table 1    Adaptive Work Calls for Leadership

| Responsibilities | Situation | |
| --- | --- | --- |
| | **Technical or Routine** | **Adaptive** |
| Direction | Define problems and provide solutions | Identify the adaptive challenge and frame key questions and issues |
| Protection | Shield the organization from external threats | Let the organization feel external pressures within a range it can stand |
| Orientation | Clarify roles and responsibilities | Challenge current roles and resist pressure to define new roles quickly |
| Managing Conflict | Restore order | Expose conflict or let it emerge |
| Shaping Norms | Maintain norms | Challenge unproductive norms |

without getting too anxious himself. Employees as well as colleagues and customers will carefully observe verbal and nonverbal cues to a leader's ability to hold steady. He needs to communicate confidence that he and they can tackle the tasks ahead.

## Maintain Disciplined Attention

Different people within the same organization bring different experiences, assumptions, values, beliefs, and habits to their work. This diversity is valuable because innovation and learning are the products of differences. No one learns anything without being open to contrasting points of view. Yet managers at all levels are often unwilling—or unable—to address their competing perspectives collectively. They frequently avoid paying attention to issues that disturb them. They restore equilibrium quickly, often with work avoidance maneuvers. A leader must get employees to confront tough trade-offs in values, procedures, operating styles, and power.

That is as true at the top of the organization as it is in the middle or on the front line. Indeed, if the executive team cannot model adaptive work, the organization will languish. If senior managers can't draw out and deal with divisive issues, how will people elsewhere in the organization change their behaviors and rework their relationships? As Jan Carlzon, the legendary CEO of Scandinavian Airlines System (SAS), told us, "One of the most interesting missions of leadership is getting people on the executive team to listen to and learn from one another. Held in debate, people can learn their way to collective solutions when they understand one another's assumptions. The work of the leader is to get conflict out into the open and use it as a source of creativity."

Because work avoidance is rampant in organizations, a leader has to counteract distractions that prevent people from dealing with adaptive issues. Scapegoating, denial, focusing only on today's technical issues, or attacking individuals rather than the perspectives they represent—all forms of work avoidance—are to be expected when an organization undertakes adaptive work. Distractions have to be identified when they occur so that people will regain focus.

When sterile conflict takes the place of dialogue, a leader has to step in and put the team to work on reframing the issues. She has to deepen the debate with questions, unbundling the issues into their parts rather than letting conflict remain polarized and superficial. When people preoccupy themselves with blaming external forces, higher management, or a heavy workload, a leader has to sharpen the team's sense of responsibility for carving out the time to press forward. When the team fragments and individuals resort to protecting their own turf, leaders have to demonstrate the need for collaboration. People have to discover the value of consulting with one another and using one another as resources in the problem-solving process. For example, one CEO we know uses executive meetings, even those that focus on operational and technical issues, as opportunities to teach the team how to work collectively on adaptive problems.

Of course, only the rare manager *intends* to avoid adaptive work. In general, people feel ambivalent about it. Although they want to make progress on hard problems or live up to their renewed and clarified values, people also want to avoid the associated distress. Just as millions of U.S. citizens want to reduce the federal budget deficit, but not by giving up their tax dollars or benefits or jobs, so, too, managers may consider adaptive work a priority but have difficulty sacrificing their familiar ways of doing business.

People need leadership to help them maintain their focus on the tough questions. Disciplined attention is the currency of leadership.

## Give the Work Back to People

Everyone in the organization has special access to information that comes from his or her particular vantage point. Everyone may see different needs and opportunities. People who sense early changes in the marketplace are often at the periphery, but the organization will thrive if it can bring that information to bear on tactical and strategic decisions. When people do not act on their special knowledge, businesses fail to adapt.

All too often, people look up the chain of command, expecting senior management to meet market challenges for which they themselves are responsible. Indeed, the greater and more persistent distresses that accompany adaptive work make such dependence worse. People tend to become passive, and senior managers who pride themselves on being problem solvers take decisive action. That behavior restores equilibrium in the short term but ultimately leads to complacency and habits of work avoidance that shield people from responsibility, pain, and the need to change.

Getting people to assume greater responsibility is not easy. Not only are many lower-level employees comfortable being told what to do, but many managers are accustomed to treating subordinates like machinery requiring control. Letting people take the initiative in defining and solving problems means that management needs to learn to support rather than control. Workers, for their part, need to learn to take responsibility.

Jan Carlzon encouraged responsibility taking at SAS by trusting others and decentralizing authority. A leader has to let people bear the weight of responsibility. "The key is to let them discover the problem," he said. "You won't be successful if people aren't carrying the recognition of the problem and the solution within themselves." To that end, Carlzon sought widespread engagement.

For example, in his first two years at SAS, Carlzon spent up to 50% of his time communicating directly in large meetings and indirectly in a host of innovative ways: through workshops, brainstorming sessions, learning exercises, newsletters, brochures, and exposure in the public media. He demonstrated through a variety of symbolic acts—for example, by eliminating the pretentious executive dining room and burning thousands of pages of manuals and handbooks—the extent to which rules had come to dominate the company. He made himself a pervasive presence, meeting with and listening to people both inside and outside the organization. He even wrote a book, *Moments of Truth* (Ballinger, 1987), to explain his values, philosophy, and strategy. As Carlzon noted, "If no one else read it, at least my people would."

A leader also must develop collective self-confidence. Again, Carlzon said it well: "People aren't born with self-confidence. Even the most self-confident people can be broken. Self-confidence comes from success, experience, and the organization's environment. The leader's most important role is to instill confidence in people. They must dare to take risks and responsibility. You must back them up if they make mistakes."

## Protect Voices of Leadership from Below

Giving a voice to all people is the foundation of an organization that is willing to experiment and learn. But, in fact, whistle-blowers, creative deviants, and other such original voices routinely get smashed and silenced in organizational life. They generate disequilibrium, and the easiest way for an organization to restore equilibrium is to neutralize those voices, sometimes in the name of teamwork and "alignment."

The voices from below are usually not as articulate as one would wish. People speaking beyond their authority usually feel self-conscious and sometimes have to generate "too much" passion to get themselves geared up for speaking out. Of course, that often makes it harder for them to communicate effectively. They pick the wrong time and place, and often bypass proper channels of communication and lines of authority. But buried inside a poorly packaged interjection may lie an important intuition that needs to be teased out and considered. To toss it out for its bad timing, lack of clarity, or seeming unreasonableness is to lose potentially valuable information and discourage a potential leader in the organization.

That is what happened to David, a manager in a large manufacturing company. He had listened when his superiors encouraged people to look for problems, speak openly, and take responsibility. So he raised an issue about one of the CEO's pet projects—an issue that was "too hot to handle" and had been swept under the carpet for years. Everyone understood that it was not open to discussion, but David knew that proceeding with the project could damage or derail key elements of the company's overall strategy. He raised the issue directly in a meeting with his boss and the CEO. He provided a clear description of the problem, a rundown of competing perspectives, and a summary of the consequences of continuing to pursue the project.

The CEO angrily squelched the discussion and reinforced the positive aspects of his pet project. When David and his boss left the room, his boss exploded: "Who do you think you are, with your holier-than-thou attitude?" He insinuated that David had never liked the CEO's pet project because David hadn't come up with the idea himself. The subject was closed.

David had greater expertise in the area of the project than either his boss or the CEO. But his two superiors showed no curiosity, no effort to investigate David's reasoning, no awareness that he was behaving responsibly with the interests of the company at heart. It rapidly became clear to David that it was more important to understand what mattered to the boss than to focus on real issues. The CEO and David's boss together squashed the viewpoint of a leader from below and thereby killed his potential for leadership in the organization. He would either leave the company or never go against the grain again.

Leaders must rely on others within the business to raise questions that may indicate an impending adaptive challenge. They have to provide cover to people who point to the internal contradictions of the enterprise. Those individuals often have the perspective to provoke rethinking that people in authority do not. Thus, as a rule of thumb, when authority figures feel the reflexive urge to glare at or otherwise silence someone, they should resist. The urge to restore social equilibrium is quite powerful, and it comes on fast. One has to get accustomed to getting on the balcony, delaying the impulse, and asking, What *really* is this guy talking about? Is there something we're missing?

## Doing Adaptive Work at KPMG Netherlands

The highly successful KPMG Netherlands provides a good example of how a company can engage in adaptive work. In 1994, Ruud Koedijk, the firm's chairman, recognized a strategic challenge. Although the auditing, consulting, and tax-preparation partnership was the industry leader in the Netherlands and was highly profitable, growth opportunities in the segments it served were limited. Margins in the auditing business were being squeezed as the market became more saturated, and competition in the consulting business was increasing as well. Koedijk knew that the firm needed to move into more profitable growth areas, but he didn't know what they were or how KPMG might identify them.

Koedijk and his board were confident that they had the tools to do the analytical strategy work: analyze trends and discontinuities, understand core competencies, assess their competitive position, and map potential opportunities. They were considerably less certain that they could commit to implementing the strategy that would emerge from their work. Historically, the partnership had resisted attempts to change, basically because the partners were content with the way things were. They had been successful for a long time, so they saw no reason to learn new ways of doing business, either from their fellow partners or from anyone lower down in the organization. Overturning the partners' attitude and its deep impact on the organization's culture posed an enormous adaptive challenge for KPMG.

Koedijk could see from the balcony that the very structure of KPMG inhibited change. In truth, KPMG was less a partnership than a collection of small fiefdoms in which each partner was a lord. The firm's success was the cumulative accomplishment of each of the individual partners, not the unified result of 300 colleagues pulling together toward a shared ambition. Success was measured solely in terms of the profitability of individual units. As one partner described it, "If the bottom line was correct, you were a 'good fellow.'" As a result, one partner would not trespass on another's turf, and learning from others was a rare event. Because independence was so highly valued, confrontations were rare and conflict was camouflaged. If partners wanted to resist firmwide change, they did not kill the issue directly. "Say yes, do no" was the operative phrase.

Koedijk also knew that this sense of autonomy got in the way of developing new talent at KPMG. Directors rewarded their subordinates for two things: not making mistakes and delivering a high number of billable hours per week. The emphasis was not on creativity or innovation. Partners were looking for errors when they reviewed their subordinates' work, not for new understanding or fresh insight. Although Koedijk could see the broad outlines of the adaptive challenges facing his organization, he knew that he could not mandate behavioral change. What he could do was create the conditions for people to discover for themselves how they needed to change. He set a process in motion to make that happen.

To start, Koedijk held a meeting of all 300 partners and focused their attention on the history of KPMG, the current business reality, and the business issues they could expect to face. He then raised the question of how they would go about changing as a firm and asked for their perspectives on the issues. By launching the strategic initiative through dialogue rather than edict, he built trust within the partner ranks. Based on this emerging trust and his own credibility, Koedijk persuaded the partners to release 100 partners and nonpartners from their day-to-day responsibilities to work on the strategic challenges. They would devote 60% of their time for nearly four months to that work.

Koedijk and his colleagues established a strategic integration team of 12 senior partners to work with the 100 professionals (called "the 100") from different levels and disciplines. Engaging people below the rank of partner in a major strategic initiative was unheard of and signaled a new approach from the start: many of these people's opinions had never before been valued or sought by authority figures in the firm. Divided into 14 task forces, the 100 were to work in three areas: gauging future trends and discontinuities, defining core competencies, and grappling with the adaptive challenges facing the organization. They were housed on a separate floor with their own support staff, and they were unfettered by traditional rules and regulations. Hennie Both, KPMG's director of marketing and communications, signed on as project manager.

As the strategy work got under way, the task forces had to confront the existing KPMG culture. Why? Because they literally could not do their new work within the old rules. They could not work when strong respect for the individual came at the expense of effective teamwork, when deeply held individual beliefs got in the way of genuine discussion, and when unit loyalties formed a barrier to cross-functional problem solving. Worst of all, task force members found themselves avoiding conflict and unable to discuss those problems. A number of the task forces became dysfunctional and unable to do their strategy work.

To focus their attention on what needed to change, Both helped the task forces map the culture they desired against the current culture. They discovered very little overlap. The top descriptors of the current culture were: develop opposing views, demand perfection, and avoid conflict. The top characteristics of the desired culture were: create the opportunity for self-fulfillment, develop a caring environment, and maintain trusting relations with colleagues. Articulating this gap made tangible for the group the adaptive challenge that Koedijk saw facing KPMG. In other words, *the people who needed to do the changing had finally framed the adaptive challenge for themselves:* How could KPMG succeed at a competence-based strategy that depended on cooperation across multiple units and layers if its people couldn't succeed in these task forces? Armed with that understanding, the task force members could become emissaries to the rest of the firm.

On a more personal level, each member was asked to identify his or her *individual* adaptive challenge. What attitudes, behaviors, or habits did each one need to change, and what specific actions would he or she take? Who else needed to be involved for individual change to take root? Acting as coaches and consultants, the task force members gave one another supportive feedback and suggestions. They had learned to confide, to listen, and to advise with genuine care.

Progress on these issues raised the level of trust dramatically, and task force members began to understand what adapting their behavior meant in everyday terms. They understood how to identify an adaptive issue and developed a language with which to discuss what they needed to do to improve their collective ability to solve problems. They talked about dialogue, work avoidance, and using the collective intelligence of the group. They knew how to "call" one another on dysfunctional behavior. They had begun to develop the culture required to implement the new business strategy.

Despite the critical breakthroughs toward developing a collective understanding of the adaptive challenge, regulating the level of distress was a constant preoccupation for Koedijk, the board, and Both. The nature of the work was distressing. Strategy work means broad assignments with limited instructions; at KPMG, people were accustomed to highly structured assignments. Strategy work also means being creative. At one breakfast meeting, a board member stood on a table to challenge the group to be more creative and toss aside old rules. This radical and unexpected behavior further raised the distress level: no one had ever seen a partner behave this way before. People realized that their work experience had prepared them only for performing routine tasks with people "like them" from their own units.

The process allowed for conflict and focused people's attention on the hot issues in order to help them learn how to work with conflict in a constructive manner. But the heat was kept within a tolerable range in some of the following ways:

- On one occasion when tensions were unusually high, the 100 were brought together to voice their concerns to the board in an Oprah Winfrey-style meeting. The board sat in the center of an auditorium and took pointed questions from the surrounding group.

- The group devised sanctions to discourage unwanted behavior. In the soccer-crazy Netherlands, all participants in the process were issued the yellow cards that soccer referees use to indicate "foul" to offending players. They used the cards to stop the action when someone started arguing his or her point without listening to or understanding the assumptions and competing perspectives of other participants.

- The group created symbols. They compared the old KPMG to a hippopotamus that was large and cumbersome, liked to sleep a lot, and became aggressive when its normal habits were disturbed. They aspired to be dolphins, which they characterized as playful, eager to learn, and happily willing to go the extra mile for the team. They even paid attention to the statement that clothes make: it surprised some clients to see managers wandering through the KPMG offices that summer in Bermuda shorts and T-shirts.

- The group made a deliberate point of having fun. "Playtime" could mean long bicycle rides or laser-gun games at a local amusement center. In one spontaneous moment at the KPMG offices, a discussion of the power of people mobilized toward a common goal led the group to go outside and use their collective leverage to move a seemingly immovable concrete block.

- The group attended frequent two- and three-day off-site meetings to help bring closure to parts of the work.

These actions, taken as a whole, changed attitudes and behaviors. Curiosity became more valued than obedience to rules. People no longer deferred to the senior authority figure in the room; genuine dialogue neutralized hierarchical power in the battle over ideas. The tendency for each individual to promote his or her pet solution gave way to understanding other perspectives. A confidence in the ability of people in different units to work together and work things out emerged. The people with the most curious minds and interesting questions soon became the most respected.

As a result of confronting strategic and adaptive challenges, KPMG as a whole will move from auditing to assurance, from operations consulting to shaping corporate vision, from business-process reengineering to developing organizational capabilities, and from teaching traditional skills to its own clients to creating learning organizations. The task forces identified $50 million to $60 million worth of new business opportunities.

Many senior partners who had believed that a firm dominated by the auditing mentality could not contain creative people were surprised when the process unlocked creativity, passion, imagination, and a willingness to take risks. Two stories illustrate the fundamental changes that took place in the firm's mind-set.

We saw one middle manager develop the confidence to create a new business. He spotted the opportunity to provide KPMG services to virtual organizations and strategic alliances. He traveled the world, visiting the leaders of 65 virtual organizations. The results of his innovative research served as a resource to KPMG in entering this growing market. Moreover, he represented the new KPMG by giving a keynote address discussing his findings at a world forum. We also saw a 28-year-old female auditor skillfully guide a group of older, male senior partners through a complex day of looking at opportunities associated with implementing the firm's new strategies. That could not have occurred the year before. The senior partners never would have listened to such a voice from below.

## Leadership as Learning

Many efforts to transform organizations through mergers and acquisitions, restructuring, reengineering, and strategy work falter because managers fail to grasp the requirements of adaptive work. They make the classic error of treating adaptive challenges like technical problems that can be solved by tough-minded senior executives.

The implications of that error go to the heart of the work of leaders in organizations today. Leaders crafting strategy have access to the technical expertise and the tools they need to calculate the benefits of a merger or restructuring, understand future trends and discontinuities, identify opportunities, map existing competencies, and identify the steering mechanisms to support their strategic direction. These tools and techniques are readily available both within organizations and from a variety of consulting firms, and they are very useful. In many cases, however, seemingly good strategies fail to be implemented. And often the failure is misdiagnosed: "We had a good strategy, but we couldn't execute it effectively."

In fact, the strategy itself is often deficient because too many perspectives were ignored during its formulation. The failure to do the necessary adaptive work during the strategy development process is a symptom of senior managers' technical orientation. Managers frequently derive "their" solution to a problem and then try to "sell" it to some colleagues and bypass or sandbag others in the commitment-building process. Too often, leaders, their team, and consultants fail to identify and tackle the adaptive dimensions of the challenge and to ask themselves, Who needs to learn what to develop, understand, commit to, and implement the strategy?

The same technical orientation entraps restructuring and business-process-reengineering initiatives, in which consultants and managers have the know-how to do the technical work of framing the objectives, designing a new work flow, documenting and communicating results, and identifying the activities to be performed by people in the organization. In many instances, reengineering falls short of the mark because it treats process redesign as a technical problem: managers neglect to identify the adaptive work and involve the people who have to do the changing. Senior executives fail to invest their time and their soul in understanding these issues and guiding people through the transition. Indeed, *engineering* is itself the wrong metaphor.

In short, the prevailing notion that leadership consists of having a vision and aligning people with that vision is bankrupt because it continues to treat adaptive situations as if they were technical: the authority figure is supposed to divine where the company is going, and people are supposed to follow. Leadership is reduced to a combination of grand knowing and salesmanship. Such a perspective reveals a basic misconception about the way businesses succeed in addressing adaptive challenges. Adaptive situations are hard to define and resolve precisely because they demand the work and responsibility of managers and people throughout the organization. They are not amenable to solutions provided by leaders; adaptive solutions require members of the organization to take responsibility for the problematic situations that face them.

Leadership has to take place every day. It cannot be the responsibility of the few, a rare event, or a once-in-a-lifetime opportunity. In our world, in our businesses, we face adaptive challenges all the time. When an executive is asked to square conflicting aspirations, he and his people face an adaptive challenge. When a manager sees a solution to a problem—technical in many respects except that it requires a change in the attitudes and habits of subordinates—she faces an adaptive challenge. When an employee close to the front line sees a gap between the organization's purpose and the objectives he is asked to achieve, he faces both an adaptive challenge and the risks and opportunity of leading from below.

Leadership, as seen in this light, requires a learning strategy. A leader, from above or below, with or without authority, has to engage people in confronting the challenge, adjusting their values, changing perspectives, and learning new habits. To an authoritative person who prides himself on his ability to tackle hard problems, this shift may come as a rude awakening. But it also should ease the burden of having to know all the answers and bear all the load. To the person who waits to receive either the coach's call or "the vision" to lead, this change may also seem a mixture of good news and bad news. The adaptive demands of our time require leaders who take responsibility without waiting for revelation or request. One can lead with no more than a question in hand.

# PART

III

# 1
# Speed, Simplicity, Self-Confidence: An Interview with Jack Welch

## Noel M. Tichy and Ram Charan

John F. Welch, Jr., chairman and CEO of General Electric, leads one of the world's largest corporations. It is a very different corporation from the one he inherited in 1981. GE is now built around 14 distinct businesses—including aircraft engines, medical systems, engineering plastics, major appliances, NBC television, and financial services. They reflect the aggressive strategic redirection Welch unveiled soon after he became CEO.

By now the story of GE's business transformation is familiar. In 1981, Welch declared that the company would focus its operations on three "strategic circles"—core manufacturing units such as lighting and locomotives, technology-intensive businesses, and services—and that each of its businesses would rank first or second in its global market. GE has achieved world market-share leadership in nearly all of its 14 businesses. In 1988, its 300,000 employees generated revenues of more than $50 billion and net income of $3.4 billion.

GE's strategic redirection had essentially taken shape by the end of 1986. Since then, Welch has embarked on a more imposing challenge: building a revitalized "human engine" to animate GE's formidable "business engine."

His program has two central objectives. First, he is championing a companywide drive to identify and eliminate unproductive work in order to energize GE's employees. It is neither realistic nor useful, Welch argues, to expect employees of a decidedly leaner corporation to complete all the reports, reviews, forecasts, and budgets that were standard operating procedure in more forgiving times. He is developing procedures to speed decision cycles, move information through the organization, provide quick and effective feedback, and evaluate and reward managers on qualities such as openness, candor, and self-confidence.

Second, and perhaps of even greater significance, Welch is leading a transformation of attitudes at GE—struggling, in his words, to release "emotional energy" at all levels of the organization and encourage creativity and feelings of ownership and self-worth. His ultimate goal is to create an enterprise that can tap the benefits of global scale and diversity without the stifling costs of bureaucratic controls and hierarchical authority and without a managerial focus on personal power and self-perpetuation. This requires a transformation not only of systems and procedures, he argues, but also of people themselves.

HBR: *What makes a good manager?*

Jack Welch: I prefer the term business leader. Good business leaders create a vision, articulate the vision, passionately own the vision, and relentlessly drive it to completion. Above all else, though, good leaders are open. They go up, down, and around their organization to reach people. They don't stick to the established channels. They're informal. They're straight with people. They make a religion out of being accessible. They never get bored telling their story.

Real communication takes countless hours of eyeball to eyeball, back and forth. It means more listening than talking. It's not pronouncements on a videotape, it's not announcements in a newspaper. It is human beings coming to see and accept things through a constant interactive process aimed at consensus. And it must be absolutely relentless. That's a real challenge for us. There's still not enough candor in this company.

*What do you mean by "candor"?*

I mean facing reality, seeing the world as it is rather than as you wish it were. We've seen over and over again that businesses facing market downturns, tougher competition, and more demanding customers inevitably make forecasts that are much too optimistic. This means they don't take advantage of the opportunities change usually offers. Change in the marketplace isn't something to fear; it's an enormous opportunity to shuffle the deck, to replay the game. Candid managers—leaders—don't get paralyzed about the "fragility" of the organization. They tell people the truth. That doesn't scare them because they realize their people know the truth anyway.

We've had managers at GE who couldn't change, who kept telling us to leave them alone. They wanted to sit back, to keep things the way they were. And that's just what they did—until they and most of their staffs had to go. That's the lousy part of this job. What's worse is that we still don't understand why so many people are incapable of facing reality, of being candid with themselves and others.

But we are clearly making progress in facing reality, even if the progress is painfully slow. Take our locomotive business. That team was the only one we've ever had that took a business whose forecasts and plans were headed straight up, and whose market began to head straight down, a virtual collapse, and managed to change the tires while the car was moving. It's the team that forecast the great locomotive boom, convinced us to invest $300 million to renovate its plant in Erie, and then the market went boom all right—right into a crater. But when it did, that team turned on a dime. It reoriented the business.

Several of our other businesses in the same situation said, "Give it time, the market will come back." Locomotive didn't wait. And today, now that the market *is* coming back, the business looks great. The point is, what determines your destiny is not the hand you're dealt; it's how you play the hand. And the best way to play your hand is to face reality—see the world the way it is—and act accordingly.

*What makes an effective organization?*

For a large organization to be effective, it must be simple. For a large organization to be simple, its people must have self-confidence and intellectual self-assurance. Insecure managers create complexity. Frightened, nervous managers use thick, convoluted planning books and busy slides filled with everything they've known since childhood. Real leaders don't need clutter. People must have the self-confidence to be clear, precise, to be sure that every person in their organization—highest to lowest—understands what the business is trying to achieve. But it's not easy. You can't believe how hard it is for people to be simple, how much they fear being simple. They worry that if they're simple, people will think they're simpleminded. In reality, of course, it's just the reverse. Clear, tough-minded people are the most simple.

*Soon after you became CEO, you articulated GE's now-famous strategy of "number one or number two globally." Was that an exercise in the power of simplicity?*

Yes. In 1981, when we first defined our business strategy, the real focus was Japan. The entire organization had to understand that GE was in a tougher, more competitive world, with Japan as the cutting edge of the new competition. Nine years later, that competitive toughness has increased by a factor of five or ten. We face a revitalized Japan that's migrated around the world—to Thailand, Malaysia, Mexico, the United States—and responded successfully to a massive yen change. Europe is a different game today. There are great European businesspeople, dynamic leaders, people who are changing things. Plus you've got all the other Asian successes.

So being number one or number two globally is more important than ever. But scale alone is not enough. You have to combine financial strength, market position, and technology leadership with an organizational focus on speed, agility, and simplicity. The world moves so much faster today. You can be driving through Seoul, talking to France on the phone and making a deal, and have a fax waiting for you when you get back to the United States with the deal in good technical shape. Paolo Fresco, senior vice president of GE International, has been negotiating around-the-clock for the past two days on a deal in England. Last night I was talking with Larry Bossidy, one of our vice chairmen, who was in West Germany doing another deal. We never used to do business this way. So you can be the biggest, but if you're not flexible enough to handle rapid change and make quick decisions, you won't win.

*How have you implemented your commitment to simplicity at the highest levels of GE, where you can have the most direct impact on what happens?*

First, we took out management layers. Layers hide weaknesses. Layers mask mediocrity. I firmly believe that an overburdened, overstretched executive is the best executive because he or she doesn't have the time to meddle, to deal in trivia, to bother people. Remember the theory that a manager should have no more than 6 or 7 direct reports? I say the right number is closer to 10 or 15. This way you have no choice but to let people flex their muscles, let them grow and mature. With 10 or 15 reports, a leader can focus only on the big important issues, not on minutiae.

We also reduced the corporate staff. Headquarters can be the bane of corporate America. It can strangle, choke, delay, and create insecurity. If you're going to have simplicity in the field, you can't have a big staff at home. We don't need the questioners and the checkers, the nitpickers who bog down the process, people whose only role is to second-guess and kibitz, the people who clog communication inside the company. Today people at headquarters are experts in taxes, finance, or some other key area that can help people in the field. Our corporate staff no longer just challenges and questions; it assists. This is a mind-set change: staff essentially reports to the field rather than the other way around.

*So many CEOs disparage staff and middle management—you know, "If only those bureaucrats would buy into my vision." When you talk about "nitpickers" and "kibitzers," are you talking about lousy people or about good people forced into lousy jobs?*

People are not lousy, period. Leaders have to find a better fit between their organization's needs and their people's capabilities. Staff people, whom I prefer to call individual contributors, can be tremendous sources of added value in an organization. But each staff person has to ask, "How do I add value? How do I help make people on the line more effective and more competitive?" In the past, many staff functions were driven by control rather than adding value. Staffs with that focus have to be eliminated. They sap emotional energy in the organization. As for middle managers, they can be the stronghold of the organization. But their jobs have to be redefined. They have to see their roles as a combination of teacher, cheerleader, and liberator, not controller.

*You've dismantled GE's groups and sectors, the top levels of the corporate organization to which individual strategic business units once reported. That certainly makes the organization chart more simple—you now have 14 separate businesses reporting directly to you or your two vice chairmen. How does the new structure simplify how GE operates on a day-to-day basis?*

Cutting the groups and sectors eliminated communications filters. Today there is direct communication between the CEO and the leaders of the 14 businesses. We have very short cycle times for decisions and little interference by corporate staff. A major investment decision that used to take a year can now be made in a matter of days.

We also run a Corporate Executive Council, the CEC. For two days every quarter, we meet with the leaders of the 14 businesses and our top staff people. These aren't stuffy, formal strategic reviews. We share ideas and information candidly and openly, including programs that have failed. The important thing is that at the end of those two days everyone in the CEC has seen and discussed the same information. The CEC creates a sense of trust, a sense of personal familiarity and mutual obligation at the top of the company. We consider the CEC a piece of organizational technology that is very important for our future success.

*Still, how can it be "simple" to run a $50 billion enterprise? Doesn't a corporation as vast as GE need management layers, extensive review systems, and formal procedures—if for no other reason than to keep the business under control?*

People always overestimate how complex business is. This isn't rocket science; we've chosen one of the world's more simple professions. Most global businesses have three or four critical competitors, and you know who they are. And there aren't that many things you can do with a business. It's not as if you're choosing among 2,000 options.

You mentioned review systems. At our 1986 officers' meeting, which involves the top 100 or so executives at GE, we asked the 14 business leaders to present reports on the competitive dynamics in their businesses. How'd we do it? We had them each prepare one-page answers to five questions: What are your market dynamics globally today, and where are they going over the next several years? What actions have your competitors taken in the last three years to upset those global dynamics? What have you done in the last three years to affect those dynamics? What are the most dangerous things your competitor could do in the next three years to upset those dynamics? What are the most effective things you could do to bring your desired impact on those dynamics?

Five simple charts. After those initial reviews, which we update regularly, we could assume that everyone at the top knew the plays and had the same playbook. It doesn't take a genius. Fourteen businesses each with a playbook of five charts. So when Larry Bossidy is with a potential partner in Europe, or I'm with a company in the Far East, we're always there with a competitive understanding based on our playbooks. We know exactly what makes sense; we don't need a big staff to do endless analysis. That means we should be able to act with speed.

Probably the most important thing we promise our business leaders is fast action. Their job is to create and grow new global businesses. Our job in the executive office is to facilitate, to go out and negotiate a deal, to make the acquisition, or get our businesses the partners they need. When our business leaders call, they don't expect studies—they expect answers.

Take the deal with Thomson, where we swapped our consumer electronics business for their medical equipment business. We were presented with an opportunity, a great solution to a serious strategic problem, and we were able to act quickly. We didn't need to go back to headquarters for a strategic analysis and a bunch of reports. Conceptually, it took us about 30 minutes to decide that the deal made sense and then a meeting of maybe two hours with the Thomson people to work out the basic terms. We signed a letter of intent in five days. We had to close it with the usual legal details, of course, so from beginning to end it took five months. Thomson had the same clear view of where it wanted to go—so it worked perfectly for both sides.

Another of our jobs is to transfer best practices across all the businesses, with lightning speed. Staff often put people all over the place to do this. But they aren't effective lightning rods to transfer best practice; they don't have the stature in the organization. Business leaders do. That's why every CEC meeting deals in part with a generic business issue—a new pay plan, a drug-testing program, stock options. Every business is free to propose its own plan or program and present it at the CEC, and we put it through a central screen at corporate, strictly to make sure it's within the bounds of good sense. We don't approve the details. But we want to know what the details are so we can see which programs are working and immediately alert the other businesses to the successful ones.

*You make it sound so easy.*

Simple *doesn't* mean easy, especially as you try to move this approach down through the organization. When you take out layers, you change the exposure of the managers who remain. They sit right in the sun. Some of them blotch immediately; they can't stand the exposure of leadership.

We now have leaders in each of the businesses who *own* those businesses. Eight years ago, we had to sell the idea of ownership.

Today the challenge is to move that sense of ownership, that commitment to relentless personal interaction and immediate sharing of information, down through the organization. We're very early in this, and it's going to be anything but easy. But it's something we have to do.

*From an organizational point of view, how are the 14 businesses changing? Are they going through a de-layering process? Are their top people communicating as the CEC does?*

In addition to locomotives, which I've already discussed, we've had major delayering and streamlining in almost all of our businesses, and they have made significant improvements in total cost productivity.

The CEC concept is flowing down as well. For example, each of the businesses has created its own executive committee to meet on policy questions. These committees meet weekly or monthly and include the top staff and line people from the businesses. Everyone in the same room, everyone with the same information, everyone buying into the targets. Each business also has an operations committee. This is a bigger group of maybe 30 people for each business: 5 staffers, 7 people from manufacturing, 6 from engineering, 8 from marketing, and so on. They get together every quarter for a day and a half to thrash out problems, to get people talking across functions, to communicate with each other about their prospects and programs. That's 30 people in 14 businesses, more than 400 people all together, in a process of instant communication about their businesses and the company.

You see, I operate on a very simple belief about business. If there are six of us in a room, and we all get the same facts, in most cases, the six of us will reach roughly the same conclusion. And once we all accept that conclusion, we can force our energy into it and put it into action. The problem is, we don't get the same information. We each get different pieces. Business isn't complicated. The complications arise when people are cut off from information they need. That's what we're trying to change.

*That brings us to Work-Out, which you've been championing inside GE since early this year. Why are you pushing it so hard?*

Work-Out is absolutely fundamental to our becoming the kind of company we must become. That's why I'm so passionate about it. We're not going to succeed if people end up doing the same work they've always done, if they don't feel any psychic or financial impact from the way the organization is changing. The ultimate objective of Work-Out is so clear. We want 300,000 people with different career objectives, different family aspirations, different financial goals, to share directly in this company's vision, the information, the decision-making process, and the rewards. We want to build a more stimulating environment, a more creative environment, a freer work atmosphere, with incentives tied directly to what people do.

Now, the business leaders aren't particularly thrilled that we're so passionate about Work-Out. In 1989, the CEO is going to every business in this company to sit in on a Work-Out session. That's a little puzzling to them. "I own the business, what are you doing here?" they say. Well, I'm not there to tell them how to price products, what type of equipment they need, whom to hire; I have no comments on that.

But Work-Out is the next generation of what we're trying to do. We had to put in a process to focus on and change how work gets done in this company. We have to apply the same relentless passion to Work-Out that we did in selling the vision of number one and number two globally. That's why we're pushing it so hard, getting so involved.

*What is the essence of Work-Out, the basic goal?*

Work-Out has a practical and an intellectual goal. The practical objective is to get rid of thousands of bad habits accumulated since the creation of General Electric. How would you like to move from a house after 112 years? Think of what would be in the closets and the attic—those shoes that you'll wear to paint next spring, even though you know you'll never paint again. We've got 112 years of closets and attics in this company. We want to flush them out, to start with a brand new house with empty closets, to begin the whole game again.

The second thing we want to achieve, the intellectual part, begins by putting the leaders of each business in front of 100 or so of their people, eight to ten times a year, to let them hear what their people think about the company, what they like and don't like about their work, about how they're evaluated, about how they spend their time. Work-Out will expose the leaders to the vibrations of their business—opinions, feelings, emotions, resentments, not abstract theories of organization and management.

Ultimately, we're talking about redefining the relationship between boss and subordinate. I want to get to a point where people challenge their bosses every day: "Why do you require me to do these wasteful things? Why don't you let me do the things you shouldn't be doing so you can move on and create? That's the job of a leader—to create, not to control. Trust me to do my job, and don't make me waste all my time trying to deal with you on the control issue."

Now, how do you get people communicating with each other with that much candor? You put them together in a room and make them thrash it out.

These Work-Out sessions, and I've already done several of them, create all kinds of personal dynamics. Some people go and hide. Some don't like the dinner in the evening because they can't get along with the other people. Some emerge as forceful advocates. As people meet over and over, though, more of them will develop the courage to speak out. The norm will become the person who says, "Dammit, we're not doing it. Let's get on with doing it." Today the norm in most companies, not just GE, is not to bring up critical issues with a boss, certainly not in a public setting, and certainly not in an atmosphere where self-confidence has not been developed. This process will create more fulfilling and rewarding jobs. The quality of work life will improve dramatically.

*It's one thing to insist that the people who report directly to you, or who work one or two layers below you, become forceful advocates and criticize the status quo. They've got your support. But what about people lower in the organization, people who have to worry how their bosses will react?*

You're right on the hottest issue—when a boss reacts to criticism by saying, "I'll get that guy." Now, hopefully, that guy is so good he quits that same week and shows the boss where that attitude gets him. That's not the best result for GE, of course, but that's what it may take to shake people up.

It's not going to be easy to get the spirit and intent of Work-Out clear throughout the company. I had a technician at my house to install some appliances recently. He said "I saw your videotape on Work-Out. The guys at my level understand what you're talking about: we'll be free to enjoy our work more, not just do more work, and to do more work on our own. But do you know how our supervisors interpreted it? They pointed to the screen and said, 'You see what he's saying, you guys better start busting your butts.'" We have a long way to go!

The potential for meanness in an organization, for a variety of reasons, is often in inverse proportion to level. People at the top have more time and resources to be fair. I wasn't trained to be a judge, but I spend a lot of time worrying about fairness. The data I get generally favor the manager over the employee. But we have two people at headquarters, fairness arbitrators so to speak, who sift the situation. So when I get a problem, I can smell it and feel it and try to figure out what's really happening. Managers down in the organization don't have the time or help for that. They too often say, "This is how we do it here, go do it." Work-Out is going to break down those attitudes. Managers will be in front of their people, challenged in a thousand different ways, held to account.

*To change behavior, you must also change how people are compensated and rewarded. Are those systems being changed at GE?*

We let every business come up with its own pay plan. It can create bonus plans in any way that makes sense. We're also doing all kinds of exciting things to reward people for their contributions, things we've never done before. For example, we now give out $20 to $30 million in management awards every year—cash payments to individuals for outstanding performance. We're trying desperately to push rewards down to levels where they never used to be. Stock options now go to 3,000 people, up from 400 ten years ago, and that's probably still not enough.

*Another way to influence behavior is to promote people based on the characteristics you want to encourage. How can you evaluate executives on qualities as subjective as candor and speed?*

Not only can we do it, we *are* doing it. Again, we're starting at the top of the company and, as the new systems prove themselves, we'll drive them down. We took three years to develop a statement on corporate values, what we as a company believe in. It was a brutal process. We talked to 5,000 people at our management development center in Crotonville. We sweated over every word. This will be the first year that our Session C meetings, the intensive process we use to evaluate the officers of the company, revolve around that value statement. We've told the business leaders that they must rank each of their officers on a scale of one to five against the business and individual characteristics in that statement [see the GE Value Statement]. Then I, Larry Bossidy, and Ed Hood, our other vice chairman, will rate

## *Exhibit I.   GE Value Statement*

| BUSINESS CHARACTERISTICS | INDIVIDUAL CHARACTERISTICS |

**BUSINESS CHARACTERISTICS**

**Lean**
What – Reduce tasks and the people required to do them.
Why – Critical to developing world cost leadership.

**Agile**
What – De-layering.
Why – Create fast decision making in rapidly changing world through improved communication and increased individual response.

**Creative**
What – Development of new ideas—innovation.
Why – Increase customer satisfaction and operating margins through higher-value products and services.

**Ownership**
What – Self-confidence to trust others. Self-confidence to delegate to others the freedom to act while, at the same time, self-confidence to involve higher levels in issues critical to the business and the corporation.
Why – Supports concept of more individual responsibility, capability to act quickly and independently. Should increase job satisfaction and improve understanding of risks and rewards. While delegation is critical, there is a small percentage of high-impact issues that need or require involvement of higher levels within the business and within the corporation.

**INDIVIDUAL CHARACTERISTICS**

**Reality**
What – Describe the environment as it is — not as we hope it to be.
Why – Critical to developing a vision and a winning strategy, and to gaining universal acceptance for their implementation.

**Leadership**
What – Sustained passion for and commitment to a proactive, shared vision and its implementation.
Why – To rally teams toward achieving a common objective.

**Candor/Openness**
What – Complete and frequent sharing of information with individuals (appraisals, etc.) and organization (everything).
Why – Critical to employees knowing where they, their efforts, and their business stand.

**Simplicity**
What – Strive for brevity, clarity, the "elegant, simple solution"— less is better.
Why – Less complexity improves everything, from reduced bureaucracy to better product designs to lower costs.

## Exhibit I.   GE Value Statement *(continued)*

| BUSINESS CHARACTERISTICS | INDIVIDUAL CHARACTERISTICS |
|---|---|
| **Reward**<br>What – Recognition and compensation commensurate with risk and performance — highly differentiated by individual, with recognition of total team achievement.<br>Why – Necessary to attract and motivate the type of individuals required to accomplish GE's objectives. A #1 business should provide #1 people with #1 opportunity. | **Integrity**<br>What – Never bend or wink at the truth, and live within both the spirit and letter of the laws of every global business arena.<br>Why – Critical to gaining the global arenas' acceptance of our right to grow and prosper. Every constituency: shareowners who invest; customers who purchase; community that supports; and employees who depend on, expect, and deserve our unequivocal commitment to integrity in every facet of our behavior.<br><br>**Individual Dignity**<br>What – Respect and leverage the talent and contribution of every individual in both good and bad times.<br>Why – Teamwork depends on trust, mutual understanding, and the shared belief that the individual will be treated fairly in any environment. |

the officers and see where we agree or disagree with the business leaders.

We had a long discussion about this in the CEC. People said just what you said: "How can you put a number on how open people are, on how directly they face reality?" Well, they're going to have to—the best numbers they can come up with, and then we'll argue about them. We have to know if our people are open and self-confident, if they believe in honest communication and quick action, if the people we hired years ago have changed. The only way to test our progress is through regular evaluations at the top and by listening to every audience we appear before in the company.

*All corporations, but especially giant corporations like GE, have implicit social and psychological contracts with their employees—mutual responsibilities and loyalties by which each side abides. What is GE's psychological contract with its people?*

Like many other large companies in the United States, Europe, and Japan, GE has had an implicit psychological contract based on perceived lifetime employment. People were rarely dismissed except for cause or severe business downturns, like in Aerospace after Vietnam. This produced a paternal, feudal, fuzzy kind of loyalty. You put in your time, worked hard, and the company took care of you for life.

That kind of loyalty tends to focus people inward. But given today's environment, people's emotional energy must be focused outward on a competitive world where no business is a safe haven for employment unless it is winning in the marketplace. The psychological contract has to change. People at all levels have to feel the risk-reward tension.

My concept of loyalty is not "giving time" to some corporate entity and, in turn, being shielded and protected from the outside world. Loyalty is an affinity among people who want to grapple with the outside world and win. Their personal values, dreams, and ambitions cause them to gravitate toward each other and toward a company like GE that gives them the resources and opportunities to flourish.

The new psychological contract, if there is such a thing, is that jobs at GE are the best in the world for people who are willing to compete. We have the best training and development resources and an environment committed to providing opportunities for personal and professional growth.

*How deeply have these changes penetrated? How different does it feel to be a GE manager today versus five years ago?*

It depends how far down you go. In some old-line factories, they probably feel it a lot less than we would like. They hear the words every now and then, but they don't feel a lot of difference. That's because the people above them haven't changed enough yet. Don't forget, we built much of this company in the 1950s around the blue books and POIM: plan, organize, integrate, measure. We brought people in buses over to Crotonville and drilled it into them. Now we're saying, "liberate, trust," and people look up and say, "What?" We're trying to make a massive cultural break. This is at least a five-year process, probably closer to ten.

*What troubles you about what's happened to date?*

First, there's a real danger of the expectation level getting ahead of reality. I was at Crotonville recently, talking about Work-Out, and someone said, "I don't feel it yet." Well, we're only a few months into it, it's much too early.

No matter how many exciting programs you implement, there seems to be a need for people to spend emotional energy criticizing the administration of the programs rather than focusing on the substance. I can sit in the Crotonville pit and ask, "How many of you are part of a new pay plan?" More than half the hands go up. "How many of you have received a management award in the last year?" More than 90% of the hands go up. "How many of you are aware of stock options?" All the hands go up. And yet many of these people don't see what we're trying to do with the programs, why we've put them in place. The emotional energy doesn't focus often enough on the objectives of the bonus plan or the excitement of the management award; it focuses on the details. The same is true of Work-Out. We'll have too much discussion on the Work-Out "process" and not enough on the "objective" to instill speed, simplicity, and self-confidence in every person in the organization.

*When will we know whether these changes have worked? What's your report card?*

A business magazine printed an article about GE that listed our businesses and the fact that we were number one or number two in virtually all of them. That magazine didn't get one complaint from our competitors. Those are the facts. That's what we said we wanted to do, and we've done it.

Ten years from now, we want magazines to write about GE as a place where people have the freedom to be creative, a place that brings out the best in everybody. An open, fair place where people have a sense that what they do matters, and where that sense of accomplishment is rewarded in both the pocketbook and the soul. That will be our report card.

## Work-Out: A Case Study

GE Medical Systems (GEMS) is the world leader in medical diagnostic imaging equipment, including CT scanners, magnetic resonance equipment, and X-ray mammography. Its more than 15,000 employees face formidable international competition. Despite positive financial results, GEMS is working to transform its human organization. Work-Out is designed to identify sources of frustration and bureaucratic inefficiency, eliminate unnecessary and unproductive work, and overhaul how managers are evaluated and rewarded.

Work-Out began when some 50 GEMS employees attended a five-day offsite session in Lake Lawn, Wisconsin. The participants included senior vice president and group executive John Trani, his staff, six employee relations managers, and informal leaders from technology, finance, sales, service, marketing, and manufacturing. Trani selected these informal leaders for their willingness to take business risks, challenge the status quo, and contribute in other key ways to GEMS. We participated as Work-Out faculty members and have participated in follow-up sessions that will run beyond 1989.

The Lake Lawn session took place after two important preliminary steps. First, we conducted in-depth interviews with managers at all levels of GEMS. Our interviews uncovered many objections to and criticisms of existing procedures, including measurement systems (too many, not focused enough on customers, cross-functional conflicts); pay and reward systems (lack of work goals, inconsistent signals); career development systems (ambiguous career paths, inadequate performance feedback); and an atmosphere in which blame, fear, and lack of trust overshadowed team commitments to solving problems. Here are some sample quotes from interviews:

- "I'm frustrated. I simply can't do the quality of work that I want to do and know how to do. I feel my hands are tied. I have no time. I need help on how to delegate and operate in this new culture."
- "The goal of downsizing and de-layering is correct. The execution stinks. The concept is to drop a lot of 'less important' work. This just didn't happen. We still have to know all the details, still have to follow all the old policies and systems."
- "I'm overwhelmed. I can and want to do better work. The solution is not simply adding new people; I don't even want to. We need to team up on projects and work. Our leaders must stop piling on more and help us set priorities."

Second, just before the first Work-Out session, Jack Welch traveled to GEMS headquarters for a half-day roundtable with the Work-Out participants. Here are some sample quotes from middle managers:

- To senior management: "Listen! Think carefully about what the middle managers say. Make them feel like they are the experts and that their opinions are respected. There appear to be too many preconceived beliefs on the part of Welch and Trani."

- To senior management: "Listen to people, don't just pontificate. Trust people's judgment and don't continually second-guess. Treat other people like adults and not children."

- About themselves: "I will recommend work to be discontinued. I will try to find 'blind spots' where I withhold power. Any person I send to speak for me will 'push' peers who resist change."

- About themselves: "I will be more bold in making decisions. I will no longer accept the status quo. I will ask my boss for authority to make decisions. In fact, I will make more decisions on my own."

The five-day Work-Out session was an intense effort to unravel, evaluate, and reconsider the complex web of personal relationships, cross-functional interactions, and formal work procedures through which the business of GEMS gets done. Cross-functional teams cooperated to address actual business problems. Each functional group developed a vision of where its operations are headed.

John Trani participated in a roundtable where he listened and responded to the concerns and criticisms of middle managers. Senior members of the GEMS staff worked to build trust and more effective communication with the functional managers. All the participants focused on ways to reorganize work and maximize return on organization time, on team time, and on individual time.

The five-day session ended with individuals and functional teams signing close to 100 written contracts to implement the new procedures. There were contracts between functional teams, contracts between individuals, contracts between function heads and their staffs, and businesswide contracts with John Trani and his staff.

Work-Out has picked up steam since Lake Lawn. Managers from different product lines have participated in workshops to review and implement the attitudes, values, and new work procedures discussed at Lake Lawn. A Work-Out steering committee has held cross-functional information meetings for field employees around the world. Managers throughout GEMS are reviewing and modifying their reward and measurement systems. And Welch continues to receive regular briefings on Work-Out's progress.

No two GE businesses approach Work-Out in the same way; a process this intensive can't be "cloned" successfully among vastly different businesses. But Work-Out at GEMS offers a glimpse of the change process taking place throughout General Electric.

—Noel M. Tichy and Ram Charan

# 2
# To Build a Winning Team:
# An Interview with Head Coach Bill Walsh

### Richard Rapaport

Joining the august company of Knute Rockne, Paul Brown, and Vince Lombardi, former San Francisco 49ers and current Stanford University football coach Bill Walsh is recognized as one of the most important figures in football history. Walsh, like other coaching legends, has done far more than produce consistently winning teams: in his case, three Super Bowl championships for the 49ers in eight years and an organization enshrined in the press as "The Team of the '80s." During his ten-year career with the 49ers and as a coach at the high school, college, and professional levels, Walsh developed a uniquely thoughtful style of play and a successful system of team management that has become one of the most respected in the modern game.

Less of a psychologist than Rockne, and never a disciplinarian like Lombardi, Walsh nevertheless produces winners through a business-like approach to maximizing the potential of players and coaches. His ability to coolly analyze opponents, matching their weaknesses with his teams' strengths, has made come-from-behind wins a Walsh football hallmark.

Believed to be too cerebral for a top position for which extreme macho was long considered an ineluctable quality, for years Walsh was forced to content himself with assistant coaching positions. Prized nonetheless for his skills on offense, Walsh was honored for honing All-Pro quarterbacks Dan Fouts, Kenny Anderson, and Greg Cook.

In 1977, at age 47, Walsh became Stanford's head football coach. That year, he took a moderately talented Stanford team to a national ranking and a win in the Bluebonnet Bowl. In 1979, Walsh was named head coach and general manager of a dreadful 49ers team that had been virtually dismembered in the late 1970s by mismanagement and horrendous personnel decisions.

Walsh immediately began to develop long-range strategic and personnel plans for the 49ers. He also focused on what other coaches had considered the minutiae of the game: minute-by-minute choreographing of practices, breaking down individual and group tactics into parts, and defining responsibilities and setting objectives for both players and coaches.

This season, Walsh has been paid the ultimate accolade for a coach: former Walsh assistants are NFL head coaches in Tampa Bay, Minnesota, Green Bay, New York (Jets), and San Francisco.

Retiring after his third Super Bowl victory in January 1989, Walsh signed on as a football analyst for NBC Sports, eschewing numerous bids to coach professionally before stunning the football world in 1992 by returning as head coach at Stanford.

HBR: *Do you see a link between managing and coaching?*

Bill Walsh: I see coaches and executives who have more similar skills today than ever before. When I was with the 49ers, I was both head coach and general manager, so my duties were more business oriented than those of a lot of NFL head coaches. Today's NFL is a very complex world, and great football knowledge alone won't get your team to the Super Bowl.

Historically in sports, there has been one central figure in the organization whose presence dominates everything and whose judgments people identify with. That one person is the dictator, and everyone else simply does whatever he says. In a lot of ways, the old system was much easier for all involved. The dictator gave orders and everyone else just followed them.

Now working successfully with the people in the organization demands more from the coach or the executive. In coaching, I think of it as the coach's ability to condition the athletes' minds and to train them to think as a unit, while at the same time, making sure each athlete approaches his own game with total concentration, intensity, and skill. There should never be a moment on the football field when a player doesn't feel challenged both physically and intellectually. That is why the old bludgeon approach is leaving football the same way it is leaving business.

*What is replacing the old approach?*

Management today recognizes that to have a winning organization, it has to be more knowledgeable and competent in dealing with and developing people. That is the most fundamental change. The real task in sports is to bring together groups of people to accomplish something. In the old days, the approach was rather crude. The organization would simply discard a player who did not fit a specific, predefined mold. If a player did not conform to the way management wanted him to behave, or if he made the organization uncomfortable, it got rid of him. That was the typical response.

Today, in sports as elsewhere, individualism is the general rule. Some of the most talented people are the ones who are the most independent. That has required from management a fundamental change in the art and skill of communication and in organizational development. Most important, there has been much more recognition and acknowledgment of the uniqueness of each individual and the need that people have for some degree of security.

*How does that translate into winning teams?*

Those teams that have been most successful are the ones that have demonstrated the greatest commitment to their people. They are the ones that have created the greatest sense of belonging. And they are the ones that have done the most in-house to develop their people. That commitment has come through in the personality of the organizations. It is true of the Redskins, the Raiders, and, of course, the 49ers.

*What is the biggest obstacle to creating this kind of organization?*

The coach must account for his ego. He has to drop or sidestep the ego barrier so that people can communicate without fear. They have to be comfortable that they will not be ridiculed if they turn out to be mistaken or if their ideas are not directly in line with their superior's. That is where the breakthrough comes. That is what it takes to build a successful, winning organization.

That approach was certainly critical to the success of the 49ers. It contributed to an environment where our team could be more flexible and adaptable in responding to the unexpected moves of our opponents.

I tried to remove the fear factor from people's minds so they could feel comfortable opening their mouths. They knew they could be wrong one time and then, when they got a little more information, change their opinion and not be demeaned for it. In fact, I made a point of reminding our coaching staff that I expected them to change their opinions and impressions over time. It's quite natural: the more information you develop, the faster things can change.

*But having enormous self-confidence seems essential for a leader—especially in pro sports. What is the role of healthy versus unhealthy ego in a competitive organization like a football team?*

English is a marvelous language until it comes to the word "ego." We Americans throw that around, using that one word to cover a broad spectrum of meanings: self-confidence, self-assurance, and as-sertiveness—attributes that most people think of as positive.

But there is another side that can wreck a team or an organization. That is being distracted by your own importance. It can come from your insecurity in working with others. It can be the need to draw attention to yourself in the public arena. It can be a feeling that others are a threat to your own territory. These are all negative manifesta-tions of ego, and if you are not alert to them, you get diverted and your work becomes diffused. Ego in these cases makes people insen-sitive to how they work with others and ends up interfering with the real goal of any group efforts.

*What do you think are the essential management skills of a successful head coach?*

The role of the head coach begins with setting a standard of com-petence. You have to exhibit a strong working knowledge of the game. The head coach must be able to function effectively and decisively in the most stressful situations. And the head coach must demonstrate resourcefulness—in particular, he is responsible for designing a system of football that is not simplistic. The head coach's system should never reduce the game to the point where he can blame his players for success or failure simply because they did not physically overwhelm the opponents.

Successful coaches realize that winning teams are not run by single individuals who dominate the scene and reduce the rest of the group to marionettes. Winning teams are more like open forums in which everyone participates in the decision-making process, coaches and players alike, until the decision is made. Others must know who is in command, but a head coach must behave democratically. Then, once a decision is made, the team must be motivated to go ahead and execute it.

*What does it take to create a decision-making process in which people feel they can participate?*

It starts with the expectations the head coach sets. It is part of the job to expect everyone in the organization to be an expert in his or her particular area of responsibility, to refine their skills continually, and to be physically and intellectually committed to the team. The head coach has to make it clear that he expects everyone to participate and volunteer his or her thoughts, impressions, and ideas. The goal is to create a communication channel that allows important information to get from the bottom to the top.

During 49ers games, my coaches and I always tried to respond to what the players said. We knew that we needed their input. And it often made a difference. For example, in a game against New Orleans in 1987, I told the team at halftime that we would call one particular pass play when we got inside the Saints 30-yard line. In the stress of the moment, when we got there, I simply didn't think of sending in the play. But on the sideline, Steve Young, our backup quarterback, immediately reminded me of it. He wasn't a bit hesitant. I called it, and we scored.

I couldn't worry about being embarrassed because I had forgotten what I said in the locker room. We were after results. We all wanted to win.

*If that is what it takes to be a successful coach, what are the qualities that define the modern football player?*

The key to being a modern football player is the ability to respond quicker, both mentally and physically, than the other player. Some people are naturally quicker physically. But to win, you need to be quicker as a team. You must beat your opposition to the punch every time.

Physical strength and speed are important advantages, but even more advantageous is having the training that permits you to respond intelligently to whatever confronts you. That means more precision, better execution, and quicker response than your opponents. Under the extreme stress of game conditions, a player must condense his intellect and focus it on thinking more quickly and clearly than the opposition.

*How do you achieve that quickness and responsiveness in your teams?*

It is all in the way you prepare. Preparation allows us to overcome the fact that we might not be the most physically talented team. During the 1980s, the 49ers may not have been as talented as the New York Giants or Chicago Bears, who had measurable advantages in speed or strength. But we were able to compensate in the way we prepared for a game.

Some coaches rely on relatively simplistic plans. When their plans don't work, they say that it was the players who did not block hard enough, did not run hard enough, or just were not tough enough. We have gone beyond that pattern of failure and finger-pointing. The responsibility for the success of the team starts with the coach, who develops the plan that is then executed by the players—who are extremely well-prepared.

Being prepared starts with identifying the essential skills our team needs to compete effectively. The next step is to create a format to teach those skills. Here at Stanford, our practices and game plans are far more detailed than those used by most of our opponents. There is more to learn with our schemes, so we demand more mental commitment and concentration from the players.

*How do you approach the job of structuring practices so your players will be prepared?*

I believe in extremely precise, minute-by-minute, tightly structured practices. We focus far more intellect and put far more thought into what we do in practice than other teams do. We have five or six skills or techniques that we want each of our players to be able to use in carrying out his assignment, where our opponents usually will have only one or two.

Take an offensive lineman, for example. Before the ball is snapped, that guard or tackle might have only three or four seconds to decide what kind of blocking technique to use on the man in front of him. Say there are four blocking techniques he can use. By the way his man is positioned, by the situation in the game, by what he has learned to expect from his opponent, he will be able to select one of those techniques.

Many other teams take a more simplistic approach. They teach their players one approach, one technique. Our approach gives our players more dimension. When we are playing powerhouses like Notre Dame, Texas A&M, or Washington, we have to use our extra dimensions to compensate for being physically outmanned. That is the intellectual part of the game. That is the area in which we ask more of our players than our opponents are asking of theirs.

*How do you teach those skills?*

The most important tool for getting things done is the drill. For example, we work on drills to teach running backs about pass protection against blitzing linebackers. You have to identify the 6 different situations that can occur. Then you have to allocate the time to work on those 6 situations and also the 20 techniques that you want your running backs to be able to apply. In teaching those skills, sometimes you want to have your guards and tight ends participate, or even the entire offensive unit. All of that requires preparation, discipline, and focus from both coaches and players.

The way I coach, I know ahead of time how I am going to run the whole season's worth of practices. I have established the priorities for what we need to accomplish and allocated the time in which to teach the necessary skills.

I establish the program long before we take the field so I can use most efficiently the time available for learning and so the players do not get bored or distracted. The players must know clearly and at all times exactly what it is that they have to get out of any given drill. After 35 years of coaching, I have found that you can't do anything in less than 10 minutes or in more than 20 minutes.

Another distinction in drills is between those skills and techniques that can be taught individually and those that require groups. It is also critical to allocate time for team play and to build in practice segments that focus on the execution of particular plays and particular game situations that you want to be ready for.

*Why is it important to prepare so many skills for so many contingencies?*

Making judgments under severe stress is the most difficult thing there is. The more preparation you have prior to the conflict, the more you can do in a clinical situation, the better off you will be. For that reason, in practice I want to make certain that we have accounted for every critical situation, including the desperate ones at the end of a game when we may have only one chance to pull out a victory. Even in that circumstance, I want us to have a play prepared and rehearsed. Say it is the last 20 seconds of a game and we're losing. We have already practiced 6 plays that we can apply in that situation. That way, we know what to do, and we can calmly execute the plays. We'll have no doubt in our minds, we will have more poise, and we can concentrate without falling prey to desperation.

*Can you recall a specific instance where this actually paid off for one of your teams?*

In 1987, we were down 26-20 against Cincinnati. We got the ball back on their 25-yard line with two seconds left in the game. It could have been a hopeless situation. We put three receivers to the left and Jerry Rice to the right. Joe Montana got the ball, looked left, pump faked, and then threw right, where Rice was covered man-to-man in the end zone. It was a touchdown, and it won an important game for us. But it would not have happened if we had not been prepared.

You need to have a plan even for the worst scenario. It doesn't mean that it will always work; it doesn't mean that you will always be successful. But you will always be prepared and at your best.

But the same applies to virtually every situation at every point in the game. Say you are on the defense and inside your own 25-yard line. The situation can vary, so there are a number of particulars you need to prepare for. You have third down and inches. Third down and feet. Third down and yards. Inside the 15-yard line, all that changes, and inside the 5 it changes again. Each situation is different, and for each you might have 15 different game situations to practice. You have to allocate time for all of them, you have to practice plays, and you have to work with individuals. And then all of the separate situations have to be pulled together to give a continuity to the team's play.

*One of the most impressive attributes of your 49ers teams was their ability to take what some people might consider a disadvantage and use it to their advantage. Did you work on developing this skill?*

I can think of several cases where we consciously tried to work on the players to reverse what in football are usually crippling disadvantages. One was playing on the road. In football, the home-field advantage is often decisive. But we were able to bond together, play in enemy territory, and feed on the emotions of the situation, without being intimidated by the other teams or their fans.

To accomplish that, I would condition the 49ers to adversity. We would talk about how it feels to fly into enemy territory. We would discuss what crosses your mind when you take the field. It allowed us to turn our status as outsiders into our advantage. When I talked with the team, I would use examples from the early days of World War II as illustrations of the desperate and heroic fights we could emulate. By talking about what could be a disadvantage, we turned our people on. We made it an advantage.

The other example is the injury factor. Some teams come unraveled when a star player gets injured. With the 49ers, an injury often served to arouse the team to play harder. Again, my approach was to talk about it openly. I would make the point that reserve players always had to be prepared, and that when they got the chance, they should actually improve on the performance of the injured player. Again, I used historical examples from warfare. For instance, in the Civil War, the best trained people, the front line and even generals, were often the first to fall. Often it was the reserves who would achieve victory. So when our reserves took the field, they were conditioned to feel this way and they knew what was expected. They would feel much more positive about going into the game.

*In teaching skills to your players, how do you organize your own thinking about the players you are trying to reach?*

Take a group of ten players. The top two will be supermotivated. Superstars will usually take care of themselves. Anybody can coach them. The next four, with the right motivation and direction, will learn to perform up to their potential. The next two will be marginal. With constant attention, they will be able to accomplish something of value to the team. The last two will waste your time. They won't be with you for long. Our goal is to focus our organizational detail and coaching on the middle six. They are the ones who most need and benefit from your direction, monitoring, and counsel.

*How do you achieve a balance between group skills and discipline on the one hand and player individuality on the other?*

They go together in defining the two directions you need to pursue at the same time. First, you develop within the organization and the players an appreciation for the role each athlete plays on the team. You talk to each player and let each one know that, at some point, he will be in a position to win or lose a game. It may be one play in an entire career for a certain player or many plays each game for a Joe Montana. But the point is that everyone's job is essential. Everyone has a specific role and specific responsibilities. And each player has to be prepared both mentally and physically to the utmost to play that role.

Second, you talk to each player and indicate the importance of everyone's participation in the process—that it is important for everyone to express himself, to offer ideas, explanations, solutions, formulas. You want everyone to enter into the flow of ideas, even ideas that may seem extreme in their creativity.

You are actually striving for two things at the same time: an organization where people understand the importance of their jobs and are committed to living within the confines of those jobs and to taking direction; and an organization where people feel creative and adaptive and are willing to change their minds without feeling threatened. It is a tough combination to achieve. But it's also the ultimate in management.

*Is there a situation with a player that exemplifies this balance between giving explicit direction and permitting individual creativity?*

Take Joe Montana, for example. He is a perfect combination of the two vital aspects that are necessary for developing greatness as a quarterback.

The formula for the success of the 49ers offense was a highly disciplined, very structured form of utilizing the forward pass. To make our system work, Joe had to master the disciplines to know which receiver to throw to, when, and why. The success of the team depended on Joe's ability to work within that framework. Consequently, the job of the coach was to use drills and repetition so that Joe developed almost automatic moves and decision-making ability.

But there is an extra quality that it takes for a quarterback to become a world champion—or, in Joe's case, the best ever. And that is an instinctive, spontaneous, natural response to situations that arise in games. Part of Montana's greatness was that 10% to 15% of the time his spontaneous instincts would break loose and make a phenomenal difference in the outcome of a game.

It is the job of the coach to find the best of both sides. We had to have a very structured system of football, and we also wanted instinctive and spontaneous play.

*How do you go about the job of coaching a player like Montana to develop that kind of balance?*

Early on, we had to encourage Joe to trust his spontaneous instincts. We were careful not to criticize him when he used his creative abilities and things did not work out. In practice, we worked with Joe repeatedly on specific plays. When he was placed in a game, we called only those plays because we knew that he should be confident that he could execute them. But we didn't jump him the minute he would break the pattern. Instead, we nurtured him to use his instincts. We had to allow him to be wrong on occasion and to live with it.

Of course, with different players the problem takes on a different look. In the case of quarterback Steve Young, it was almost the opposite. We had to work with him to be disciplined enough to live within the strict framework of what we were doing. Steve is a great spontaneous athlete and a terrific runner. But we found that we had to reduce the number of times he would use his instincts and increase his willingness to stay within the confines of the team concept.

For example, we would be at a point in a game where we had designed a special play to break the defense wide open and score a touchdown. In his early days, Steve might not have had the discipline to wait for that play to develop. Instead, he would see an opening and run with the ball for a five-yard gain. He would let his instincts and emotions affect his patience with the play and his confidence that the entire team could execute.

*As a coach, how do you know what it takes to bring out the best in a young player's abilities?*

Unfortunately, there is nothing exact about it. Experience is really the only teacher. I was 47 years old when I became an NFL head coach. Typically, that job comes to people when they are between the ages of 35 and 40. I was in a subordinate role as an assistant coach for a longer period of time than most, so I was forced to analyze, evaluate, and learn to appreciate the roles that other people play more than I might have. In retrospect, I was lucky.

*But if developing your players is an inexact art, there are bound to be mistakes. How do you deal with them?*

Again and again in the development and selection of personnel, you have to account for miscalculation. In professional sports, the person who is best at dealing with personnel is the person who recognizes his or her errors and deals with them the quickest and most effectively. That could mean adopting a long-term approach, or it could mean the release of a player.

Take our drafting of John Taylor in 1986. John came to the 49ers as a wide receiver from Delaware State. He had great physical talent, but not a lot of background in playing sophisticated football. We simply miscalculated how long it would take John to be ready to play in the NFL. Consequently, we were disappointed in him. John was not adapting well to the competition, he appeared confused and frustrated, and he had lost his enthusiasm.

But instead of giving up on him, we took a longer term, more patient approach. We waited an extra year to allow him to mature and grow into this level of competition and into the role we wanted him to play. Now he is an All-Pro and one of the great receivers in the game.

The other side to that would be the decision I made with Thomas "Hollywood" Henderson. He was a very bright, articulate, charming person, but he also had an uncontrollable drug habit. I made a calculated choice that involved a high risk when we acquired him from Dallas—that I could personally nurture and rehab and influence Thomas into once again becoming a great linebacker. It was a miscalculation on my part. I gave it every chance to work, but finally I had to decide that it simply was not going to.

When you reach that point, you have to make a controlled and well-planned retreat. You regret the decision that you made, but you have to live with it, and you have to work yourself out of it. That is one important facet of good management: deciding how to acknowledge your mistakes.

Do you simply gloss over them? Do you blame someone else? Are you so insecure that your ego will not let you do anything but maintain that your original decision was correct? I could have kept Thomas Henderson on the team, but then the 49ers would not have become world champs. Or I could have had the public blaming Thomas or blaming an assistant coach. But none of those approaches would have helped the team.

In this case, I did not want to publicly embarrass Thomas, but I did want to show the team that I was still in control and that drug abuse would not be tolerated. We simply had to move as smoothly as possible to release Thomas for any number of reasons, remove him from the picture. I made a mistake, acknowledged it, and decided what to do about it.

*If the personnel issue is so overriding, do you have a methodology for the way you evaluate players?*

We use a five-bracket ranking system to categorize people we are looking at. The first is the star player who cannot miss. The second is a player who will someday be a starter and play for a number of years. The third will make the team, and the fourth has an isolated specialty—covering kickoffs or fielding punts. The fifth is someone who will make the squad and help you by playing solidly in a backup role.

You want as many superstars as you can get. The more stars, the better. But the difference between winning and losing is the bottom 25% of your people. Most coaches can deliver the top 75%. But the last 25% only blossoms in the details, in the orchestration of skills, in the way you prepare.

*When you go into a draft, what are the particulars you are looking for in a player?*

It is always a combination of factors that add up to the right person. It's his level of natural ability. It's his competitive instincts. It's also the history of that athlete; his ability to learn, retain, and apply what he has learned; and his ability to work under stress with other people.

Then you have to be able to project those qualities into the slot or role that athlete would play for your team. And you have to do that over time, thinking about the short, middle, and long term. For example, a player could come in and play a certain role in his first year, and then in his second year that role could develop or be enhanced. After a number of years, that player might end up in a feature role, and then revert back to the role in which he started as the wear and tear of the game begins to take its toll.

*You have said that one of the most important attributes of any organization is the way it treats its people. In pro football, with frequent trading and the yearly competition from rookies for veterans' jobs, cutting a veteran player or convinc-*

*ing him to retire is a big part of your job. How do you handle that part of the personnel issue?*

Any good coach or manager has got to be responsible for phasing his people through the organization. It may be the most emotionally difficult part of the job. When you do it, you often end up as the most unpopular person in the organization. Yet it is part of the role that the leader must play. It has to be done and done continually. You have to be prepared to use your own professional judgment as to when and why it is time for one of your players to call it quits.

As the head coach, I forced myself to deal with this process rather than turn my back on it or hand it off to the assistant coaches. In fact, in this area you can only listen to the assistant coaches so much because, typically, they would rather have veteran players on the team. It makes their coaching job easier. Subconsciously, I think assistant coaches feel much more comfortable with ten-year players than with the rookies. The coaches have become friends with the veterans, they have great faith in them, they understand each other. And the veterans already know what the coaches want done out on the field.

In sports, there is an arc of utilization that describes most athletes' careers. By that I mean a curve that a coach can use to project what a player can do now, next year, and ten years from now. A player may be a superstar this year, but with minor injuries nicking at him and starting to add up, he won't be a superstar three years from now. And then in the next phase you have to begin thinking about replacing him.

Most people don't realize it, but the players who get all the attention are usually the ones on the downside of their careers. Ironically, the organization is often paying the most money to the team members who are on the descending curve as players. When players are starting to wind down their careers but are still playing effectively, you have to remind yourself how to use them. You have to gauge how they practice, what you ask them to do on the field, what kinds of situations you use them in, how much playing time they get. These are all factors that ultimately lead to the point where you judge that a younger player could do the job as well. That younger player is on an ascending curve on the arc. That is when you have to make your move.

*How do you go about making that move without dealing the veteran player a crushing blow?*

There will be some suffering, and there is no way to avoid it. It's simply part of the process. There will be agonizing, frustration, and anger. But the coach has to make the decision to improve the team. The real danger is if the decision aimed at improving the team leads to so much bitterness that the fallout causes other players to take sides. When the team becomes divided, the decision has done more harm than good.

That is why managing people's emotions is such an important part of the coach's job. You begin by acknowledging that your decision will cause some suffering. Then you do whatever you can to soften the edges, to reduce the anguish and frustration, to communicate your own sensitivity, and, in a sense, even to manipulate the player.

*You recommend manipulating people rather than being honest?*

The easiest thing is to be truly honest and direct. In fact, it sounds just great to say that you are going to be honest and direct. But insensitive, hammer-like shots that are delivered in the name of honesty and openness usually do the greatest damage to people. The damage ends up reverberating throughout the entire organization. Over time, people will lose the bonding factor they need for success. And over time, that directness will isolate you from the people with whom you work.

The real task is to lead people through the troubled times, when they are demoted or find themselves at the end of their playing days, and to help them maintain as much of their self-esteem as possible. These are the tasks that really define the job of the manager. A manager's job is not simply having a desk filled with family pictures and a wall covered by plaques for good behavior. It's developing the skills to understand and deal with people.

*You have described a variety of tasks that the coach has to be sensitive to, including the ability to make tough decisions and the need to soften the edges when it comes to dealing with people. What has made your system so successful?*

The bottom line in professional sports is winning. Everything has to focus on that product: winning football games. Other offshoots—the public relations, the merchandising, the high-sounding philosophical approach—mean little compared with being successful on the playing field.

But winning does not necessarily mean being a victor in every game. It's not winning every game at any cost. We have to remind ourselves that it's not just a single game that we are trying to win. It is a season and a series of seasons in which the team wins more games than it loses and each team member plays up to his potential. If you are continually developing your skills and refining your approach, then winning will be the final result.

But I have seen coaches who are simply too sentimental, who allow themselves to be too maudlin about "breaking up the old family." They are going to lose sight of the bottom line. And there is another kind who are severe, tough, and hard-hitting. But they sacrifice the loyalty of the people around them. In that situation, people are always afraid that they are going to be the next to go. These coaches rarely have sustained success.

Somewhere in the middle are the coaches who know that the job is to win, who know that they must be decisive, that they must phase people through their organizations, and at the same time they are sensitive to the feelings, loyalties, and emotions that people have toward one another. If you don't have these feelings, I do not know how you can lead anyone.

I have spent many sleepless nights trying to figure out how I was going to phase out certain players for whom I had strong feelings, but that was my job. I wasn't hired to do anything but win.

## The Turnaround CEO

By 1979, when I came to the 49ers, things were about as bad with the team as they could get. The 49ers fans had been let down so far that they had become indifferent to what was happening with the team. I knew we couldn't take them down even farther by telling them, "Now we're really rebuilding." They had been handed that line from the previous management and coaching staff for the past several years. We couldn't tear the team apart and expect people to come to the games, see a competitive contest, and enjoy themselves.

I didn't have a master plan. It was simply a matter of staying afloat while we prepared for the future. We had to field an entertaining and competitive team, but what we really had in mind was building toward a championship future.

I knew we couldn't get there simply by spending money. Money is an important facet, of course, but you need skill, confidence, and training to win football games. When the 49ers breakthrough season came in 1981, we won our first championship with the lowest salary schedule in the NFL.

My first two seasons taught me that even in defeat you can make progress if you have confidence, patience, a plan, and a timetable. One of the biggest problems in coaching is the people around you who don't understand what it takes to get the job done or who lose their nerve. There are always quick fixes and instant criticisms that get written up in the sports pages. Head coaches get pressure from ownership, from fans, from the press, from assistant coaches, and from players. They may think you are moving too fast or not fast enough. The owners are often the worst. The team is their investment, so nerves and ego get in the way. They have to feel they have you under their thumbs when they hire you and when they fire you.

With 49ers owner Eddie DeBartolo, Jr., I tried to make sure that he had something in writing in front of him, a plan that we had developed and were implementing. I wrote an operations manual, a personnel manual, a budget manual, and an overall set of job descriptions. I outlined the job of each player, evaluated each member of the team, and set down our goals and expectations for where we were and where we wanted to be. A high degree of documentation gives an owner the feeling that his or her investment is in good hands. Fortunately for me, Eddie never interfered with the changes I wanted to make. He listened and was enthusiastic—at least in the early years. Later he didn't listen quite so well.

In the face of all that, you have got to be resolute in where you are heading and how you plan to get there. And even though you might fail, even though it might not develop, you never panic. A lot of people bring on failure in the way they react to pressure. Most coaches lose their nerve late in the game. When they do, players will turn on each other and try to protect themselves from criticism. The minute that happens, you have people working against their own best interests.

The coach who has the nerve to stay with a program right up to the bitter end is the one who most often will have the best results.

## On Organized Labor

I've always believed there should be a football players' association. But sometimes the association has worked against the best interests of the rank and file. That was the story of the 1983 NFL players strike. There were certain players' needs that should have been addressed and were not. Things like their safety, medical services, and the condition of the fields. But the union didn't think these things were important. It was just pure dollars to them. It was an example of the players being led by and obligated to follow people who didn't understand the important issues.

Players rely heavily on the business advice of agents and lawyers—often these advisers run every aspect of the players' lives. And sometimes the players accept the judgments of people who take advantage of their emotions and suspicions. I suppose it's not so surprising that there are even some union leaders in professional sports who use the union as a way to fulfill their own needs at the expense of the members.

But even though a strike might be misdirected, it would be a terrible mistake to underestimate the power that is inherent in people grouping together. The players develop a tremendous loyalty to each other, and that bonding won't let them cave in to the owners.

During the 1983 strike, the 49ers did one of the best jobs in the NFL of working around the strike and healing the team afterwards. When you face an issue like a strike, you have to be sensitive without demonstrating weaknesses or vacillating. I didn't lose communication with the striking players. I had empathy for them, and I wasn't confrontational. I was willing to do whatever it took to keep the team together. And although I felt the union leadership was wrong, I understood that the players were obligated to follow it.

## College Football: The Professional Approach

Part of the agreement that brought Bill Walsh back to Stanford in 1992 was that he be allowed to pick his assistant coaches. Of the nine assistants, one, Fred vonAppen, is a former 49ers coach, and four, Bill Ring, Mike Wilson, Tom Holmoe, and Keena Turner, are former 49ers players. Turner, an outside linebacker who played on all four 49ers Super Bowl championship teams, was known as a "player's leader." As Walsh puts it, "Keena's inner strength and quiet, unobtrusive leadership most exemplified the 49ers personality."

Walsh's respect for players continues at Stanford, where, according to Turner, one of Walsh's greatest strengths is his ability to encourage communication and a sense of affinity among the players. "Coach Walsh is not an authority figure bellowing out commands," Turner insists. "Instead, he promotes closeness. One of the primary concerns that Bill passes on to his assistants is that we never demean a player, that we don't even holler. We must coach in a way that is respectful."

But during the first few months of Stanford practices, Turner was also made aware that the mythology and expectations that had been building up around Walsh could be as misleading and detrimental as they were potentially animating. "Where people get lost concerning Bill is that 'genius' label he has been saddled with. It's not always true that Bill's way is the only way that works, and he knows that too. And I don't want to paint him like a saint. He encourages the assistants to respect the players, but it's not as if he's never gone off on a guy."

One factor that continues to amaze Turner is Walsh's organizing scheme. "Bill has a plan for everything. For example, take our game at Notre Dame last October. At halftime, we were down by 16 points, and I'm sure everyone watching had written us off. But in the locker room, there was no sense of panic. We had a calm, thoughtful discussion on how to get it done. The players handled it because Bill had laid the groundwork. He had prepared us to be 16 points down. All he had to ask was, 'Do you pack it up or figure out how to win?'"

The response was decidedly the latter. In the second half, a determined Stanford team, quite reminiscent of the Walsh 49ers, marched on the field and methodically crushed Notre Dame 33 to 16.

# 3

# The CEO as Coach: An Interview with AlliedSignal's Lawrence A. Bossidy

## Noel M. Tichy and Ram Charan

In July 1991, Lawrence A. Bossidy became chairman and CEO of AlliedSignal, the $13 billion industrial supplier of aerospace systems, automotive parts, and chemical products. The company's story since then appears to be that of a classic slash-and-burn turnaround: head count has been reduced, assets have been sold, restructurings have occurred, and earnings and market value have risen dramatically. But the view from inside is far more interesting for anyone grappling with what it takes to build and lead a competitive organization capable of sustained performance over the long term.

Bossidy is known as a straight-shooting, tough-minded, results-oriented business leader. But he also is a charismatic and persistent coach, determined to help people learn and thereby to provide his company with the best-prepared employees. In this interview, he discusses what he does to "coach people to win."

The 60-year-old Bossidy is no stranger to corporate transformation. As vice chairman of General Electric, he helped CEO Jack Welch reposition the $65 billion industrial giant. Bossidy's career at GE began in 1957, when he joined the finance staff. In the late 1970s and early 1980s, he led GE Capital Corporation, creating a world-class financial service organization.

HBR: *How can one person approach the job of changing a large organization?*

Lawrence A. Bossidy: I believe in the "burning platform" theory of change. When the roustabouts are standing on the offshore oil rig and the foreman yells, "Jump into the water," not only won't they jump but they also won't feel too kindly toward the foreman. There may be sharks in the water. They'll jump only when they themselves see the flames shooting up from the platform. Chrysler's platform was visibly burning; the company changed. IBM's platform was not visibly burning; it didn't.

The leader's job is to help everyone see that the platform is burning, whether the flames are apparent or not. The process of change begins when people decide to take the flames seriously and manage by fact, and that means a brutal understanding of reality. You need to find out what the reality is so that you know what needs changing.

*What was the reality you found at AlliedSignal?*

It was a company that had grown rapidly through mergers and acquisitions but whose earnings had stalled. We had 58 business units, each guarding its own turf. It was an inner-directed company, focused mainly on itself. Management made all the decisions, and employees' ideas were rarely solicited and therefore rarely offered.

*So what was your burning platform, and how did you use it to get people mobilized?*

In 1991, we were hemorrhaging cash. That was the issue that needed focus. I traveled all over the company with the same message and the same charts, over and over. Here's what I think is good about us. Here's what I'm worried about. Here's what we have to do about it. And if we don't fix the cash problem, none of us is going to be around. You can keep it simple: we're spending more than we're taking in. If you do that at home, there will be a day of reckoning.

In the first 60 days, I talked to probably 5,000 employees. I would go to Los Angeles and speak to 500 people, then to Phoenix and talk to another 500. I would stand on a loading dock and speak to people and answer their questions. We talked about what was wrong and what we should do about it. And as we talked, it became clear to me that there hadn't been a good top-down enunciation of the company's problem.

I knew intuitively that I needed support at the bottom right from the outset. Go to the people and tell them what's wrong. And they knew. It's remarkable how many people know what's really going on in their company. I think it's important to try to get effective interaction with everybody in the company, to involve everyone.

It's something I continue to do. Besides talking to large groups, whenever I go to a location I host smaller, skip-level lunches, where I meet with groups of about 20 employees without name tags and without their bosses. I think the combination of talking to a lot of people in an interactive setting and doing skip-levels and conducting periodic attitude surveys gives you a pretty good handle on how people think about things.

Also, there was a context to our burning platform. I mentioned IBM a few moments ago. People here had observed difficulties at IBM, Kodak, and other companies, so the environment was ripe for change. They didn't want what had happened there to happen here. The restructurings and displacements all around us had made people more acutely aware of the value of a good job.

Interestingly, the situation at AlliedSignal was very different from the one that GE faced. Fifteen years ago, GE was preeminent. There was no visible burning platform, but the company had to change. So Jack Welch's idea was to try to make people more humble. At Allied-Signal, our people had been humbled. Our job was to promote our employees' ability to win. But I think that the steps you take to accomplish change aren't dramatically different in either instance.

*Can you elaborate a bit more about how you build support in the organization? For example, how do you field tough questions in the large meetings?*

First, we want to create an environment in which people will speak up. Every question is interesting and important. When I conduct interactive sessions, I don't walk out after three questions. I make it clear that I'm going to be there until the last question is asked. When employees point out things that aren't right, I'm the first to say, "Yes, that's one we need to do something about, and here's what we're going to do." Or, "I don't know the answer to that, but I'll look into it"—and then I'd better follow up. But let's assume someone asks a question that's critical of what we're doing. The whole room hears it, which I think is positive. That gets it on the table and permits response. And I think it's healthy to let all the frustration get aired. It's good if people go home at night and say, "I told that son of a bitch what I thought about him today."

You have to deal with tough questions honestly. I'll give you an example. A guy in aerospace got up and asked me, "Are we going to have layoffs?" "Here's the issue," I answered. "We're in aerospace. We're in an environment that's weakening. We all know that. Defense expenditures are down. The commercial aviation industry is in recession. And we have too much capacity to begin with. So we're going to have layoffs."

I just try to answer the questions. I don't know if I ever will pull it off, but I think the idea of getting some support from the bottom is powerful. It gets the people in the middle on the horse faster. We need to work on this every day.

*During your first 60 days, in addition to getting support from the bottom, you also spent a lot of time team building at the top. Were you focusing on culture change with that group?*

I think you don't change a culture. I think you coach people to win. Basically, people want to be successful. They want to go home at night and feel that they've made a contribution. At AlliedSignal, each of our three major sectors had its own history as an independent company, its own distinct culture. We didn't want to change that. It makes the company stronger.

But we had to unite ourselves with vision and values. And that effort begins with the team at the top. In November 1991, we had an off-site meeting with the top 12 managers of the company. We spent two days arguing—and I mean arguing—about values. That was helpful because at the end of the meeting, we not only had the values, we also had a specific definition of each of those values. The seven values we settled on are simple: customers, integrity, people, teamwork, speed, innovation, and performance. They're not unique. But they're important because they give all our people a view of what behavior is expected of them. And if you're a leader in this company, you risk being labeled a hypocrite if you don't behave according to those values. And you're going to get some heat—and I think that's terrific.

Let me explain it another way. We made a major commitment to use total quality as the vehicle to drive change. Everybody in the world has TQ or something like it. I want AlliedSignal to be the people who do it, not the people who talk about it. TQ does not replace goals; it's the vehicle to facilitate progress toward your goals. And here's where the question of values comes in. TQ tests us because we're going to encounter four types of people. We're going to have people who embrace TQ and make their numbers. We're going to want to promote them. We're going to have people who don't like TQ and don't make their numbers. That's easy: we're going to suggest they leave. We're going to have people who love TQ and don't make their numbers. We're going to try to move them someplace so they can continue to contribute. And we're going to have people who don't like TQ and make their numbers. Those are the people who will test our resolve about whether the process is going to go forward, because they have to go, too. Think about it. Anybody who makes his numbers and says, "I don't need TQ," has to walk the plank or change. Some people have changed, and some are gone.

Besides values, you have to have clear goals. People have to know where they're going. What is victory? Where do you want to be? Every year, we set three goals that we put in front of everybody. It creates focus. In 1994, for example, the goals were: make the numbers, reduce cycle times, and make growth happen. Wherever I go in the company, people know what our three goals are. That's important. Because every time I go to a factory, I conduct a review with those three goals in mind. Are we making the numbers? Are we making quantum gains with cycle-time reduction? Are we growing? People need to be focused on what we're trying to do. We want them to believe that the goals we're talking about are real, that we can do it.

The day when you could yell and scream and beat people into good performance is over. Today you have to appeal to them by helping them see how they can get from here to there, by establishing some credibility, and by giving them some reason and some help to get there. Do all those things, and they'll knock down doors.

*So you begin by creating values and putting an emphasis on goals. But how do you teach people how to win?*

You have to create clarity about the issues you're dealing with, and here I mean the business issues. Before joining AlliedSignal, I looked at the company from afar and thought it had strikingly good market positions in its industries that were not at all matched by margins or profitability. During my first 60 days, I spent a lot of time looking in depth at the businesses and the management processes, and talking to a lot of people. Then I went to the board with my observations, both positive and negative.

I think we all pretty much knew the problems. We were focused internally rather than on customers, and there was way too much organization. Those two generally go hand in hand because layers of organization get in the way. I have the view that you centralize paper and you decentralize people. At AlliedSignal, we had it backward. We had centralized all the people and decentralized all the paper. That created enormous cost. We had far too many purchasing departments, payroll departments, and software systems. In addition, we were being drowned in capital projects—too many projects chasing too little money. The expected payback was unclear. There was no emphasis on margins. We were holding on to underperforming nonstrategic assets.

We felt we could address many of our business issues through TQ. The nice thing about TQ is that it has only three elements: sensitivity to customers, continuous improvement in productivity, and the involvement of all employees. The three are linked, but if we don't satisfy customers, you can pull the curtains. It's over.

TQ can be unifying, it can be positive, it can give self-confidence, and it can get all the players on the field. But to work, it has to yield results. We required every TQ team to have a specific business project to work on and to get something done. So while people are learning new skills, they are also completing projects that make the company better.

*In your first 60 days, you also managed to get out and talk to customers. What did you learn, and how did you bring back what you learned to the organization?*

I made an effort to talk to customers early on, but that's something you need to do all the time, not just in the first 60 days. I visited a lot of customers, and in my first few months I really got an earful. I tried to get examples in every sector—and I still do. In those early days, we looked at some interesting measurements. While we were saying that we were delivering an order-fill rate of 98%, our customers thought we were at 60%. The irony was, we seemed to think we had to justify why we were right and the customers were wrong, instead of spending time trying to address their complaints. So we changed that. The customers are right, regardless, and we began to use their measurements.

I'll never forget one session in Phoenix with our field salespeople. They were the ones who were getting beaten up every day out there by our customers. We asked them, as a constructive exercise, to tell us what their customers thought about us in each of their territories. I mean, they just colored the air blue.

So we said, "Okay, we're going to do something about this." And we went to the customers and said, "Hey, we have a lot of problems, and we'd like to have you team with us so we can get them identified and solved." Almost to a customer, they agreed to do that. We now have hundreds of multifunctional teams in place, and they have helped give our customers higher-quality products and faster turn-around time.

The benefits of the teams go beyond solving specific problems. People often underestimate the importance of having face time with customers. I noticed that our people in the field weren't asking me to speak with customers. In my former incarnation at GE, I spoke frequently at customer meetings of one sort or another. Why? Because customers have events and they need speakers and no one wants to speak. I raised my hand. Why? Because I'm Mario Cuomo? No. Because it gives me two hours to spend with a customer's organization. That's a chance of a lifetime. Invite me, for heaven's sake. I'm not bad. Invite some of the other leaders whose titles can help you. Use us. Don't resent it; don't protect turf. We want a lot of coverage on customers—up and down the organization. We want contacts. Have seminars for them. Have whatever it takes to get quality time with them. And when you visit them, ask, "How are we doing?" You know, they are the only customers we have, so we'd better love them.

*Let's get down to specifics about how you've managed change. In your three and a half years at AlliedSignal, you've focused on improving three common core operating processes. In our experience, those three processes—operations, strategy, and human resources—can be bureaucratic, highly staged exercises.*

Frankly, we were disappointed with all three of those core processes. We had to strengthen them and make them more robust. As a leader, you can influence only three things. You can influence people, you can influence your strategy, and you can influence operations. In my judgment, that's all you do. And if you don't work on those three things all the time, you might be having fun, but nothing's going to happen.

Anyone reading this interview will say, "Big deal! We have those three processes, too!" But the fact is that 90% of all companies don't work them or push them to the ultimate to get value. So it's not enough just to have the processes. You have to work intensely to make them better and better and involve everybody in them.

*How do you become better at managing the operating plan?*

One of the first things that struck me when I came here was that it was more or less accepted practice that you put a plan together and

## Table 1.  *AlliedSignal's Numbers Improve*

|  | Net Income* (in millions) | Operating Margin* | Working- Capital Turns* | Market Value† (in millions) |
|---|---|---|---|---|
| June 30, 1991 | $359 | 4.4% | 4.1 | $4,506 |
| June 30, 1992‡ | $457 | 6.0% | 4.3 | $7,584 |
| June 30, 1993 | $592 | 7.3% | 4.5 | $9,416 |
| June 30, 1994 | $708 | 8.5% | 5.0 | $9,792 |

\* For 12-month period
† At period's end
‡ Before restructuring charges and accounting changes

Since July 1991, when Lawrence A. Bossidy assumed leadership, AlliedSignal has combined business units, closed factories, increased working-capital turns, and generated substantial free cash flow. Bossidy and his team have maintained capital spending, coordinated companywide functions such as purchasing and information systems, reduced the number of suppliers from 9,000 to 3,000, pruned 19,000 salaried jobs from the payroll, and refocused research and development spending.

then missed it. First revelation: people routinely miss their numbers. We don't need meaningless budgets. We need an operating plan that recognizes that underlying assumptions are often wrong and that provides options when that happens. From day one, I made it clear that the people in this organization will be known for meeting commitments. Period.

Here, as at many other companies, we didn't appreciate the contribution that good finance people can make—good in the sense of well-rounded businesspeople who contribute to business solutions, not just scorekeepers. We had a terrific senior vice president of finance, but his job had been limited to running a good corporate finance function. So we had a lot of financial analysis at the corporate level but very little at the business level. And I wanted the opposite. When he had the chance to broaden his interest and take responsibility for the quality of the finance function throughout the company, dramatic things happened.

Good finance people are the ones who can help give real meaning to operating plans. When you say you're going to get a 6% improvement in productivity, they're the ones who are supposed to ask where. What are the projects? When are they going to be done? How much money are they going to be providing? If we're going to grow by 5%, they ask the tough questions: Where are we going to grow? What products are going to grow by 5%? How are we going to get price increases? Good financial involvement is critical in constructing a sound operating plan; it really drives at the particulars.

And then, if our assumptions are wrong, what are the contingencies? Are we going to have to take out more people? Are we going to have to kill this project? Capable, involved finance people should be monitoring the operating plan constantly. I take it as a given that each one is a good accountant, but they must be more than that. To contribute to the business, they have to interpret financial results in a way that helps us run operations. It's imperative that finance people really understand what's happening in the factories.

*Are there specific measures of operating performance that you watch more closely than others?*

Productivity is critical. We have to have 6% per year from everybody. Why? Because if we have cost inflation of 3% to 4% per year and little or no ability to raise prices, that can translate into poor margins. That's why productivity is the rule of the day around here. We define productivity change from one year to the next as sales excluding price increases divided by cost excluding inflation. Although initially we worked the cost side hard, we know that eventually you need to get productivity from both unit-volume growth and cost reduction. It isn't easy, but the most successful companies in the world in the 1990s will be those that sustain productivity. It's essential to our survival, not to mention our prosperity.

In my view, productivity is an important part of TQ. TQ must mean results. Managers get results by improving processes, but I'm not interested in process improvement for its own sake. That's where productivity comes in. If we're doing all this stuff and our productivity isn't getting any better, we're kidding ourselves.

We also look at working-capital turnover. Why? Very simple: we need money to grow the company. In 1991, we had a 40% debt-to-capital ratio and no cash. We sold off some assets and cut costs. Working-capital turns were at about four. I said we needed to improve fast. And when we hit five, we raised the hurdle to ten. At first, people asked, "Why is he so interested in cash?" It's just like your checkbook. If there's none there, we can't invest in growth. We worry about cash every day.

Margins are also critical. Every year, we'll miss some plans, not necessarily because we're deficient but because we won't read markets, we won't foresee all the unknowns. That's okay. But in my view, a real professional maintains margins. When you see you're going to miss a plan, I regard it as an obligation to do what you have to do to make your margin commitments.

A lot of people didn't know what their competitors' margins were. I would say to them, "You know, if they have 12 points of margin and we have 8, that's $300 million of cost we have to take out of this business to be competitive. Now, how the hell are we going to do that?" And, bang! You get focused real fast.

*Earlier, you mentioned that one of your concerns was that the company was inwardly focused. When you ask about competitors' margins, is that part of a larger effort to get people to look outside?*

Absolutely. When we did our large restructuring in 1991, I asked the leadership committee—the top 12—to come back to me with a plan to de-layer the organization and reduce head count. They came back with a plan that I thought was too modest. So I said, "I think you made a sincere effort, but I have to take this public now, and I'm going to make your plan far more ambitious because I don't want to have to come back a year from now and restructure all over again. If we're going to take a charge, I want to take a big one." That was my challenge to them. "As a test," I said, "go back and look at the margins of your best competitors and then see what your margin is, and figure out what you have to do to make that margin." We do that kind of benchmarking continually. You can't say, "Well, we're done. We benchmarked." You have to say, "We benchmark every day."

Our people have worked hard to improve working-capital turnover. But now we have to do even better. If someone says, "I don't know how to do it," my job is to say, "Wait a minute. Let's talk about that." Again, I go to the competition. "Ford Motor turns working capital more than 20 times. Now, what's the difference between its business and yours?" I carry charts around showing who has made the particular goals we're working on; they don't have to be in our businesses. I ask people to get out there and talk with these folks and figure out what they're doing, and then come back and we'll talk.

We have to assume that every company does at least one thing better than we do. Benchmarking is not industrial tourism. It is looking at specific practices, getting the benefit of expertise, bringing it back, and having no inhibitions about adopting it and letting people know where it came from.

We bounce around depending on where we think the expertise is, and we benchmark many companies. For new-product development, 3M has done a good job. For acquisitions, it might be Emerson Electric. In manufacturing and inventory management, we've looked at Motorola; and for receivables, American Express.

I ask my senior managers to go to as many companies as they can, and I also do it myself.

*What about another of those core operating processes—strategic planning? What sorts of things have you done to improve that process?*

The strategic planning process was under way when I arrived, so rather than try to change it, I let it happen. It was the kind of thing I'm sure everyone has seen before: a series of big books, show and tell, and then the books were relegated to the shelf and life went on. It was all highly orchestrated. During the sessions, I listened a lot, but then we talked about it and agreed we wanted something different.

I don't believe strategic planning should be a onetime annual event. It's important to have a good, concentrated thought period. But then you have to live with that strategy every day. Whenever we do an operating review, we have to be calibrating against our strategy. When we talk about competition or market share in our operating reviews, we're working on strategy in real time. That means we ask ourselves whether we're doing what we said we'd do and, if we aren't, what happened.

Today the business heads make the presentations and answer the questions. And look, there's no rocket science to strategy, but you're supposed to know where you are, where your competition is, what your cost position is, and where you want to go. If you don't know those four things, you're not going to have a very effective effort. We needed a better database—key measures such as market share over time, for example—followed by issue identification and some options for solutions.

So we put together a corporate training program to expose people to a more external way of approaching strategy. The result is a much more exciting conversation. And after every strategy review we have, I write a three- or four-page letter to the business head that solidifies our agreement about what the issues are and what we're going to do about them.

I brought in a new person to take charge of the strategic plan, and an important part of his job is to make sure people are learning how to do strategy better. I did the same with the two other important management processes: I put the CFO in charge of the operating plan, and the head of human resources is responsible for the management-resource review. We continually rethink what we want those three processes to yield. We also want to make sure we have good coaching in all of them so that we can continue to improve.

*That brings us to the third process: human resources. What do you do to strengthen it?*

One of the worst things we do in corporate America is not tell people what we think of them. Every appraisal looks the same. Basically, you get a star if you don't say anything offensive. That's no way to foster development. I think you have a responsibility to make people as good as you can make them. And if you identify a trait that interferes with their being better, you have an obligation to point it out and to try to do something about it with them. I don't think you should approach the job gingerly. I don't want people dreading the day they get their appraisals. But I do say to myself, Gee, if I think John Doe is as good as I'm going to get in that job, then I have to see if I can make him as good as I can make him.

People tend to flinch when it comes to certain words to describe employees: saying that they're not aggressive enough or not results-oriented enough or not outgoing enough, or that they don't have communication skills or they're not analytically inclined or they don't like customers. But you have to say those things if you want to help them.

*Describe what you do in performance appraisals.*

I don't have a sophisticated appraisal. I write down what I think is good and what should get better. Pluses and minuses. The first thing I do is give you a copy and ask you to read it. Then I talk frankly, spending more time on the areas for improvement. The sessions usually take about an hour. Then I give the appraisal to you and say, "If you want to think about it and come back and talk again, that's fine." Most don't; some do.

I want to stress how important it is to put the appraisal in writing. I don't want people to go home and say, "He said something else—I just heard him wrong." Some people are complicated and want to rationalize these things. Putting it in writing helps them learn to live with it.

When I sit down with someone 6 or 12 months later, I want to see some of those minuses erased. Sometimes that doesn't happen. Recently, one guy said, "Well, I don't care if I'm going to limit my potential; I've gone as far as I want to anyway." I said, "No, no, you've got it wrong. You have to keep growing just to stay where you are. And you've demonstrated that you can't do it yourself, so you have to get some help." Then I offered him some suggestions and said, "We're not going to sit here and have the same discussion every year."

*Since you took over at AlliedSignal, how many of the key players have you changed?*

Of the top 12, 4 have left; the other 8 are still here. But of the 140 senior managers, about 75% are new to their jobs. We hired 40 new people from the outside, and the rest were moved from other jobs in the company. I didn't replace the head of finance, as I mentioned earlier, but we needed an enormous number of new finance people. I told the people filling a corporate role that they had to be involved in the field. I said to the CFO, "I'm going to measure you not just on who works for you here at headquarters. Every finance person in the business who doesn't perform, I'm going to blame on you."

If you don't have the best people, you hurt everyone in the organization. You have to be sensitive and compassionate to people, and you have to extend your hand to help them, but you have to have the best people.

As tough as it is to cut a lot of employees, I kept coming back to one item that showed up in our employee attitude survey. People in great numbers were saying that we tolerated mediocrity. Now, that's quite an indictment. So at every review meeting, we talk about people and whether they are meeting their goals, and what they are doing to fix weaknesses that have been pointed out. Do they like our values, share our enthusiasm? Do they support TQ? And what's their understanding of the businesses? Do they understand strategy, people, and operations? So I wasn't the one saying, "It's time for Joe to go." Instead, they'd say, "Hey, look. Joe's not going to make it." And I told them, "Let's get this done sooner rather than later. Because no matter how well it's done, it's negative, and you might as well get it behind you and get positive."

Another tendency we've changed was to take people who weren't cutting it and move them somewhere else in the company. We've stopped doing that. I think you have to get those people out of the organization. Give them some time—not a pink slip on Friday afternoon. Err on the side of giving them more time. But get them out of here. Credibility matters.

*If having the best people is so important, can you describe what kind of people you're looking for?*

Today's corporation is a far cry from the old authoritarian vertical hierarchy I grew up in. The cross-functional ties among individuals and groups are increasingly important. They're channels of activity and communication. The traditional bases of managerial authority are eroding. In the past, we used to reward the lone rangers in the corner offices because their achievements were brilliant even though their behavior was destructive. That day is gone. We need people who are better at persuading than at barking orders, who know how to coach and build consensus. Today, managers add value by brokering with people, not by presiding over empires. That has a big impact on how you think about who the "best" people are.

Don't get me wrong. We're not looking for backslapping nice guys, however dumb they might be. Competition is tough, and it takes brains to win. But today we look for smart people with an added dimension: they have an interest in other people and derive psychic satisfaction from working with them.

I am convinced that nothing we do is more important than hiring and developing people. At the end of the day, you bet on people, not on strategies. Strategies are intellectually simple; their execution is not. Your strategies will not make you a better company. Of course, you want to have a good idea of where you're going, but that's not enough. The question is, Can you execute? That's what differentiates one company from another.

To execute, you need people who can lead. Managers have to understand that they don't *manage* anybody. That is especially true in a freedom-loving country like the United States. We all hate to be managed. I like the way Teddy Roosevelt put it: "The best executive is the one who has sense enough to pick good men to do what he wants done, and self-restraint enough to keep from meddling with them while they do it."

*You've invested a lot of money and management time on training, and you've accomplished it at a faster pace and wider scope than anyone else we've seen. Why?*

The only way to bridge the gap between where we are and where we want to go is education. We put every one of our 80,000 people through TQ training within two years. All our business leaders, including me, go through all the training. And I visit as many classes as I can whenever I'm on location. We want people on the factory floor to feel as good about training as top-level managers do.

Beyond formal training programs, we also need to provide tools. Let me give you an example. We need to be more global. Specifically, we want to be major factors in China, India, and Mexico. In order to get there, people need help in understanding those markets. For example, we've put together an Asia council so that the people who are undertaking initiatives at the business-unit level have an opportunity to get together, share market intelligence, and compare notes. It gives people access to information they need, and it helps them stay current about what people in other sectors are doing in that country. So there's a support network to help people tackle something new.

Everyone has to get on board with the importance of learning new skills. I'll give you an example. When I go to a factory, I always look up the union leader and say, "Look, you're responsible for keeping these jobs as much as I am. If you turn down TQ, you're refusing to let these people be trained, and you're going to have to be accountable for it." They don't want to hear that. They know that jobs are an important factor in their life. I don't do it to excoriate them, but I make sure everyone understands.

*You've mentioned a number of times the reviews you have for each of the three core management processes. How do they work?*

Each process review is separate, so each business leader can expect to go through three reviews with me a year—one for people, one for strategy, and one for operations. Right now, I want to get to a lot of employees, so we tend to include more people in the meetings. I want everyone to know what we think about market share and productivity. When you pack the room, you lose some candor. You have to be more careful. You don't want to embarrass anybody. But you do get to communicate with five times as many people.

How do the review sessions work? Take operations, for example. Before the review, I send the business leader a letter to explain what I want him to emphasize. Then we have the review. It covers both my issues and his. It's a candid discussion about operations and not about people or strategy. When it's over, I write a letter setting down what the goals are. Then the head of the business writes me a letter telling me what he is doing to meet those goals. That closes the loop—and serves as a starting point for the next review.

The process is the same for strategy and for human resources. I don't want to make too much of the letters. They aren't a bureaucratic exercise. But they are a useful operating mechanism. They eliminate a lot of questions and tension and misunderstandings about what we agreed to do. They save us from spending the first half hour of every meeting trying to determine who said what to whom. They help us focus on the work we need to get done.

Then, coming off the meetings, my mantra is, Make the numbers. By that I mean not just financial targets but all the goals we agreed on.

*Where are you today in the change process?*

People's mind-sets have changed. Employees are interested in our stock price now. You go into the lobbies where we've installed monitors, and people are tracking AlliedSignal. Not just their sector but the whole company. The chief achievement of all that we're talking about, and it's not finished yet, is that people are thinking differently about their jobs. We still have a long way to go. We're still far from achieving our vision of becoming a premier company, but I think our people are now motivated to get there and, more important, they know what they have to do to get there.

I think you have to position organizations to continue to take steps up. Companies don't change incrementally. They change in quantum jumps. If you shoot for anything less, you don't get any change. You may fall short, but still you've made a big difference.

I think that the closer you come to the customers, the more you appreciate the need to change. And the more inwardly focused you are, the less you understand that need. As we get more and more customer focused, we don't have to preach about the need to change. People know it.

# 4

# What Holds the Modern Company Together?

## Rob Goffee and Gareth Jones

The organizational world is awash with talk of corporate culture—and for good reason. Culture has become a powerful way to hold a company together against a tidal wave of pressures for disintegration, such as decentralization, de-layering, and downsizing. At the same time, traditional mechanisms for integration—hierarchies and control systems, among other devices—are proving costly and ineffective.

Culture, then, is what remains to bolster a company's identity as one organization. Without culture, a company lacks values, direction, and purpose. Does that matter? For the answer, just observe any company with a strong culture—and then compare it to one without.

But what is corporate culture? Perhaps more important, is there one right culture for every organization? And if the answer is no—which we firmly believe—how can a manager change an organization's culture? Those three questions are the subject of this article.

Culture, in a word, is community. It is an outcome of how people relate to one another. Communities exist at work just as they do outside the commercial arena. Like families, villages, schools, and clubs, businesses rest on patterns of social interaction that sustain them over time or are their undoing. They are built on shared interests and mutual obligations and thrive on cooperation and friendships. It is because of the commonality of all communities that we believe a business's culture can be better understood when viewed through the same lens that has illuminated the study of human organizations for nearly 150 years.

*Exhibit I.*

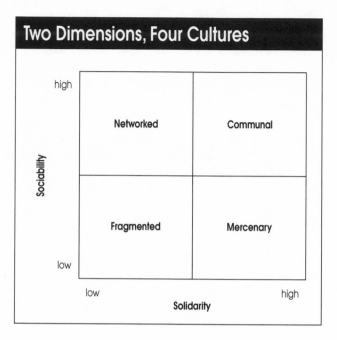

## Two Dimensions, Four Cultures

high

Sociability

Networked            Communal

Fragmented           Mercenary

low

low                              high

**Solidarity**

That is the lens of sociology, which divides community into two types of distinct human relations: sociability and solidarity. Briefly, *sociability* is a measure of sincere friendliness among members of a community. *Solidarity* is a measure of a community's ability to pursue shared objectives quickly and effectively, regardless of personal ties. These two categories may at first seem not to capture the whole range of human behaviors, but they have stood the test of close scrutiny, in both academia and the field.

What do sociability and solidarity have to do with culture? The answer comes when you plot the dimensions against each other. The result is four types of community: networked, mercenary, fragmented, and communal. (See the matrix "Two Dimensions, Four Cultures.") None of these cultures is "the best." In fact, each is appropriate for different business environments. In other words, managers need not begin the hue and cry for one cultural type over another. Instead, they must know how to assess their own culture and whether it fits the competitive situation. Only then can they consider the delicate techniques for transforming it.

## Sociability and Solidarity in Close Focus

Sociability, like the laughter that is its hallmark, often comes naturally. It is the measure of emotional, noninstrumental relations (those in which people do not see others as a means of satisfying their own ends) among individuals who regard one another as friends. Friends tend to share certain ideas, attitudes, interests, and values and usually associate on equal terms. In its pure form, sociability represents a type of social interaction that is valued for its own sake. It is frequently sustained through continuing face-to-face relations characterized by high levels of unarticulated reciprocity. Under these circumstances, there are no prearranged "deals." We help one another, we talk, we share, we laugh and cry together—with no strings attached.

In business communities, the benefits of high sociability are clear and numerous. First, most employees agree that working in such an environment is enjoyable, which helps morale and esprit de corps. Sociability also is often a boon to creativity because it fosters teamwork, sharing of information, and a spirit of openness to new ideas, and allows the freedom to express and accept out-of-the-box thinking. Sociability also creates an environment in which individuals are more likely to go beyond the formal requirements of their jobs. They work harder than is technically necessary to help their colleagues—that is, their community—look good and succeed.

But there also are drawbacks to high levels of sociability. The prevalence of friendships may allow poor performance to be tolerated. No one wants to rebuke or fire a friend. It's more comfortable to accept—and excuse—subpar performance in light of an employee's personal problems. In addition, high-sociability environments are often characterized by an exaggerated concern for consensus. That is to say, friends are often reluctant to disagree with or criticize one another. In business settings, such a tendency can easily lead to diminished debate over goals, strategies, or simply how work gets done. The result: the best *compromise* gets applied to problems, not the best *solution.*

In addition, high-sociability communities often develop cliques and informal, behind-the-scenes networks that can circumvent or, worse, undermine due process in an organization. This is not to say that high-sociability companies lack formal organizational structures. Many of them are very hierarchical. But friendships and unofficial networks of friendships allow people to pull an end run around the hierarchy. For example, if a manager in sales hates the marketing department's new strategic plan, instead of explaining his or her opposition at a staff meeting, the manager might talk it over directly (over drinks, after work) to an old friend, the company's senior vice president. Suddenly the plan might be canceled without the marketing department's ever knowing why. In a best-case scenario, this kind of circumvention of systems lends a company a certain flexibility: maybe the marketing plan was lousy, and canceling it through official routes might have taken months. But in the worst case, it can be destructive to loyalty, commitment, and morale. In other words, networks can function well if you are an insider—you know the right people, hear the right gossip. Those on the outside often feel lost in the organization, mistreated by it, or simply unable to affect processes or products in any real way.

Solidarity, by contrast, is based not so much in the heart as in the mind, although it, too, can come naturally to groups in business settings. Its relationships are based on common tasks, mutual interests, or shared goals that will benefit all involved parties. Labor unions are a classic example of high-solidarity communities. Likewise, the solidarity of professionals—doctors and lawyers, for example—may be swiftly and ruthlessly mobilized if there is an outside competitive threat, such as proposed government regulations that could limit profitability. But, just as often, solidarity occurs between unlike individuals and groups and is not sustained by continuous social relations.

Consider the case of a Canadian clothing maker that wanted to identify strategies to expand internationally. Although its leaders were aware that the company's design, manufacturing, and marketing divisions had a long history of strained relations, they assigned two managers from each to a strategy SWAT team. Despite very little socializing and virtually no extraneous banter, the team worked fast and well together—and for good reason: each manager's bonus was based on the team's performance. After the group's report was done—its analysis and recommendations were top-notch—the managers returned to their jobs, never to associate again. In other words, solidarity can be demonstrated discontinuously, as the need arises. In contrast to sociability, then, it can be expressed both intermittently and contingently. It does not require daily display, nor does it necessarily rest upon a network of close friendships.

The organizational benefits of solidarity in a business community are many. Solidarity generates a high degree of strategic focus, swift response to competitive threats, and intolerance of poor performance. It also can result in a degree of ruthlessness. If the organization's strategy is correct, this kind of focused intent and action can be devastatingly effective. The ruthlessness, by the way, can itself reinforce solidarity: if everyone has to perform to strict standards, an equality-of-suffering effect may occur, building a sense of community in shared experience. Finally, when all employees are held to the same high standards, they often develop a strong sense of trust in the organization. This company treats everyone fairly and equally, the thinking goes; it is a meritocracy that cuts no special deals for favored or connected employees. In time, this trust can translate into commitment and loyalty to the organization's goals and purpose.

But, like sociability, solidarity has its costs as well. As we said above, strategic focus is good as long as it zeroes in on the right strategy. But if the strategy is not the right one, it is the equivalent of corporate suicide. Organizations can charge right over the cliff with great efficiency if they do the wrong things well. In addition, cooperation occurs in high-solidarity organizations only when the advantage to the individual is clear. Before taking on assignments or deciding how hard to work on projects, people ask, "What's in it for me?" If the answer is not obvious or immediate, neither is the response.

Finally, in high-solidarity organizations, roles (that is, job definitions) tend to be extremely clear. By contrast, in cultures where people are very friendly, roles and responsibilities tend to blur a bit. Someone in sales might become deeply involved in a new R&D project—a collaboration made possible by social ties. This kind of overlap usually doesn't happen in high-solidarity environments. Indeed, such environments are often characterized by turf battles, as individuals police and protect the boundaries of their roles. Someone in sales who tried to become involved in an R&D effort would be sent packing—and quickly.

Although our discussion separates sociability and solidarity, many observers of organizational life confuse the two, and it is easy to see why. The concepts can, and often do, overlap. Social interaction at work may reflect the sociability of friends, the solidarity of colleagues, both, or—sometimes—neither. Equally, when colleagues socialize outside work, their interaction may represent an extension of workplace solidarity or an expression of intimate or close friendship. Yet to identify a community's culture correctly and to assess its appropriateness for the business environment, it is more than academic to assess sociability and solidarity as distinct measures. Asking the right questions can help in this process. (See the questionnaire "What Is Your Organization's Culture?")

It is critical, before completing the form, to select the parameters of

*Exhibit II.*

## What Is Your Organization's Culture?

| To assess your organization's level of sociability, answer the following questions: | low | medium | high |
|---|---|---|---|
| 1. People here try to make friends and to keep their relationships strong | ☐ | ☐ | ☐ |
| 2. People here get along very well | ☐ | ☐ | ☐ |
| 3. People in our groups often socialize outside the office | ☐ | ☐ | ☐ |
| 4. People here really like one another | ☐ | ☐ | ☐ |
| 5. When people leave our group, we stay in touch | ☐ | ☐ | ☐ |
| 6. People here do favors for others because they like one another | ☐ | ☐ | ☐ |
| 7. People here often confide in one another about personal matters | ☐ | ☐ | ☐ |

| To assess your organization's level of solidarity, answer the following questions: | low | medium | high |
|---|---|---|---|
| 1. Our group (organization, division unit, team) understands and shares the same business objectives | ☐ | ☐ | ☐ |
| 2. Work gets done effectively and productively | ☐ | ☐ | ☐ |
| 3. Our group takes strong action to address poor performance | ☐ | ☐ | ☐ |
| 4. Our collective will to win is high | ☐ | ☐ | ☐ |
| 5. When opportunities for competitive advantage arise, we move quickly to capitalize on them | ☐ | ☐ | ☐ |
| 6. We share the same strategic goals | ☐ | ☐ | ☐ |
| 7. We know who the competition is | ☐ | ☐ | ☐ |

the group you will be evaluating; for instance, you might assess your entire company with all its divisions and subgroups or a unit as small as a team. Either is fine, as long as you do not change horses in midstream. Our unit of analysis here is primarily the corporation, but we recognize that executives may use the framework to look inside their own organizations, comparing units, divisions, or other groups with one another.

Such an exercise can indeed be instructive. One of the great errors of the recent literature on corporate culture has been to assume that organizations are homogeneous. Just as one organization differs from another, so do units within them. For example, the R&D division of a pharmaceutical company might differ markedly from the manufacturing division in both solidarity and sociability. In addition, there are often hierarchical differences within a single company: senior managers may display an entirely different culture from middle managers, and different still from blue-collar workers.

Is this variation good news or bad news? The answer depends on the situation and requires managerial judgment. Radically different cultures inside a company may very well explain conflict and suggest that intervention is necessary. Similarly, one type of culture throughout a corporation may be a signal that some forms need to be adjusted to account for differing business environments.

## The Networked Organization: High Sociability, Low Solidarity

It is perhaps the rituals of what we call networked organizations that are most noticeable to outsiders. People frequently stop to talk in the hallways; they wander into one another's offices with no purpose but to say hello; lunch is an event in which groups often go out and dine together; and after-hours socializing is not the exception but the rule. Many of these organizations celebrate birthdays, field softball teams, and hold parties to honor an employee's long service or retirement. There may be nicknames, in-house jokes, or a common language drawn from shared experiences. (At one networked company, for instance, employees tease one another with the phrase "Don't pull a Richard," in reference to an employee who once fell asleep during a meeting. Richard himself uses the jest as well.) Employees in networked organizations sometimes act like family, attending one another's weddings, anniversary parties, and children's confirmations and bar mitzvahs. They may even live in the same towns.

Inside the office, networked cultures are characterized not by a lack of hierarchy but by a profusion of ways to get around it. Friends or cliques of friends make sure that decisions about issues are made before meetings are held to discuss them. People move from one position to another without the "required" training. Employees are hired without going through official channels in the human resources department—they know someone inside the network. As we have said, this informality can lend flexibility to an organization and be a healthy way of cutting through the bureaucracy. But it also means that the people in these cultures have developed two of the networked organization's key competencies: the ability to collect and selectively disseminate soft information, and the ability to acquire sponsors or allies in the company who will speak on their behalf both formally and informally.

What are the other hallmarks of networked organizations? Their low levels of solidarity mean that managers often have trouble getting functions or operating companies to cooperate. At one large European manufacturer, personal relations among senior executives of businesses in France, Italy, the United Kingdom, and Germany were extremely friendly. Several executives had known one another for years; some even took vacations together. But when the time came for corporate headquarters to parcel out resources, those same executives fought acrimoniously. At one point, they individually subverted attempts by headquarters to introduce a Europe-wide marketing strategy designed to combat the entry of U.S. competition.

Finally, a networked organization is usually so political that individuals and cliques spend much of their time pursuing personal agendas. It becomes hard for colleagues to agree on priorities and for managers to enforce them. It is not uncommon to hear frequent calls for strong leadership to overcome the divisions of subcultures, cliques, or warring factions in networked organizations.

In addition, because there is little commitment to shared business objectives, employees in networked organizations often contest performance measures, procedures, rules, and systems. For instance, at one international consumer-products company with which we have worked, the strategic planning process, the structural relationship between corporate headquarters and operating companies, and the accounting and budgetary control systems were heavily and continually criticized by executives in country businesses. Indeed, the criticism even took on an element of sport, increasing sociability among employees but doing nothing for the already diminished levels of solidarity.

Generally speaking, few organizations start their life cycle in the networked quadrant. By definition, sociability is built up over time. It follows, then, that many organizations migrate there from other quadrants. And despite the political nature of this kind of community, there are many examples of successful networked corporations. These organizations have learned how to overcome the negatives of sociability, such as cliques, gossip, and low productivity, and how to reap its benefits, such as increased creativity and commitment. One method of maximizing the benefits of a networked culture is to move individuals regularly between functions, businesses, and countries in order to limit excessive local identification and help them develop a wider strategic view of the organization. Later on, these individuals often become the primary managers of the networked organization's political processes, and they keep them healthy.

High levels of sociability usually go hand in hand with low solidarity because close friendships can inhibit the open expression of differences, the criticism of ideas, and forceful dissent. Constructive conflict, however, is often a precondition for developing and maintaining a shared sense of purpose—that is, solidarity. It would not be surprising, then, to find that well-meaning management interventions to increase strategic focus often consolidate workplace friendships but do little for organizational solidarity. That could account for at least some of the frustrations of those who complain, for example, that the outdoor team-building weekend was great fun but not remotely connected to the daily work of ensuring that the different parts of the business are integrated.

As we have noted, each type of corporate culture has its most appropriate time and place. We have observed that the networked organization functions well under the following business conditions:

- When corporate strategies have a long time frame. Sociability maintains allegiance to the organization when short-term calculations of interest do not. Consider the case of a company expanding into Vietnam. It might be years before such an effort is profitable, and in the meantime the process of getting operations running may be difficult and frustrating. In a networked culture, employees are often willing to put up with risk and discomfort. They are loyal to their colleagues in an open-ended way. The enjoyment of friendship on a daily basis is its own reward.

- When knowledge of the peculiarities of local markets is a critical success factor. The reason is that networked organizations are low on solidarity: members of one unit don't willingly share ideas or information with members of another. This would certainly be a strategic disadvantage if success came from employees having a broad, big-picture perspective. But when success is driven by deep and intense familiarity with a unit's home turf, low solidarity is no hindrance.

- When corporate success is an aggregate of local success. Again, this is a function of low solidarity. If headquarters can do well with low levels of interdivisional communication, then the networked culture is appropriate.

## The Mercenary Organization: Low Sociability, High Solidarity

At the other end of the spectrum from the networked organization, the mercenary community is low on hallway hobnobbing and high on data-laden memos. Indeed, almost all communication in a mercenary organization is focused on business matters. The reason: individual interests coincide with corporate objectives, and those objectives are often linked to a crystal clear perception of the "enemy" and the steps required to beat it. As a result, mercenary organizations are characterized by the ability to respond quickly and cohesively to a perceived opportunity or threat in the marketplace. Priorities are decided swiftly—generally by senior management—and enforced throughout the organization with little debate.

Mercenary organizations are also characterized by a clear separation of work and social life. (Interestingly, these cultures often consist of people whose work takes priority over their private life.) Members of this kind of business community rarely fraternize outside the office, and if they do, it is at functions organized around business, such as a party to celebrate the defeat of a competitor or the successful implementation of a strategic plan.

Because of the absence of strong personal ties, mercenary organizations are generally intolerant of poor performance. Those who are not contributing fully are fired or given explicit instructions on how to improve, with a firm deadline. There is a hard-heartedness to this aspect of mercenary cultures, and yet the high levels of commitment to a common purpose mean it is accepted, and usually supported, in the ranks. If someone has not performed, you rarely hear, for instance, "It was a shame we had to let John go—he was so nice." John, the thinking would be, wasn't doing his part toward clearly stated, shared strategic objectives.

Finally, the low level of social ties means that mercenary organizations are rarely bastions of loyalty. Employees may very well respect and like their organizations; after all, these institutions are usually fair to those who work hard and meet standards. But those feelings are not sentimental or tied to affectionate relationships between individuals. People stay with high-solidarity companies for as long as their personal needs are met, and then they move on.

Without a doubt, the advantages of a mercenary organization can sound seductive in the performance-driven 1990s. What manager would not want his or her company to have a heightened sense of competition and a strong will to win? In addition, because of their focused activity, many mercenary organizations are very productive. Moreover, unhindered by friendships, employees are not reluctant to compete, further enhancing performance as standards get pushed ever higher.

But mercenary communities have disadvantages as well. Employees who are busy chasing specific targets are often disinclined to cooperate, share information, or exchange new or creative ideas. To do so would be a distraction. Cooperation between units with different goals is even less likely. Consider the example of Warner Brothers, the entertainment conglomerate. The music and film divisions, each with its own strategic targets, have trouble achieving synergy—for example, with sound tracks. (Musicians recording on a Warner record label, for instance, might be called on to score a Warner movie.) Compare this situation with that at Disney, a major competitor, which relentlessly and profitably exploits synergies between its movie characters—from Snow White to Simba—and its merchandising divisions.

The mercenary organization works effectively under the following business conditions:

- When change is fast and rampant. This type of situation calls for a rapid, focused response, which a mercenary organization is able to mount.
- When economies of scale are achieved, or competitive advantage is gained, through creating corporate centers of excellence that can impose processes and procedures on operating companies or divisions. For example, the Zürich-based diversified corporation ABB Asea Brown Boveri builds worldwide centers of excellence for product groups. Its Finnish subsidiary Stromberg has become the world leader in electric drives since its acquisition in 1986, and it now sets the standard for the ABB empire.
- When corporate goals are clear and measurable, and there is therefore little need for input from the ranks or for consensus building.
- When the nature of the competition is clear. Mercenary organizations thrive when the enemy—and the best way to defeat it—are obvious. The mercenary organization is most appropriate when one enemy can be distinguished from many. Komatsu, for example, made *Maru-C*—translated as "Encircle Caterpillar"—its war cry back in 1965 and focused all

its strategic efforts during the 1970s and early 1980s on doing just that, aided effectively by a high-solidarity culture. By contrast, IBM zigzagged strategically for years, unable to identify its competition until the game was nearly up. Its cultural type during that time is not known to us, but we can guess with confidence that it wasn't mercenary.

## The Fragmented Organization: Low Sociability, Low Solidarity

Few managers would volunteer to work for or, perhaps harder still, run a fragmented organization. But like strife-ridden countries, unfriendly neighborhoods, and disharmonious families, such communities are a fact of life. What are their primary characteristics in a business setting?

Perhaps most notably, employees of fragmented organizations display a low consciousness of organizational membership. They often believe that they work for themselves or they identify with occupational groups—usually professional. Asked at a party what he does for a living, for instance, a doctor at a major teaching hospital that happens to have this kind of culture might reply, "I'm a surgeon," leaving out the name of the institution where he is employed. Likewise, organizations that have this kind of culture rarely field softball teams—who would want to wear the company's name on a T-shirt?— and employees engage in none of the extracurricular rites and rituals that characterize high-sociability cultures, considering them a waste of time.

This lack of affective interrelatedness extends to behavior on the job. People work with their doors shut or, in many cases, at home, going to the office only to collect mail or make long-distance calls. They are often secretive about their projects and progress with coworkers, offering information only when asked point-blank. In extreme cases, members of fragmented organizations have such low levels of sociability that they attempt to sabotage the work of their "colleagues" through gossip, rumor, or overt criticism delivered to higher-ups in the organization.

This culture also has low levels of solidarity: its members rarely agree about organizational objectives, critical success factors, and performance standards. It's no surprise, then, that high levels of dissent about strategic goals often make these organizations difficult to manage top-down. Leaders often feel isolated and routinely report feeling as if there is no action they can take to effect change. Their calls fall on deaf ears.

Low sociability also means that individuals may give of themselves on a personal level only after careful calculation of what they might get in return. Retirement parties, for example, are often sparsely attended. Indeed, any social behavior that is discretionary is unlikely to take place.

We realize it must sound as if fragmented organizations are wretched places to work—or at least appeal only to the hermits or Scrooges of the business world. But situations do exist that invite, or even benefit from, such a culture, and further, this kind of environment is attractive to individuals who prefer to work alone or to keep their work and personal lives entirely separate.

In our research, we have seen fragmented organizations operate successfully in several forms. First, the culture functions well in manufacturing concerns that rely heavily on the outsourcing of piecework. Second, the culture can succeed in professional organizations, such as consulting and law firms, in which highly trained individuals have idiosyncratic work styles. Third, fragmented cultures often accompany organizations that have become virtual: employees work either at home or on the road, reporting in to a central base mainly by electronic means. Of course, fragmented organizations sometimes reflect dysfunctional communities in which ties of sociability or solidarity have been torn asunder by organizational politics, downsizing, or other forms of disruption. In these cases, the old ties of friendship and loyalty are replaced by an overriding concern for individual survival, unleashing a war of all against all.

The last unhealthy scenario aside, however, a fragmented culture is appropriate under the following business conditions:

- When there is little interdependence in the work itself. This might occur, for example, in a company in which pieces of furniture or clothing are subcontracted to individuals who work out of their homes and then assembled at another site. A second example might be a firm composed of tax lawyers, each working for different clients.

- When significant innovation is produced primarily by individuals rather than by teams. (This, it should be noted, is becoming increasingly rare in business, as cross-disciplinary teams demonstrate the power of *unlike* minds working together.)

- When standards are achieved by input controls, not process controls. In these organizations, time has proven that management's focus should be on recruiting the right people; once they have been hired and trained, their work requires little supervision. They are their own best judges, their own harshest taskmasters.

- When there are few learning opportunities between individuals or when professional pride prevents the transfer of knowledge. In an international oil-trading company we have worked with, for example, employees who traded Nigerian oil never shared market information with employees trading Saudi crude. For one thing, they weren't given any incentive to take the time to do so; for another, each group of traders took pride in knowing more than the other. To give away information was to give away the prestige of being at the top of the field—a market insider.

## The Communal Organization: High Sociability, High Solidarity

A communal culture can evolve at any stage of a company's life cycle, but when we are asked to illustrate this form, we often cite the characteristics of a typical small, fast-growing, entrepreneurial start-up. The founders and early employees of such companies are close friends, working endless hours in tight quarters. This kinship usually flows into close ties outside the office. In the early days of Apple Computer, for instance, employees lived together, commuted together, and spent weekends together, too. At the same time, the sense of solidarity at a typical start-up is sky high. A tiny company has one or at most two products and just as few goals (the first usually being survival). Because founders and early employees often have equity in the start-up, success has clear, collective benefits. In communal organizations, everything feels in sync.

But, as we have said, start-ups don't own this culture. Indeed, communal cultures can be found in mature companies in which employees have worked together for decades to develop both friendships and mutually beneficial objectives.

Regardless of their stage of development, communal organizations share certain traits. First, their employees possess a high, sometimes exaggerated, consciousness of organizational identity and membership. Individuals may even link their sense of self with the corporate identity. Some employees at Nike, it is said, have the company's trademark symbol tattooed above their ankles. Similarly, in the early days of Apple Computer, employees readily identified themselves as "Apple people."

Organizational life in communal companies is punctuated by social events that take on a strong ritual significance. The London office of the international advertising agency J. Walter Thompson, for instance, throws parties for its staff at exciting, even glamorous, locations; recent events were held at the Hurlingham Club and the Natural History Museum in London. The company also offers its employees a master class on creativity that features a speech by a celebrity. Dave Stewart, former guitarist of the rock band the Eurythmics, even played a set during his presentation. And finally, Thompson holds an annual gala awards ceremony for the company's best creative teams. Winners go to lunch in Paris. Other communal companies celebrate entrance into their organizations and promotions with similar fanfare.

The high solidarity of communal cultures is often demonstrated through an equitable sharing of risks and rewards among employees. Communal organizations, after all, place an extremely high value on fairness and justice, which comes into sharp focus particularly in hard times. For example, during the 1970 recession, rather than lay people off, Hewlett-Packard introduced a 10% cut in pay and hours across every rank. It should be noted that the company's management did not become demonized or despised in the process. In fact, what happened at Hewlett-Packard is another characteristic of communal companies: their leaders command widespread respect, deference, and even affection. Although they invite dissent, and even succeed in receiving it, their authority is rarely challenged.

Solidarity also shows itself clearly when it comes to company goals and values. The mission statement is often given front-and-center display in a communal company's offices, and it evokes enthusiasm rather than cynicism.

Finally, in communal organizations, employees are very clear about the competition. They know which companies threaten theirs—what they do well, how they are weak—and how they can be overcome. And not only is the external competition seen clearly, its defeat is also perceived to be a matter of competing values. The competition has as much to do with an organization's purpose—the reason it exists—as it has with winning market share or increasing operating margins.

Given all these characteristics, it is perhaps not surprising that many managers see the communal organization as the ideal. Solidarity alone may be symptomatic of excessive instrumentalism. Employees may withdraw their cooperation the moment they become unable to identify shared advantage. In some cases, particularly where there are well-established performance-related reward systems, this attitude may be reflected in an exaggerated concern with those activities that produce measurable outcomes. By contrast, organizations that are characterized primarily by sociability may lose their sense of purpose.

However, where both sociability and solidarity are high, a company gets the best of both worlds—or does it? The answer is that the communal culture may be an inappropriate and unattainable ideal in many business contexts. Our research suggests that it seems to work best in religious, political, and civic organizations. It is much harder to find commercial enterprises in this quadrant. The reason is that many businesses that achieve the communal form find it difficult to sustain. There are a number of possible explanations. First, high levels of sociability and solidarity are often formed around particular founders or leaders whose departure may weaken either or both forms of social relationship. Second, the high-sociability half of the communal culture is often antithetical to what goes on inside an organization during periods of growth, diversification, or internationalization. These massive and complex change efforts require focus, urgency, and performance—the stuff of solidarity in its undiluted form.

More profoundly, though, there may be a built-in tension between relationships of sociability and solidarity that makes the communal business enterprise an inherently unstable form. The sincere geniality of sociability doesn't usually coexist—it can't—with solidarity's dispassionate, sometimes ruthless focus on achievement of goals. When the two do coexist, as we have said, it is often in religious or volunteer groups. Perhaps one reason is that people tend to join these groups after they've become familiar with, and agree with, their objectives. (A church's policies, procedures, beliefs, and goals, for instance, are made well known to prospective members before they join. Once inside the organization, members find little "strategic" dissension to get in the way of friendship.) By contrast, when people consider employment at a business enterprise, they may not know what the organization's beliefs and values are—or they may know them and disagree with them but join the organization anyway for financial or career reasons. Over time, their objections may manifest themselves in low-solidarity behaviors.

In their attempts to mimic the virtues of communal organizations, many senior managers have failed to think through whether high levels of both sociability and solidarity are, in fact, what they need. Again, from our research, it is clear that the desirable mix varies according to the context. In what situations, then, does a communal culture function well?

- When innovation requires elaborate and extensive teamwork across functions and perhaps locations. Increasingly, high-impact innovation cannot be achieved by isolated specialists. Rather, as the knowledge base of organizations deepens and diversifies, many talents need to combine (and combust) for truly creative change. For example, at the pharmaceutical company Glaxo Wellcome, research projects are undertaken by teams from different disciplines—such as genetics, chemistry, and toxicology—and in different locations. Without such teamwork, drug development would be much slower and competitive advantage would be lost.

- When there are real synergies among organizational subunits and real opportunities for learning. We emphasize the word *real* because synergy and learning are often held up as organizational goals without hard scrutiny. Both are good—in theory. In practice, opportunities for synergy and learning among one company's divisions may not actually exist or be worth the effort. However, when they do exist, a communal culture unquestionably helps.

- When strategies are more long-term than short-term. That is to say, when corporate goals won't be reached in the foreseeable future, managerial mechanisms are needed to keep commitment and focus high. The communal culture provides high sociability to bolster relationships (and the commitment that accompanies them) and high solidarity to sustain focus. Indeed, we have seen communal cultures help enormously as organizations have gone global—a long and often tortuous process during which strategies have a tendency to be open ended and emergent, as opposed to the sum of measurable milestones.

- When the business environment is dynamic and complex. Although many organizations claim to be in such an environment, it is perhaps most pronounced in sectors like information technology, telecommunications, and pharmaceuticals. In these industries, organizations interface with their environment through multiple connections involving technology, customers, the government, competition, and research institutes. A communal culture is appropriate in this kind of environment because its dynamics aid in the synthesis of information from all these sources.

## Changing the Culture

There is clearly an implied argument here that organizations should strive for a form of community suited to their environment. Reality is never so neat. In fact, managers continually face the challenge of adjusting their corporate community to a changing environment. Our research suggests that over the last decade, a number of large, well-established companies with strong traditions of loyalty and collegiality have been forced, mostly through competitive threat, to move from the networked to the mercenary form. To describe the process as tricky does not do it justice. It is perhaps one of the most complex and risk-laden changes a manager can face.

Consider the example of chairman and president Jan D. Timmer of the Dutch electronics company Philips. Once a monumentally successful company, Philips lost its competitive edge in the mid-1980s and even came close to collapse. Timmer (and many observers) attributed much of the company's troubles to its corporate culture. Sociability was so extreme that highly politicized cliques ruled and healthy information flow stopped, particularly between R&D and marketing. (During this period, many of Philips's new products flopped; critics said the reason was that they provided technology that consumers didn't particularly want.) Meanwhile, authority was routinely challenged, as were company goals and strategies. Management's lack of control allowed many employees to relax on the job. They had little concern with performance standards and no sense of competitive threat. In short, Philips demonstrated many of the negative consequences of a networked organization. However, given the industry's primary success factors—innovation, market focus, and fast product rollout—Philips needed a mercenary or communal culture to stay even, not to mention get ahead.

Timmer attempted just such a transformation, first by trying to lower managers' comfort level. He implemented measurable, ambitious performance targets and held individuals accountable to them. In the process, many long-serving executives left the company or were sidelined. Timmer also conducted frequent management conferences, at which the company's objectives, procedures, and values were clearly communicated. He demanded commitment to these goals, and those employees who did not conform were let go. In this way, solidarity was increased, and Philips's performance began to show it.

As performance began to improve markedly, Timmer made efforts to restore some of the company's sociability, which had been lost during the turnaround—thus moving the company from mercenary toward communal. Meetings began to focus on the company's values and on gaining consensus. In short, Timmer was trying to reestablish loyalty to Philips and connections among its members. Timmer was scheduled to retire in October, and it remains to be seen in what direction his successor, Cor Boonstra, will take the company.

Boonstra's challenge is formidable. Once organizations try to reduce well-established ties of sociability, they can inadvertently unleash a process that is difficult to control. Unpicking emotional relationships may make solidarity difficult, too. The result: organizations can devolve toward an inappropriate fragmented form. From there, recovery can be difficult.

This precise phenomenon, in fact, can be seen in the uncomfortable transition now occurring in the British Broadcasting Corporation. Its director general, John Birt, has tried to focus the organization—long known for its quality programming and public service—on efficiency and productivity. In the process, strict performance standards have been set, and colleagues have had to vie against one another for scarcer resources. As sociability has diminished, talented individuals who once saw themselves as part of a communal culture have railed against what they consider target-oriented changes. Some have decided to stay and stubbornly defend their own interests; others have chosen to leave. With its communal culture heading toward a fragmented one, the BBC faces no alternative but to reinvent itself.

How, then, does an organization change its culture from one type to another without wreaking too much damage? How does a manager tweak levels of sociability or solidarity?

Clearly, the tools required to manipulate each dimension are different. And using them involves understanding why a culture has taken its current form in the first place—why, that is, a culture possesses its present levels of sociability and solidarity. Neighborhoods, book clubs, and *Fortune* 100 companies can all be friendly for myriad reasons—the example set by a leader, the personalities of certain members, the physical setting of the organization or its history, or simply the amount of cash in the bank. Likewise, solidarity can arise for many reasons. Our purpose here has been not to analyze *why* organizations have different levels of sociability and solidarity but to examine *what happens* to their culture when they do, and what that means for managers who seek satisfied employees and strong performance. However, before attempting to change levels of sociability or solidarity, a manager needs to think a bit like a doctor taking on a new patient. The patient's past and current conditions are not only relevant but also critically important to assessing the best future treatment.

Our research shows that to increase sociability, managers can take the following steps:

**Promote the sharing of ideas, interests, and emotions by recruiting compatible people—people who naturally seem likely to become friends.** Before hiring a candidate, for instance, a manager might arrange for him or her to have lunch with several current employees in order to get a sense of the chemistry among them. This kind of activity need not be covert. Trying to find employees who share interests and attitudes can even be stated as an explicit goal. In itself, such an announcement may signal that management seeks to increase sociability.

**Increase social interaction among employees by arranging casual gatherings inside and outside the office, such as parties, excursions—even book clubs.** These events might be awkward at first, as employees question their purpose or simply feel odd associating outside a business setting. One way around this problem is to schedule such gatherings during work hours so that attendance is essentially mandatory. It is also critical to make these interactions enjoyable so that they create their own positive, self-reinforcing dynamic. The hard news for managers is that sometimes this orchestrated socializing requires spending money, which can be difficult to rationalize to the finance department. However, if the business environment demands higher levels of sociability, managers can consider the expenditure a good investment in long-term profitability.

**Reduce formality between employees.** Managers can encourage informal dress codes, arrange offices differently, or designate spaces where employees can mingle on equal terms, such as the lunchroom or gym.

**Limit hierarchical differences.** There are several means to this end. For one, the organization chart can be redesigned to eliminate layers and ranks. Also, hierarchy has a hard time coexisting with shared facilities and open office layouts. Some companies have narrowed hierarchical differences by ensuring that all employees, regardless of rank, receive the same package of benefits, park in the same lot (with no assigned spaces), and get bonuses based on the same formula.

**Act like a friend yourself, and set the example for geniality and kindness by caring for those in trouble.** At one communal company we know of, management gave a three-month paid leave of absence to an employee whose young son was ill, and then allowed her to work on a flexible schedule until he was completely well. Sociability is increased when this caring extends beyond crisis situations—for instance, when management welcomes the families of its employees into the fold by inviting them to company picnics or outings. Indeed, many high-sociability companies hold Christmas parties for the children of employees or give each family a special holiday present.

To build solidarity, managers can take the following steps:

**Develop awareness of competitors through briefings, newsletters, videos, memos, or E-mail.** For example, as Timmer worked to move Philips toward the mercenary form, he exhorted his managers to take a new, hard look at the company's Japanese competitors. Breaking a longtime organizational taboo, he praised Japanese quality highly and compared Japanese products favorably with those his company made.

**Create a sense of urgency.** Managers can promote a sense of urgency in their people by developing a visionary statement or slogan for the organization and communicating it relentlessly. In the late 1980s, for example, Gerard van Schaik, then chairman of the board of Heineken, took his company global with the internal war cry Paint the World Green. The message was clear, focused, and action oriented. It worked. Today Heineken is the most international beer company in the world.

**Stimulate the will to win.** Managers can hire and promote individuals with drive or ambition, set high standards for performance, and celebrate success in high-profile ways. Mary Kay, the Texas-based cosmetics company, is famous for giving its top saleswomen pink Cadillacs. In most other organizations, a large check or public recognition—or both—does the same job. Similarly, an incentive system that rewards corporate performance (rather than or in addition to unit and personal performance) underscores the importance of the company's overall achievement.

**Encourage commitment to shared corporate goals.** To do so, managers can move people between functions, businesses, and countries to reduce strong subcultures and create a sense of one company. Disney, for example, identifies highfliers—candidates that show promise—and then moves them through five divisions in five years. These individuals then carry the organization's larger strategic picture and purpose with them throughout their later positions at Disney, pollinating each division in the process.

# Building the Right Community

So far, we have stressed three primary points. First, knowing how your organization measures up on the dimensions of sociability and solidarity is an important managerial competence. Second, knowing whether the company's culture fits the business environment is critical to competitive advantage. And third, there is no golden quadrant that guarantees success. We must stress, however, that our model for analyzing culture and its fit with the business context is a dynamic one. Business environments do not stay the same. Similarly, organizations have life cycles. Successful organizations need a sense not just of where they are but of where they are heading. This demands a subtle appreciation of human relations and an awareness that manipulating sociability on the one hand and solidarity on the other involves very different challenges.

Finally, we have claimed that patterns of organizational life are often conditioned by factors outside the organization, such as the competition, the industry structure, and the pace of technological change. But a company's culture is also governed by choices. Senior executives cannot avoid or deny this fact. Managers can increase the amount of sociability in their staffs by employing many of the devices listed above; similarly, they can manipulate levels of solidarity through the decisions they make. In short, these choices have the ability to affect what kinds of experiences members of an organization enjoy—and don't—on a day-to-day basis. Executives are therefore left with the job of managing the tension between creating a culture that produces a winning organization and creating one that makes people happy and allows the authentic expression of individual values. This challenge is profound and personal, and its potential for impact on performance is enormous. Culture *can* hold back the pressures for corporate disintegration if managers understand what culture means—and what it means to change it.

## Unilever: A Networked Organization

There is a frequently told story within Unilever, the Anglo-Dutch consumer-goods group with worldwide sales of roughly $50 billion. Unilever executives, it is said, recognize one another at airports, even when they've never met before. There's something about the way they look and act—something so subtle it's impossible to pin down in words yet unmistakable to those who have worked for the company for more than a few years.

Obviously, there's a bit of exaggeration in this company legend, but it underscores Unilever's tradition as a networked company—that is, one with a culture characterized by high levels of sociability. For years, the company has explicitly recruited compatible people—people with similar backgrounds, values, and interests. Unilever's managers believe that this corps of like-minded individuals is the reason why its employees work so well together despite their national diversity, why they demonstrate such strong loyalty to their colleagues, and why they embrace the company's values of cooperation and consensus.

Unilever takes other steps to reinforce and increase the sociability in its ranks. At Four Acres, the company's international-management-training center outside London, hundreds of executives a year partake in activities rich in social rituals: multicourse dinners, group photographs, sports on the lawn, and, perhaps above all, a bar that literally never closes. As former chairman Floris Maljers remarks, "This shared experience creates an informal network of equals who know one another well and usually continue to meet and exchange experiences."

In addition to the events at Four Acres, Unilever's sociability is bolstered by annual conferences attended by the company's top 500 managers. The company's leaders use these meetings to communicate and review strategy, but there is much more to them than work. (The intense fraternizing that takes place at these conferences has earned them the nickname Oh! Be Joyfuls!) Maljers notes, "Over good food and drink, our most senior people meet, exchange views, and reconfirm old friendships."

Finally, Unilever moves its young managers frequently—across borders, products, and divisions. This effort is an attempt to start Unilever relationships early, as well as to increase know-how.

Yet these carefully nurtured patterns of sociability have not always been matched by high levels of companywide solidarity. Unilever has found it hard over the years to achieve cross-company coordination and agreement on objectives. It's not that executives fight over strategy as much as "talk it to death" in the search for consensus, says one senior vice president.

Does this networked culture fit Unilever's business environment? In good part, yes. Unilever's managers hail from dozens of countries. This diversity could have been an isolating factor, hindering the flow of information and ideas. But because of the culture's high levels of sociability, there is widespread fellowship and goodwill instead. Second, a key success factor in Unilever's business is proximity to local markets. The organization's low solidarity has kept units focused on their home bases with good results. And finally, until recently, Unilever has been a highly decentralized organization. Simply put, there has been little need for strategic agreement among units.

But Unilever's environment might very well be changing with the emergence of a single European market, which would make coordination among businesses and functions imperative. Indeed, many recent organizational changes—the creation of Lever Europe in the detergents business, for example—can be interpreted as an attempt by Unilever to create higher levels of corporate solidarity, largely through a process of centralization.

In addition, Unilever faces some competitors, such as Procter & Gamble and L'Oréal, known for their high levels of solidarity around corporate goals. This asset has lent Unilever's competitors the ability to accelerate product development processes and exploit market opportunities quickly. Unilever must match those competencies or risk losing clout.

Finally, Unilever's relative lack of solidarity means that management can lose its sense of urgency—a competitive advantage in any business environment. This challenge is well known to the company's leaders. As Maljers himself notes, "Everybody may be so busy with friends elsewhere—with the interesting training program, the well-organized course, the next major conference—that complacency sets in. Unfortunately, we have seen this happen in some of our units, especially the more successful ones. It may be necessary to shake up the system from time to time."

This comment underlines one of the biggest risks of the networked organization. Employees may be so busy being friends that they lose sight of the reason they are at work in the first place.

Interestingly, Unilever's recently announced organizational restructuring is designed in part to address some of the negative consequences of the networked form. The company will be broken into 14 business groups, and, according to the plan, each will have a clear business rationale, stretch targets, and transparent accountability. In a booklet sent to all managers, the company described the changes as a means to "establish a simple, effective organization dedicated to the needs of the future. This must provide great clarity of roles, responsibilities, and decision making. . . . Under the new structure, business groups will make annual contracts on which they must deliver come 'hell or high water.'"

Similarly, in an interview in *Unilever* magazine, company chairman Niall FitzGerald identified the values of the new organization in these words: "Simplicity, clarity, and delegation of authority are intended to be the prime virtues of the new organization. A disciplined approach [is essential]—those who have been given the task of delivering results must focus on delivering."

In the terms of our model, this reorganization is clearly an effort to move toward the mercenary quadrant: less politicking (as enjoyable as it might be) and a more ruthless focus on results. But can Unilever let go of its ingrained sociability and take on the behaviors of a high-solidarity enterprise? The company's future performance will tell.

## Mastiff Wear: A Mercenary Organization

Several years ago, a senior manager at a company we'll call Mastiff Wear, an international manufacturer of popular children's clothing, invited 15 of the company's top executives to dinner at a fancy new restaurant in London. The men and women had just sat down when the host announced a challenge to be completed over dinner: devise a new advertising slogan. The best solution, the host said, would earn a bottle of Dom Pérignon. For the next three hours, the guests took to their task single-mindedly, even tearing up the elegant menus to use as working paper. The restaurant's delicacies passed before them throughout the night, and the executives ate, but few seemed to take notice of where they were. What they were doing was all that mattered.

Not long after, one of the authors of this article met with a similar group of executives at Mastiff Wear. "If I join Mastiff next Monday," he asked them, "what should I know are the rules of success at this organization?" Rule one, he was told: Arrive on Sunday. Rule two: Call your family and tell them you won't be home until next weekend.

Both of these stories illustrate a typical mercenary culture in action: members work long hours and often value work over family life. (The executives in the restaurant worked even when they could have been socializing, and no one complained—or even noticed.) In addition, the stories illustrate this form's high degree of internal competition and strong focus on the achievement of tasks.

Mastiff also embodies several other characteristics of high-solidarity cultures. There are strict standards for performance, and underachievers are dealt with ruthlessly. As one executive remarks, "Once in a while, one of us just disappears." Those who survive are well rewarded—so well that many are able to retire early. Indeed, a common strategy for a Mastiff executive is to work hard, even at the cost of his or her personal life, accumulate wealth, and then leave. Relationships with the organization exist primarily as a means for employees to promote their own interests—career, personal, or otherwise.

In some ways, this mercenary culture has been an apt fit for Mastiff in recent years. The company has had considerable success in the clearly defined distribution channels in which it operates. Internally, a fierce focus on efficiency has ensured that resources are used to the fullest. Little is wasted, and the company does only what it can do best, creating centers of corporate excellence to spread its knowledge. Externally, a strategy of targeting clearly defined sectors—primarily department stores and cata-logs—and a clearly identified "enemy" has consistently enabled Mastiff to establish dominant market positions. Most recently, this ability has been illustrated by the company's dramatic entry into the European market—a move that has inflicted considerable damage on a major competitive player there.

But mercenary cultures have their shortcomings. When you successfully occupy the number one position in many markets, as Mastiff has for many years, you may run out of enemies. As a result, you may lose the com-petitive edge that originally brought your company a sense of urgency and the collective will to win. In addition, Mastiff, like many mercenary cultures, may have suffered from excessive strategic focus. In this case, a charac-teristic concern with operational efficiencies proved barely adequate when competitors were gaining market share from new-product devel-opment. Focusing on one or two issues is a strength, of course. The danger is that you can lose sight of what's happening on the horizon.

## University Business School: A Fragmented Organization

Despite how unpleasant it sounds to work where both sociability and solidarity are lacking, there are indeed environments that invite such cultures and do no harm whatsoever to the organization, its people, or its products in the process. Still, there is the stigma of an "unfriendly" organization to contend with, which is the reason this case study uses a disguised name for its subject.

University Business School is typical of its breed: it offers an M.B.A. program and several shorter executive programs. Its other products are books, reports, and scholarly articles. The school achieves all this smoothly, with remarkably low levels of social interaction of any kind among mem-bers of the community.

Take sociability. At UBS, professors work mainly on their own, re-searching their specialty, preparing classes, writing articles, and assessing students' papers. Often this work is done at home or in the office, behind closed doors displaying Do Not Disturb signs. Many professors have demanding second jobs as consultants to industry. Therefore, when social contact does occur, it is with clients, students, or research sponsors rather than with colleagues. In fact, faculty members may actively avoid sociability on campus in order to maximize discretionary time for private consulting work and research for publication.

As for solidarity, UBS professors see themselves foremost as part of an international group of scholars, feeling no particular affinity for the institution that employs them. Their occupational group, they believe, sets the standards and controls outputs, such as journal articles. In addition, it shapes employment opportunities and determines career progress. There is no point, the professors' thinking goes, concerning themselves with the goals and strategies of an institution that does not have direct bearing on their day-to-day work or future pursuits.

As we have said, however, none of this diminished sociability or solidarity compromises the competitive position of UBS, a highly renowned institution. The reason is that many professors do indeed do their best work alone or with scholars from other institutions who share similar interests. Moreover, M.B.A. and other academic programs don't necessarily need input from groups of staff members; most professors know what to teach and are disinclined in any case to take the advice of others. Indeed, the only reason for meetings in this environment is to decide on academic appointments and promotions. This activity involves consideration of scholarship, which requires neither sociability nor solidarity. Finally, UBS need not worry that its employees are losing focus or urgency about their work—one of the biggest risks of low-solidarity organizations. On the contrary, UBS attracts a self-selecting group of highly autonomous, sometimes egocentric individuals who are motivated, not alienated, by the freedoms of the fragmented organization.

In short, the success of UBS underscores our point: there is no generic ideal when it comes to corporate community. If the culture fits, wear it.

### British-Borneo Petroleum Syndicate: A Communal Organization

Synergy is a term that gets bandied about quite a bit, as in "Wouldn't it be terrific if our divisions, operating companies, or functional areas had more synergy? Then they could learn from one another and share new ideas—even exchange market or technological information." This hope, while admirable in theory, often remains just that in practice—a hope.

Not so at British-Borneo Petroleum Syndicate, where a communal culture—combining high sociability and high solidarity—dovetails effectively with the company's strategic need for cooperation and interchange among functions and locations. Indeed, the synergy among groups at British-Borneo is perhaps its greatest competitive advantage. The London-based company, which has grown more than tenfold in the 1990s to reach a market capitalization of $550 million in 1996, explores for and produces oil and gas in the North Sea and the Gulf of Mexico. Success in this kind of endeavor arises from speed of movement, risk management, and the innovative use of technology—which in this context can come only out of cross-functional teams. Success is also linked to well-orchestrated, complex interfaces with other players in the market and with governments. And finally, success comes from employees committing to strategies that are rather long-term. The exploration phase for most ventures will take several years, and production—hence cash flow—often lags a few years beyond that.

British-Borneo's high levels of sociability can be seen in the honest and relaxed way employees interact. They talk about their feelings openly and often help one another out—without making deals. In addition, they are a team that plays together out of the office—at picnics, parties, and ball games. This conviviality is, in some part, management's doing. Managers have systematically tried to recruit compatible people with similar interests and backgrounds. And they have improved on this foundation with regular team-building events such as Outward Bound courses for all new hires, frequent social events, and active support of company softball, track, and sailing teams. Everyone in the company is invited to participate, from board members to clerks.

British-Borneo's sociability, however, has not come at the expense of solidarity. The company's employees display a strong sense of urgency and will to win. They are clearly committed to a common purpose. Indeed, in the United Kingdom, the company's strategy is known and understood by people of every rank, including secretaries and other support personnel. The widespread knowledge and acceptance of British-Borneo's objectives have come about through careful effort. The company devotes considerable time and energy to hammering out—through workshops and brainstorming sessions—a collective vision that is owned by the staff.

Interestingly, despite the company's high levels of sociability, British-Borneo employees are not reluctant to speak their mind. (Ordinarily, friendships preclude tough criticism or disagreement.) Staff members are encouraged to strip things down to reality when they communicate about the company's business. This frankness creates an atmosphere of challenge and debate, which is one of the hallmarks of a high-solidarity environment.

Finally, British-Borneo is a classic high-solidarity environment in its adherence to strict performance standards. The culture does not tolerate underachievement. Outstanding results are generously rewarded, but it is not unusual for someone who does not measure up to be asked to leave, sooner rather than later.

We've mentioned some of the sources of British-Borneo's culture, but it is critical to note that perhaps the most important source is CEO Alan Gaynor, whose charismatic leadership sets an example. Gaynor participates in the company's many social functions, for example, and is open about his feelings. At the same time, he is intolerant of subpar performance and is relentlessly focused on strategic goals.

That Gaynor is a major driver of British-Borneo's communal culture, however, is emblematic of one of this form's challenges. While a communal culture is usually difficult to attain and sustain, a strong leader can manage both to powerfully effective ends. But should the leader ever leave, the community he or she created can easily collapse. Because of its fragility, a communal culture is also difficult to export. That is the challenge Gaynor faces today, in fact, as British-Borneo's embryonic operations in Houston, Texas, go through a dramatic expansion.

# Executive Summaries

---

## Asinine Attitudes Toward Motivation

Harry Levinson

What this noted psychologist calls "the great jackass fallacy" is an unconscious managerial assumption about people and how they should be motivated. It results in the powerful treating the powerless as objects and in the perpetuation of anachronistic organizational structures that destroy the individual's sense of worth and accomplishment. And it is responsible for the "motivational crisis" that afflicts many large organizations. The author argues that in today's climate of increased pressure on organizations to become more responsive to both their members and society, it is particularly incumbent on managers to recognize the effect of the jackass fallacy on their thinking and to counter its effects in their organizations. Then he offers some suggestions for taking the first steps in this direction.

## Why Incentive Plans Cannot Work

Alfie Kohn

It is difficult to overstate the extent to which most managers and the people who advise them believe in the redemptive power of rewards. Certainly, the vast majority of U.S. corporations use some sort of program intended to motivate employees by tying compensation to one index of performance or another. But more striking is the rarely examined belief that people will do a better job if they have been promised some sort of incentive.

This assumption and the practices associated with it are pervasive, but Alfie Kohn examines a growing collection of evidence that supports an opposing view. According to numerous studies in laboratories, workplaces, classrooms, and other settings, rewards typically undermine the very processes they are intended to enhance. The findings suggest that the failure of a given incentive program is due less to a glitch in that program than to the inadequacy of the psychological assumptions that ground all such plans.

Do rewards work? The answer depends on what we mean by "work." Research suggests that, by and large, rewards succeed at securing one thing only: temporary compliance. They do not create an enduring commitment to any value or action. They merely, and temporarily, change what we do. Kohn explains why rewards fail in a six-point framework: rewards do not motivate; they punish; they rupture relationships; they ignore reasons; they discourage risk taking; and, finally, they undermine interest.

Any manager thinking about a new incentive program—or attached to an old one—would do well to consider Kohn's argument. According to Kohn, incentives—or bribes—simply can't work in the workplace.

## Rethinking Rewards

The views that Alfie Kohn expressed in the chapter "*Why Incentive Plans Cannot Work*" elicited a lively debate on the role of incentives in the workplace. In this chapter, nine experts consider Kohn's argument. Kohn then offers a general response. Some experts:

"A world without A's, praise, gold stars, or incentives? No thank you, Mr. Kohn. Communism was tried, and it didn't work."
*G. Bennett Stewart III*

"The problem is not that incentives can't work but that they work all too well."
*George P. Baker III*

"Incentives are neither all good nor all bad. Although not the right answer in all cases, they can be highly effective motivational tools and should be employed under the appropriate circumstances."
*Donita S. Wolters*

"It would be a mistake to believe that reward and recognition must always have a negative effect on performance or that creative people cannot be motivated by both money and interest in the work itself."
*Teresa M. Amabile*

## How Well Is Employee Ownership Working?

Corey Rosen and Michael Quarrey

More than eight million workers now participate in employee stock ownership plans (ESOPs) in approximately 8,100 companies. The tax incentives designed by Congress since 1974 partly explain the growth in the number of ESOP companies, but most ESOPs reflect the view that worker ownership and participation have real advantages.

How accurate is that view? How well are ESOP companies doing? To find out, the authors compared the performance of 45 ESOP companies with the performance of many other companies of similar size and in similar industries. On average, sales and employment grew at a rate 5% faster in the ESOP companies than in the non-ESOP companies during the five years after ESOPs were established. More than 73% of the ESOP companies significantly improved their performance after setting up their plans.

Moreover, there is a strong correlation between corporate performance and worker participation: ESOP companies do best when they set up programs that permit workers to have a say in corporate policy. A synergy emerges between ownership and participation; ownership provides a strong incentive for employees to work productively, and programs for participation provide channels for their ideas and talents. With ESOPs performing so well, the authors suggest, more American managers should consider adopting this approach.

## What Business Can Learn from Nonprofits

Peter F. Drucker

Every year in Florida, some 25,000 young people who have been convicted to their first term in prison enter the Salvation Army's parole program. Statistics show that if these men and women go to jail, the majority will become habitual criminals. The Salvation Army has been able to rehabilitate 80% of them through a strict work program run largely by volunteers. The program costs a fraction of what it would to keep the offenders behind bars.

This kind of effectiveness is characteristic of the best nonprofit organizations. Twenty years ago, management was a dirty word in nonprofits. Today they offer best practice in two areas, strategy and effective use of the board. And in the area that presents the biggest challenge for every enterprise—motivating knowledge workers and raising their productivity—they are truly pioneers.

In successful nonprofit enterprises, well-meaning amateurs are giving way to unpaid staff members, many of whom work as managers and professionals in their for-pay jobs. These people volunteer because they believe in the organization's mission. They stay because the organization knows how to put their competence and knowledge to work. The formula is the same, whether the employer is a church, the Girl Scouts, or a business: give people responsibility for meaningful tasks, hold them accountable for their performance, reward them with training and the chance to take on more demanding assignments.

## Power Is the Great Motivator

David C. McClelland and David H. Burnham

What makes or motivates a good manager? This HBR Classic, the McKinsey Award winner in 1976 (March-April), attempts to answer that question by using the degree of a person's need for power as a measure of success. McClelland and Burnham studied managers in large U.S. corporations who were participating in management workshops designed to improve their effectiveness. They also surveyed the managers' subordinates to determine how effective the managers were and to isolate the characteristics of those who created high morale.

Their conclusions? The better managers tended to score high in their need for power—that is, their desire to influence people—and that need outweighed their need to be liked. The authors also found that the most effective managers, whom they call *institutional managers*, disciplined and controlled their desire for power so that it was directed toward the benefit of the institution as a whole—not toward their own personal aggrandizement.

In contrast to institutional managers, the authors identified two other kinds of managers, both of whom breed low morale among subordinates. The first, *affiliative managers,* scored higher in their need to be liked than in their need for power, and the second, *personal power managers,* have a greater need for power than for affiliation but display little self-control in their actions.

In his retrospective commentary, David McClelland considers his earlier findings in light of his research into two important changes that have occurred in the workplace since HBR first published this article: large hierarchical organizations have flattened out, and female managers have entered the workplace in full force.

## Demand Better Results—and Get Them

Robert H. Schaffer

This HBR classic, first published in 1974, asks and answers one of management's most important questions: Why do so few organizations reach their productivity potential? The answer: because most senior executives fail to establish expectations of performance improvement in ways that get results. They fail because making heavy demands involves taking risks and threatens those who have the demands imposed on them. It's safer to ask for less.

To avoid facing the reality of underachievement, managers may rationalize that their subordinates are doing the best they can or that better performance requires more authority or greater resources. They may put their faith in incentive plans that don't need their personal intervention. They may actually set high goals but let subordinates escape accountability for results.

To get out of these doldrums, executives have to be willing to invest time and energy; responsibility can be delegated only so far. The key to the recovery strategy is to set a specific, modest, measurable goal pertaining to an important problem in the organization. If this goal is met, management uses the success as a springboard for more ambitious demands, each one carefully supported by plans, controls, and persistence directed from the top.

Resistance can be expected from many levels. But as the organization registers genuine achievement, consciousness-raising in the form of recognition transforms expectations into positive factors. The fact is, most people like to work in a results-oriented environment.

In a retrospective commentary, the author writes that while companies today are more impressed with the need for performance improvement, the ability to establish high expectations is still the most universally under-developed managerial skill.

## The New Managerial Work

Rosabeth Moss Kanter

As corporations restructure for greater flexibility and innovation, radical changes are taking place in the nature of managerial work. Collaborative work is increasing, hierarchy fading. Cross-divisional and cross-company ventures are multiplying, control vanishing. Change takes five key forms:

1. There are many more channels for instigating action and exerting influence.
2. These channels are more likely to function horizontally, through peers, than vertically, through the chain of command.
3. There are fewer differences between managers and the people they manage, especially in terms of information, control over assignments, and access to external relationships.
4. External relationships have become important sources of internal power and influence.
5. Career development is less structured, with fewer assured routes to promotion but more opportunities for innovation and entrepreneurial success.

Managers need to master change in two critical areas—power and motivation—in order to manage effectively in the new organization.

Hierarchy is no longer an adequate base of power. Today managers get things done by building relationships, by finding new sources of ideas and opportunity, and by brokering deals across internal and external boundaries. Effective managers are integrators and facilitators, not watchdogs.

Loss of hierarchy has deprived managers of some of their capacity to guarantee promotion, grant raises, direct work, even to protect their people (and themselves) from the perils of restructuring. As a result, they have to rely on new motivational tools. Among these are professional pride, agenda control, sharing value creation, learning, and reputation.

## The Work of Leadership

Ronald A. Heifetz and Donald L. Laurie

More and more companies today are facing *adaptive* challenges: changes in societies, markets, and technology around the globe are forcing them to clarify their values, develop new strategies, and learn new ways of operating. And the most important task for leaders in the face of such challenges is mobilizing people throughout the organization to do adaptive work.

Yet for many senior executives, providing such leadership is difficult. Why? One reason is that they are accustomed to solving problems themselves. Another is that adaptive change is distressing for the people going through it. They need to take on new roles, relationships, values, and approaches to work. Many employees are ambivalent about the sacrifices required of them and look to senior executives to take problems off their shoulders.

But both sets of expectations have to be unlearned. Rather than providing answers, leaders have to ask tough questions. Rather than protecting people from outside threats, leaders should let the pinch of reality stimulate them to adapt. Instead of orienting people to their current roles, leaders must disorient them so that new relationships can develop. Instead of quelling conflict, leaders should draw the issues out. Instead of maintaining norms, leaders must challenge "the way we do business" and help others distinguish immutable values from the historical practices that have become obsolete.

The authors offer six principles for leading adaptive work: "getting on the balcony," identifying the adaptive challenge, regulating distress, maintaining disciplined attention, giving the work back to people, and protecting voices of leadership from below.

## Speed, Simplicity, Self-confidence: An Interview with Jack Welch

Noel M. Tichy and Ram Charan

The chairman and CEO of General Electric leads a billion dollar enterprise that he believes must operate with the flexibility and agility of a small company. In this interview, John F. Welch explains how he is building a revitalized "human engine" to match GE's formidable "business engine."

Welch has two objectives. He is championing a companywide drive to eliminate unproductive work and energize employees. And he is leading a transformation of attitudes—struggling, in his words, to release "emotional energy" at all levels of GE's organization.

"For a large organization to be effective, it must be simple," Welch says. For a large organization to be simple, its people must have maximum self-confidence and intellectual self-assurance. Insecure managers create complexity. . . . Clear, tough-minded people are the most simple."

The centerpiece of Welch's transformation process is Work-Out—an intense multiyear program through which representatives of GE's 14 businesses meet regularly to identify sources of frustration and inefficiency, unnecessary reports, reviews, and forecasts, and to overhaul evaluation and reward systems.

"The ultimate objective of Work-Out is so clear," Welch says. "We want 300,000 people with different career objectives, different family aspirations, different financial goals to share directly in this company's vision, the information, the decision-making process, and the rewards. We want to build a more stimulating and creative environment, a freer work atmosphere, with incentives tied directly to what people do."

The interview was conducted by Professor Noel M. Tichy and consultant Ram Charan, both of whom have worked closely with GE for two decades.

## To Build a Winning Team: An Interview with Head Coach Bill Walsh

Richard Rapaport

Throughout his 35-year football coaching career, at the high school, college, and professional levels, Bill Walsh has produced winners with a structured and businesslike approach to maximizing the potential of players and coaches. It is his highly successful management style in the most intense competitive situations that make his organizational insights so applicable to today's corporate environment.

Taking over as head coach and general manager of a dreadful San Francisco 49ers team in 1979, Walsh immediately began to develop and chart meticulous, long-range strategic and personnel plans for the organization. He defined responsibilities for both players and coaches, with objectives and priorities set for all. His practices focused on being prepared for every possible game situation, "including the desperate ones at the end of a game when we may have only one chance to pull out a victory." The result was three Super Bowl championships in eight years for the 49ers and the distinction of being enshrined in the sports press as "The Team of the '80s."

In a profession where a player's career can be as long as the next bone-crushing tackle, Walsh developed an intricate but direct process for moving people through his organization. It begins by drafting top prospects, and then projecting what each player can do now, next year, and ten years from now. Walsh calls this the "arc of utilization," and it guides his decisions on how to best utilize a player's skills and what to do when those skills are diminishing and can no longer help the team. Replacing veteran players "may be the most emotionally difficult part of the job," Walsh explains. "Yet it is the role the leader must play. The bottom line in professional sports is winning. Everything has to focus on that."

## The CEO as Coach: An Interview with AlliedSignal's Lawrence A. Bossidy

Noel M. Tichy and Ram Charan

In July 1991, Lawrence A. Bossidy became chairman and CEO of Allied-Signal, the $13 billion industrial supplier of aerospace systems, automotive parts, and chemical products. The company's story since then appears to be the typical slash-and-burn turnaround: head count has been reduced, assets have been sold, restructurings have occurred, and earnings and market value have risen dramatically. But the view from the inside is far more interesting for anyone grappling with what it takes to lead a competitive organization and sustain its performance over the long term.

Bossidy is a straight-shooting, tough-minded, results-oriented business leader. But he is also a charismatic and persistent coach, determined to help people learn and thereby to provide his company with the best-prepared employees. In this interview, Bossidy explains his views on the leader's role in changing a large organization. He discusses how he uses values and goals to "coach people to win." And he explains his efforts to focus AlliedSignal's management on three core processes—strategy, operations, and human resources.

Bossidy is no stranger to corporate transformation. As vice chairman of General Electric, he helped CEO Jack Welch reposition the billion dollar industrial giant. Bossidy's career at GE began in 1957, when he joined the finance staff. In the late 1970s and early 1980s, he led GE Capital Corporation, creating a world-class financial service organization.

## What Holds the Modern Company Together?

Rob Goffee and Gareth Jones

The organizational world is awash with talk of corporate culture—and for good reason. Culture has become a powerful way to hold a company together against the recent tidal wave of pressures for disintegration, such as decentralization and downsizing. But what is culture? Perhaps more important, is there one *right* culture for every organization? And if the answer is no, how can a manager change an organization's culture?

Addressing those three questions, Rob Goffee and Gareth Jones begin the article with the assertion that culture is community. Moreover, they contend, because business communities are no different from communities outside the commercial arena—such as families, schools, clubs, and villages—they can and should) be viewed through the same lens that has illuminated the study of human organizations for nearly 150 years.

That is the lens of sociology, which divides community into two types of human relations: *sociability,* a measure of friendliness among members of a community, and *solidarity,* a measure of a community's ability to pursue shared objectives. Plotting these two dimensions against each other results in four types of business community: networked, mercenary, fragmented, and communal. None of these cultures is "the best," the authors say. In fact, each is appropriate for different business environments. In other words, managers need not advocate one cultural type over another. Instead, they must know how to assess their own culture and whether it fits the competitive situation. Only then can they consider the delicate techniques for transforming it.

# About the Contributors

After publishing "Power Is the Great Motivator" in the *Harvard Business Review*, **David Burnham** spent the next two decades working as a consultant to leaders in Singapore, Europe, and Australia, helping them become more like the institutional manager described in the article. Now a partner in the Boston-based Burnham Rosen Group, a consulting firm specializing in leadership training and business strategy, Burnham has just completed a five-year follow-up study to his original research. He is in the process of writing an article based upon these findings.

**Ram Charan** specializes in business strategy from conception to completion: the reality-based conversion of vision into action; developing and implementing global strategies and integrating mechanisms for effective transitional organizations; and guiding CEOs in the selection of people, succession planning, and creation of value-added boards. He has been on the faculty of the Harvard Business School and the Northwestern University Graduate School of Management, and he was named by *Business Week* as one of the Top 10 resources nationwide for in-house programs.

The Marie Rankin Clarke Professor of Social Science and Management at Claremont Graduate School, **Peter F. Drucker** is perhaps the most influential writer today on modern organizations and their management. His 27 books have been translated into more than 20 languages. Among his publications are two classics, *The Practice of Management*, and *Management: Tasks, Responsibilities, Practices*. Professor Drucker has served as consultant to numerous governments, public service institutions, and major corporations.

**Rob Goffee** is a professor of organizational behavior at London Business School and an internationally respected authority on organizational transformation. He has published six books—including *Corporate Realities: The Dynamics of Large and Small Organizations,* and *Reluctant Managers: Their Work and Lifestyles*—and more than 40 articles in scholarly and managerial journals. With Gareth Jones, he is co-founder of the London-based consulting firm Creative Management Associates, which has instituted large-scale cultural change initiatives at numerous organizations.

For the last twelve years, **Ronald A. Heifetz** has been responsible for developing a theory of leadership and a method for leadership education. He is a lecturer in public policy at Harvard University and a clinical instructor in psychiatry at Harvard Medical School. His research aims to provide leaders with an approach to political and organizational diagnosis and strategy suitable to the complex challenges facing our diverse society. His book, *Leadership Without Easy Answers,* was published by the Belknap Press of Harvard University Press in 1994. Heifetz works extensively with leaders in government and industry, and his consultations focus on the work of leaders in generating and sustaining adaptive change across political boundaries, operating units, and product divisions and functions in politics, government agencies, and international businesses.

**Gareth Jones** holds academic appointments in organizational development at both Henley Management College in the United Kingdom and at INSEAD in France. His specialties are cultural analysis, creativity, and leadership. With Rob Goffee, he is co-founder of the London-based consulting firm Creative Management Associates, which has instituted large-scale cultural change initiatives at numerous organizations.

**Rosabeth Moss Kanter** has taught at the Harvard Business School since 1986 as the Class of 1960 Professor of Business Administration, also serving as editor of the *Harvard Business Review* from 1989 to 1992. She has designed and led business renewal and change efforts for corporations, governments, and other organizations throughout the world. She is the author of numerous books, including *Rosabeth Moss Kanter on the Frontiers of Management, World Class, When Giants Learn to Dance, The Change Masters,* and *Men and Women of the Corporation.*

**Steven Kerr** is vice president of leadership development and chief learning officer for General Electric; he is responsible for GE's renowned leadership education center at Crotonville. He was previously on the faculties of Ohio State University, University of Southern California, and University of Michigan, and he was dean of the faculty of the USC business school from 1985 to 1989. From 1989 to 1990, Dr. Kerr was president of the Academy of Management. His writings on leadership, substitutes for leadership, and "the folly of rewarding A, while hoping for B" are among the most cited and reprinted in the management sciences. He is a co-author of *The Boundaryless Organization* and author of "Risky Business: The New Pay Game" in *Fortune* magazine.

**Alfie Kohn** is the author of five books, including *No Contest: The Case Against Competition* and *Punished by Rewards: The Trouble with Gold Stars, Incentive Plans, A's, Praise, and Other Bribes,* from which this article was adapted. Kohn lectures widely at universities, conferences, and corporations on management and motivation. He lives in Belmont, Massachusetts.

Founder and managing director of the management consulting firm Laurie International Limited, **Donald L. Laurie**'s work focuses on strategic management issues relevant to chairmen and chief executives. His ongoing research entitled *The Work of the Leader* involves chief executives of major corporations and has received wide acclaim by business leaders in the United States and Europe. A book detailing this research, as well as his own experiences, is forthcoming in 1998.

**Harry Levinson,** Ph.D. is chairman of The Levinson Institute and clinical professor emeritus of psychology in the Department of Psychiatry, Harvard Medical School. He is a consultant to and lecturer for many business, academic, and government organizations. In addition to numerous articles, Dr. Levinson has written more than 10 books, including *Career Mastery; Men, Management, and Mental Health; Executive;* and, with Dr. Stuart Rosenthal, *CEO: Corporate Leadership in Action.*

**David C. McClelland** is founder and chairman of the board of McBer and Co., now a part of the Hay Group. He is professor emeritus of psychology at Harvard University, and research professor of psychology at Boston University. Dr. McClelland has devoted a lifetime to research that has resulted in an internationally accepted theory of human motivation and in a widely adopted method of measuring competencies that are associated with executive success. Author of *The*

*Achieving Society, Power: The Inner Experience,* and *Human Motivation,* Dr. McClelland is widely published on human motivation and related topics. His research findings have been applied to management, small-business development, economic development, and the modernization of developing countries, as well as postsecondary education, mental health, and behavioral medicine.

**Michael Quarrey** is vice president of operations for Connor Formed Metal Products, based in Menlo Park, California. Connor is a forty-million dollar, forty-percent employee-owned manufacturer of precision metal components. He is the author, with Corey Rosen and Joseph Blasi, of *Taking Stock: Employee Ownership at Work.*

A San Francisco-based writer and contributing editor to *San Francisco Focus* and *Forbes/ASAP,* **Richard Rapaport**'s political commentary appears frequently in Knight-Ridder and other newspaper chains around the United States.

**Corey Rosen** is the executive director of the National Center for Employee Ownership, a private, nonprofit information and membership organization based in Oakland, California. Prior to co-founding the NCEO in 1981, he worked on a Senate staff, where he helped draft Employee Stock Ownership Plan (ESOP) legislation. He has co-authored four books on employee ownership and authored more than 100 articles.

**Robert H. Schaffer** founded Robert H. Schaffer & Associates and has been its head for more than 30 years. He is the originator of the firm's unique results-driven approach described in his 1988 book, *The Breakthrough Strategy,* and RHS&A employs this strategy in helping organizations achieve major performance improvement and accelerate the pace of change. In addition, Schaffer helped launch the *Journal of Management Consulting* and has served as its editor for many years. He is the author of numerous articles and several books.

**Noel M. Tichy** is a professor of organizational behavior and human resource management at the Graduate School of Business Administration, University of Michigan. Professor Tichy is also Director of the Global Leadership Program, a 36-company consortium of Japanese, European, and North American companies who are partnered to develop senior executives and conduct action research on globalization. He is founder and editor in chief of the journal *Human Resource Management,* as well as the author of numerous books and articles.

# Index